LOAD BALANCING IN PARALLEL COMPUTERS

Theory and Practice

THE KLUWER INTERNATIONAL SERIES IN ENGINEERING AND COMPUTER SCIENCE

LOAD BALANCING IN PARALLEL COMPUTERS

Theory and Practice

by

Chengzhong Xu
Wayne State University

Francis C. M. Lau
The University of Hong Kong

SPRINGER SCIENCE+BUSINESS MEDIA, LLC

Library of Congress Cataloging-in-Publication Data

A C.I.P. Catalogue record for this book is available
from the Library of Congress.

ISBN 978-1-4757-7066-7 ISBN 978-0-585-27256-6 (eBook)
DOI 10.1007/978-0-585-27256-6

Printed on acid-free paper.

Contents

Foreword

Load balancing makes a fundamental difference in the performance of parallel computers. Through many years of dedicated research in this area, Dr. C.-Z. Xu and Dr. Francis C. M. Lau have put together a comprehensive book on the theory and practice of load balancing in parallel computers.

The book starts with a simple characterization of static and dynamic schemes for load balancing. The authors formulated the performance models of various load balancing schemes. A good survey of load balancing algorithms is given in Chapter 2, covering both deterministic and stochastic algorithms.

The GDE load balancing algorithm is particularly treated in Chapters 3 and 4, followed by a characterization of the diffusion method in Chapter 5. A comparison of these two methods is given in Chapter 6. These methods are mapped on rings, meshes, and tori with illustrated simulation results.

Termination detection algorithms are treated in Chapter 7. A remapping strategy based on the GDE method for data parallel computations is given in Chapter 8. In Chapter 9, the authors apply combinatorial optimizations to load balancing. Finally, they summarize known results and identify the open problems.

I strongly recommend this book to readers who are working in the area of parallel and distributed computing. It is an excellent reference for researchers as well as for practitioners. The book is suitable for use as a textbook in graduate-level courses in Computer Science and Engineering.

Kai Hwang
The University of Hong Kong

Preface

A load would sink a navy.
—SHAKESPEARE [HENRY VIII]

"Parallel computing" is no longer a buzzword, it is synonymous with high-performance computing, it is practical. Parallel computers are here to stay. By interconnecting hundreds and thousands of the world's most advanced processors, trillion floating point operations/second (teraflop) computers will soon be a reality and they will be ready to confront the most complex problems and the grandest challenges. A notable example is the project by the U.S. Department of Energy (DOE) on building the world's first teraflop computer, which will be powered by more than 9000 Intel's Pentium Pro processors. Another project of similar scale, also involving the DOE, will use a vast number of IBM's RS/6000 processors to achieve a comparable performance. But parallel computing is not limited to massively parallel processing (MPP). Symmetric multiprocessing (SMP) is now a common trend in the server market. There is the likelihood that before too long multiprocessing will reach even the desktop. Recent advances in high speed communication networks have enabled parallel computing on clusters of workstations.

The raw power of computers has kept on increasing by leaps and bounds, but humankind's ability to harness that power does not seem to be keeping up. Perhaps we are too accustomed to solving problems sequentially, especially when using the computer. The gap must be bridged by advanced software. A huge amount of effort has been devoted by researchers worldwide to the development of software techniques for parallel computing. These researchers all share the common goal of making the use of parallel computers much less formidable and enabling the user to fully exploit the power of the parallel computer. One such essential software technique is *load balancing*, which is the subject of this book. Load balancing aims at improving the performance of parallel computers by equalizing the workloads of processors automatically during the execution of parallel programs.

This book is about load balancing in distributed memory message-passing parallel computers, also called multicomputers. Each processor has its own address space and has to communicate with other processors by message passing. In general, a direct, point-to-point interconnection network is used for the communications. Many commercial parallel computers are of this class, including the Intel Paragon, the Thinking Machine CM-5, and the IBM SP2. This book presents a comprehensive treatment of the subject using rigorous mathematical analyses and practical implementations. The focus is on nearest-neighbor load balancing methods in which every processor at every step is restricted to balancing its workload with its direct neighbors only. Nearest-neighbor methods are iterative in nature because a global balanced state could be reached through processors' successive local operations. Since nearest-neighbor methods have a relatively relaxed requirement on the spread of local load information across the system, they are flexible in terms of allowing one to control the balancing quality, effective for preserving communication locality, and can be easily scaled in parallel computers with a direct communication network.

In the design and analysis of nearest-neighbor load balancing algorithms, the two most important performance metrics are stability and efficiency. Stability measures the ability of the algorithm to coerce any initial workload distribution into a global balanced state in the static workload model and the ability to bound the variance of processors' workload in the dynamic workload model. Efficiency measures the time delay for arriving at the global balanced state or for reducing the variance to a certain level. The objective of this work is to try to design nearest-neighbor algorithms that have good stability and efficiency characteristics.

Two of the most well-known nearest-neighbor load balancing algorithms are the *dimension exchange* and *diffusion* methods. With the dimension exchange method, a processor goes around the table, balancing workload with its nearest neighbors one at a time. With the diffusion method, a processor communicates simultaneously with all its nearest neighbors in order to reach a local balance. These two methods are rigorously analyzed in this book, resulting in optimal tunings of the methods for a number of popular interconnection networks. On the practical side, these two methods are implemented on multicomputers with different characteristics and evaluated in applications with different behaviors. They are found to be effective and efficient in solving the load balancing problem.

Modeling and Analysis of Load Balancing Algorithms

The dimension exchange method equalizes a processor's workload with those of its nearest neighbors one by one, and the most recently computed value is always used in the next equalization step. It is observed that "equal splitting" of workload between a pair of processors in each balance operation does not necessarily lead to the fastest convergence rate in arriving at a global balanced state. We therefore generalize the dimension exchange method by introducing an exchange parameter into the method to control the workload splitting; it is expected that through adjusting this parameter, the load balancing efficiency may be improved. We carry out an analysis of this *generalized dimension exchange* (GDE) method using linear system theory, and derive a necessary and sufficient condition for its convergence. We also present a sufficient condition *w.r.t.* the structure of the system network for the optimality of the dimension exchange method. Among networks that have this property are the hypercube and the product of any two networks having the property.

For other popular networks, the ring, the chain, the mesh, the torus and the k-ary n-cube, we derive the optimal exchange parameters in closed form and establish several important relationships between the efficiencies of these structures using circulant matrix theory. Based on these relationships, we conclude that the dimension exchange method favors high dimensional networks.

With the diffusion method, a processor balances its workload with those of its nearest neighbors all at the same time rather than one by one as in the dimension exchange method. Its efficiency is dependent on a diffusion parameter, which characterizes the behavior of a local balance operation. We analyze the diffusion method using circulant matrix theory and derive the optimal values for the diffusion parameter for the k-ary n-cube and its variants. Through statistical simulation, we show significant improvements due to the optimal exchange and the diffusion parameters.

Furthermore, we analyze the dimension exchange and the diffusion method in different workload models and system characteristics. We show that the optimally-tuned dimension exchange algorithm outperforms the diffusion method in both one-port and all-port communication models in achieving a global balanced state. The strength of the diffusion method is in load sharing (*i.e.*, keeping all processors busy but not necessarily balancing their loads) in the all-port communication model.

Practical Implementations

On the practical side, we experiment with the dimension exchange and the diffusion methods in various applications for the purposes of global load balancing and load sharing. We implement the GDE method for periodic remapping in two time-dependent multiphase data parallel computations: a parallel Monte Carlo simulation and a parallel image thinning algorithm. The experimental results show that GDE-based remapping leads to substantial improvements in execution time for both cases. The GDE method is also implemented for parallel partitioning of unstructured finite-element graphs. Experimental results show that the GDE-based parallel refinement, coupled with simple geometric partitioning approaches, produces partitions comparable in quality to those from the best serial algorithms.

The last application is parallel combinatorial optimizations. We experiment with the dimension exchange and the diffusion methods for distributing dynamically generated workloads at run-time. Their performance is evaluated in the solution of set partitioning problems on two distributed memory parallel computers. It is found that both methods lead to an almost linear speedup in a system with 32 processors and a speedup of 146.8 in a system with 256 processors. These two methods give the best results among all the methods we tried.

Organization

Chapter 1 gives an overview of the load balancing problem, and presents a general dynamic load balancing model and the performance metrics. Chapter 2 surveys nearest-neighbor load balancing algorithms in multicomputers. Chapter 3 introduces and presents an analysis of the basic properties of the GDE method, one of the two nearest-neighbor methods covered in this book. In Chapter 4, we apply the GDE method to a number of popular interconnection networks, and derive optimal values for the exchange parameter for these various cases. We also present results of the simulation of the GDE method in these structures, which clearly show that the optimal exchange parameters do speed up the efficiency of the balancing procedure significantly. The second method, the diffusion method, is studied in Chapter 5 in a style similar to the study of the GDE method in the previous chapters. Chapter 6 compares the stability and efficiency of the GDE and diffusion methods for different machine and workload models. One important issue of implementing these methods in real parallel computers is *termination*—how do the processors know they have reached a global balanced state? This is a non-trivial problem as the two methods under study are fully distributed solutions. Chapter 7 addresses this issue and proposes an efficient solution to the termination detection problem. Chapter 8 reports on the implementation of the GDE method for remapping in two realistic data parallel applications and for parallel partitioning of unstructured finite-element graphs. These implementations incorporate the termination detection algorithm presented in Chapter 7. Chapter 9 reports on the implementation of the GDE and the diffusion methods for dynamic load distribution in parallel branch-and-bound optimizations. Chapter 10 concludes the work and gives suggestions on further work.

Acknowledgements

A large part of the materials in this book was derived from the first author's Ph.D. dissertation, which was submitted to the Department of Computer Science, The University of Hong Kong in June 1993. The experiments of graph partitioning and parallel branch-and-bound optimizations were conducted in cooperation with the AG-Monien research group while the first author was visiting the University of Paderborn and the Paderborn Center for Parallel Computing (PC^2) of Germany. The first author's thesis research was funded by a Li Ka Shing Postgraduate Scholarship, and supported in part by a Hong Kong and China Gas Company Limited Postgraduate Scholarship and a research assistantship from The University of Hong Kong. The first author's visit of Germany was supported by DFG-Forschergruppe "Effiziente Nutzung Paralleler Systeme". The second author was supported by grants from The University of Hong Kong and grants from the Research Grant Council of the Hong Kong Government.

The authors are very grateful to Burkhard Monien, Ralf Diekmann, Reinhard Lüling and Stefan Tschöke for their valuable comments and contributions to both the theoretical and experimental aspects of this research. Thanks also go to Erich Köster and other associates of the AG-Monien group for their considerate arrangements in both academic and non-academic affairs while the first author was in Germany.

Many other people have contributed to this book. We thank Professor Kai Hwang for the foreword, and Professors Dimitri P. Bertsekas, Tony Chan, Vipin Chaudhary, Henry Cheung, Francis Chin, Andrew Choi, Georege Cybenko, F. Meyer auf der Heide, David Nassimi, and Loren Schwiebert for their valuable inputs at various stages of this project. Special thanks go to our families who had suffered through many long nights of being neglected. Their love, patience and support had meant a lot to us. To Jiwen who had assisted us wholeheartedly from beginning to end, we are greatly indebted.

Chengzhong Xu
Detroit, USA

Francis C. M. Lau
Hong Kong

1

INTRODUCTION

The greatest of the human soul consists in knowing how to preserve the mean.
—PASCAL

Parallel computing has come of age. This is evident partly from the recently released top-of-the-line products offered by major computer vendors. Equipped with multiple processors, parallel computers are now dominating the server and enterprise computing markets, and moving rapidly into the domains of the desktops as well as the supercomputers. As an indication of the shift in emphasis, Intel designed its Pentium Pro chip which contains new features to make the chip a building block for easy construction of small parallel computers [46]; Cray Research, Inc., the vector supercomputer giant, released its multiprocessor systems, the T3D [107], and recently the T3E [94], for supercomputing. Recent advances in high speed communication networks are enabling practical parallel computing on clusters of workstations [6, 120, 157].

Parallel computers depart from the predominantly sequential von Neumann model and transcend low-level physical limitations to offer the promise of a quantum leap in computing power. Whether and to what extent this promise can be fulfilled, however, has yet to be fully seen because the software for parallel computers is still lagging behind. Every machine family runs a different operating system and supports a different set of programming languages and tools. Users of parallel machines not only need to write programs in unfamiliar and sometimes obscure parallel languages, but also need to tailor their programs to specific systems based on their knowledge of each system's architecture.

This situation has resulted in much attention in and effort being devoted to the development of advanced software techniques for parallel computers. New programming standards such as High-Performance Fortran (HPF) [84], PVM [72] and MPI [178, 197], and automatic parallelizing compilers such as KAP [7] and SUIF [206] represent important strides in advancing the state of affairs in this regard. *Load balancing*, the subject of this book, is among the most critical considerations in parallel programming, automatic parallelization, and run-time resource management. It aims at improving the performance of parallel computers by scheduling users' tasks appropriately on processors. More specifically, it tries to equalize the processors' workloads automatically during the execution of parallel programs so that either the execution time or the average response time of the parallel programs is minimized.

This chapter presents an overview of the load balancing problem and a general framework for systematically designing and analyzing load balancing algorithms for distributed memory parallel computers.

1.1 Parallel Computers

A parallel computer is a collection of processing elements that communicate and cooperate to solve large problems efficiently [5, 92]. Parallel computers vary in two fundamental architectural facets: (1) single-instruction-multiple-data (SIMD) versus multiple-instructions-multiple-data (MIMD), and (2) shared memory versus distributed memory [123]. SIMD computers apply a single instruction to multiple data values before moving on to the next instruction [48, 88]. All processing elements execute the same instruction but over different data sets. They proceed synchronously under the control of a single instruction stream. They are good at handling applications, like image processing and the solution of partial differential equations, which have regular data operations. Their utility, however, is limited because of their strict requirements on computational structures. MIMD computers, by contrast, allow processing elements to execute different programs over different data sets. The asynchronism provides greater flexibilities for users to program any complex applications. There are parallel computers in the market that can operate in either mode, such as the Thinking Machine CM-5 [44].

A parallel computer with a centralized memory scheme has a single common memory system, from which all processor read and to which they all write. The common memory system provides a simple shared memory programming abstraction but limits the scalability of parallel computers. By contrast, a parallel computer with a distributed memory scheme physically associates a memory system with each processor so as to alleviate the bottleneck in memory accesses.

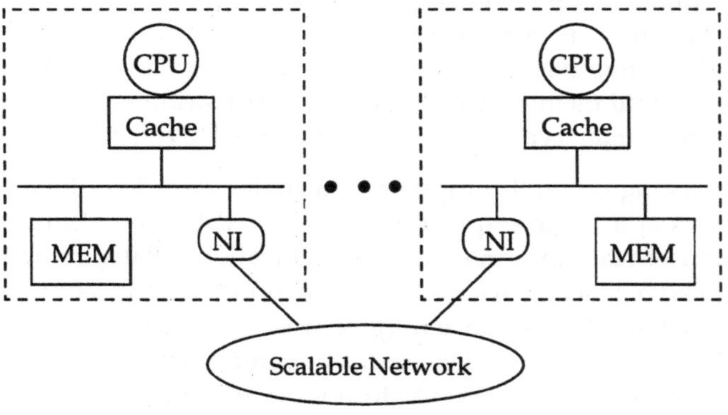

Figure 1.1: An architecture of parallel computers

The machine model assumed in this book is that of a distributed memory MIMD system, as illustrated in Figure 1.1. A parallel computer of this kind comprises a collection of processing elements interconnected by a scalable communication network. Each element consists of one processor (cpu), a memory module and a hardware interface to the network. We focus our attention on such parallel machines because of the following architectural advantages they have over other alternatives. They are cost effective because readily available processors can be used as building blocks; they can be easily scaled to fit problems to be solved or upgraded incrementally; they are also flexible in terms of integrating different types of processing nodes into one system, which is sometimes called for by particular specialized problems. Another reason for our interest in this machine model as compared to the centralized memory machine model is that the load balancing problem on the latter can be easily solved by using the centralized memory as a pool to buffer workloads among processors.

Notice that the memory module in the distributed memory machine model does not necessarily have to be private to its associated processor; it may be shared by all processors. A computer with private local memories provides disjoint memory address spaces . Processors only have direct access to their local memories. They must communicate with each other through sending messages. Since each processing element maintains a certain degree of autonomy, such a distributed memory message-passing system is referred to as a *multicomputer* [8, 167]. Examples include the IBM SP2 [2], the Intel Paragon [45], the Thinking Machine CM-5 [44], the nCUBE NCUBE2 [154], the Parsytec GCel [95] and the PowerPlus [95]. A parallel computer with a logically shared memory system provides a single global address space to all processors, and hence a shared memory programming paradigm to the users. Such a system is referred to as a distributed shared memory (DSM) machine. Cray T3D/T3E and Convex Exemplar are some DSM examples that use hardware techniques in their network interfaces to realize a shared global address space [107, 94, 151]. There are also a number of experimental software systems that provide the users with a shared memory view on physically distributed memory architectures through an intermediate run-time layer (see [159] for a survey).

Load balancing on multicomputers is a challenge due to the autonomy of the processors and the inter-processor communication overhead incurred in the collection of state information, communication delays, redistribution of loads, *etc.* Load balancing on DSM machines is no less a challenge even though the shared global address space may be used as a common pool for workloads awaiting balancing as in centralized memory systems. This is because memory accesses from a processor to remote memory banks on other processors are much more expensive than local memory accesses. An appropriate distribution of workloads across physically distributed memories helps reduce such costly remote accesses. Our solution to the workload distribution problem for distributed memory machines may also be applicable to the DSM model. Whether it is a multicomputer or a DSM machine, any interaction or accesses across processors are realized through message passing. The message passing programming paradigm on distributed memory machines is assumed throughout this book.

1.2 The Load Balancing Problem

A parallel program is composed of multiple processes, each of which is to perform one or more tasks defined by the program. A task is the smallest unit of concurrency the parallel program can exploit. A process is an abstract software entity that executes its assigned tasks on a processor. Creating a parallel program involves first decomposing the overall computation into tasks and then assigning the tasks to processes. The decomposition and assignment steps together are often called partitioning. The optimization objective for partitioning is to balance the workload among processes and to minimize the interprocess communication needs. Executing a parallel program requires mapping the processes to processors available to the program. The number of processes generated by the partitioning step may not be equal to the number of processors. Thus a processor can be idle or loaded with multiple processes. The primary optimization objective of mapping is to balance the workload of processors and to minimize the inter-processor communication cost.

Collectively, the problem of load balancing is to develop partitioning and mapping algorithms for the purpose of achieving their respective optimization objectives. In essence, the partitioning problem and the mapping problem are identical because the models they assume (task-process versus process-processor) are equivalent and their optimization objectives are identical. Unless otherwise specified, the process-processor model is assumed in the discussion of the load balancing problem in this book.

The problem of load balancing started to emerge when distributed memory multiprocessors were gaining popularity. On the other hand, a similar problem, the *load sharing* problem, has existed for as long as loosely-coupled distributed computing systems have existed [29, 39, 56, 93, 113, 173, 199, 219, 220]. A distributed system consists of a collection of autonomous computers connected by a local area network. Users generally start their processes at their host computers. The random arrival of newly created processes can cause some computers to become highly loaded while others are idle or lightly loaded. The load sharing problem is to develop process scheduling algorithms to transfer processes automatically from heavily loaded computers to lightly loaded computers. Its primary goal is to ensure that no processor is idle while there are processes waiting for services in other processors. Clearly, load balancing algorithms, which aim at equalizing the processors' workloads, represent a step beyond load sharing. Although load sharing has been proposed as an alternative to load balancing because the latter tends to be more demanding in terms of resource requirement in distributed systems [114], the situation is somewhat different in parallel computers where the overhead due to load balancing is not as significant. In fact, techniques for load sharing are adaptable for load balancing in parallel computers.

1.2.1 Static versus Dynamic

Load balancing algorithms can be broadly categorized into *static* and *dynamic*. Static load balancing algorithms distribute processes to processors at compile-time, in most cases relying on *a priori* knowledge about the processes and the system on which they run, while dynamic algorithms bind processes to processors at run-time.

A major advantage of static load balancing algorithms is that they will not cause any run-time overhead. For execution times that are random or not so predictable, there exist some theoretical results on static assignments which are optimized according to various objectives [150]. Static load balancing algorithms are attractive for parallel programs for which the execution times of processes and their communication requirements can be predicted. In some situations, static load balancing is the only choice because the size of the processes' state precludes migration of processes during run-time. Even so, however, discovering a static optimal distribution solution for a system with more than two processors is NP-hard [20, 21]. Nevertheless, under certain assumptions about processes' behavior and/or characteristics of the system, there exist some theoretical results on optimal static assignments [22, 38, 96, 148, 150, 170, 187]. On the other hand, many approximate and heuristic approaches have been proposed (see [78, 179] for surveys). The heuristic approaches, as the name implies, search for good solutions simply by some rule of thumb [133, 27, 37]. Heuristic approaches are a common practice because they are simple and fast.

Static load balancing algorithms rely on the estimated execution times of processes and interprocess communication requirements. It is not satisfactory for parallel programs that are of the dynamic and/or unpredictable kind. For example, in a parallel combinatorial search application, processes evaluate candidate solutions from a set of possible solutions to find one that satisfies a problem-specific criterion. Each process searches for optimal solutions within a portion of the solution space. The shape and size of the solution space usually change as the search proceeds. Portions that encompass the optimal solution with high probability will be expanded and explored exhaustively, while portions that have no solutions will be discarded at run-time. Consequently, processes are generated and destroyed without a pattern at run-time. To ensure parallel efficiency, processes have to be distributed at run-time, and hence the patterns of workload changes of the processors are difficult to predict.

Another example of dynamic and unpredictable program behavior is parallel simulation of molecular dynamics (MD). An MD program simulates the dynamic interactions among atoms in a system of interest for a period of time. At each time step, the simulation calculates the forces between atoms, the energy of the whole structure and the movements of atoms. Assume that each process of the program is responsible for simulating a portion of the system domain. As atoms tend to move around the system domain, the computational requirements of the processes may change from step to step. Since the processes need to be synchronized at the end of each simulation step, an imbalanced workload distribution will cause a severe penalty for some processes within the step. To improve parallel efficiency, processes' workloads have to be redistributed periodically at run-time.

Dynamic load balancing algorithms have the potential to outperform static algorithms. They would aim to equalize the workload among processors and minimize the inter-processor communication costs. Dynamic load balancing with these performance goals is sometimes called remapping or semi-dynamic load balancing because the parallel program is usually suspended during the load balancing procedure. Remapping algorithms are most applicable to time-varying multiphase data parallel computations such as parallel MD simulations.

Dynamic load balancing algorithms incur non-negligible run-time overhead. In practice, it is not always reasonable to aim at a global balanced state. Sometimes, it pays to aim a little lower by relaxing the requirement of load balancing to various degrees. At one extreme is load sharing. Load sharing algorithms are found to be well suited for such computations as parallel combinatorial optimizations where processes proceed asynchronously. Dynamic load balancing algorithms aiming for a partial balanced state between the two extremes represent a certain tradeoff between balancing quality and run-time overhead. In the absence of load balancing overhead, it was shown that additional migrations beyond those necessary to conserve work have a significant positive effect on the performance of parallel computations [114].

The success of dynamic load balancing algorithms hinges upon the likelihood of the phenomenon that a light-loaded or idle processor and some overloaded processor coexist during the execution of a computation [168].

1.2.2 Key Issues in Dynamic Load Balancing

Execution of a dynamic load balancing algorithm requires some means for maintaining a consistent view of the system state at run-time and some negotiation policy for process migrations across processors [32, 174, 203]. Generally, a dynamic load balancing algorithm consists of four components: a *load measurement rule*, an *information exchange rule*, an *initiation rule*, and a *load balancing operation*.

Load Measurement. Dynamic load balancing algorithms rely on the workload information of processors. The workload information is typically quantified by a load index—a non-negative variable taking on a zero value if the processor is idle, and taking on increasing positive values as the load increases [63]. A load index should be a good estimate of the response time of the resident processes of a processor. Generally, this is impossible without actually running the processes because their response time depends not only on their needs for cpu, memory and I/O resources, but also on their inter-processor communication requirements. Instead, we must estimate the workload based on some measurable parameters, such as the processes' grain sizes (*i.e*, the size of operations executed by a process between communication events), the amount of communication, the rate of context switching, the size of available free memory, and the number of ready processes [120]. Since the measure of load would occur frequently, its calculation must be very efficient. This rules out an exhaustive use of too many parameters. Instead, a subset of the parameters are used along with some heuristic to estimate the load. Previous studies have shown that the choice of a load index has considerable effect on the performance of load balancing and that simple load indices such as the number of ready processes are particularly effective [120, 64].

Another interesting scheme, recently proposed by Harchol-Balter and Downey [77], uses process lifetime distributions (hence assuming no *a priori* information about processes) to drive a load balancing operation. Although targeted at UNIX processes, the scheme might be applicable to processes of applications running in multicomputers.

Information Exchange. The information exchange rule specifies how to collect and maintain the workload information of processors necessary for making load balancing decisions. Ideally, a processor should keep a record of the most up-to-date workload information of others. Practically, however, this is not feasible in distributed memory message-passing machines because interprocessor communication necessary for the collection of workload information introduces non-negligible delays. This communication overhead prohibits processors from exchanging their workload information frequently. Hence, a good information exchange rule should strike a balance between incurring a low cost for the collection of systemwide load information and maintaining an accurate view of the system state. This tradeoff is captured in the following three information exchange rules:

- On-demand—Processors collect others' workload information whenever a load balancing operation is about to begin or be initiated [182, 221].
- Periodical—Processors periodically report their workload information to others, regardless of whether the information is useful to others or not [147, 212].
- On-state-change—Processors disseminate their workload information whenever their state changes by a certain degree [172, 191, 217].

The on-demand information exchange rule minimizes the number of communication messages but postpones the collection of systemwide load information till the time when a load balancing operation is to be initiated. A typical example is the bidding algorithm, in which a processor in need of load balancing calls for bids from others to determine the best partners to perform load balancing with [182, 221]. Its main disadvantage is that it results in an extra delay for load balancing operations. Conversely, the periodic rule allows processors in need of a balancing operation to initiate the operation based on the maintained workload information without any delay. The periodic rule is mostly used with periodic initiation policies [147, 213]. The problem with the periodic rule is how to set the interval for information exchange. A short interval would incur heavy communication overhead, while a long interval would sacrifice the accuracy of the workload information used in load balancing decision-making. The on-state-changing rule is a compromise of the on-demand and periodic rules.

The information exchange rules discussed above are distributed rules because all processors maintain the workload information of others by themselves. Based on this information, processors can also make load balancing decisions individually. Maintaining a global view of the system state in parallel computers based on direct networks is implemented using collective communication operations. Since the overhead of collective operations often increases linearly with the system size, global information exchange rules are impractical in large systems. A more practical approach is *local information exchange*, which restricts the workload information exchanges to a local sphere of processors. Load balancing operations are also performed within the domain.

An alternative to distributed approaches is a centralized rule, in which a dedicated processor collects and maintains the system's workload information [127, 25, 176]. Usually, this dedicated processor will also take the responsibility of making load balancing decisions and guide other individual processors to adjust their workloads accordingly during the load balancing procedure. Centralized approaches can yield good performance in small-scale systems [42, 144]. In systems with hundreds or thousands of processors, however, the dedicated processor is prone to be a communication bottleneck. A remedy for the bottleneck is hierarchical (or semi-distributed) approaches which try to combine the advantages of both centralized and fully distributed approaches [4, 3, 62, 71, 111, 203]. An example is a two-level policy proposed by Ahmad *et al.* [4, 3]. At the first level, the load is balanced among different spheres of the system. At the second level, load balancing operations are carried out within individual spheres where the scheduler of each sphere acts as a centralized controller for its own sphere.

In addition to current workload information, feedback information from previous decisions made may also be used for making new load balancing decisions [139, 140, 181]. There are also algorithms that randomly distribute the workload at run-time without relying on any workload information [103, 34].

Initiation Rule. An initiation rule dictates when to initiate a load balancing operation. The execution of a balancing operation incurs non-negligible overhead; its invocation decision must weigh its overhead cost against its expected performance benefit. An initiation policy is thus needed to determine whether a balancing operation will be profitable. An optimal invocation policy is desirable but impractical as its derivation could be complicated. In fact, the load indices are just an estimate of the actual workloads and the workload information they represent may be out of date due to communication delays and infrequent collections. Instead, primarily heuristic initiation policies are used in practice.

Generally, load balancing operations can be initiated either by an overloaded processor (*sender-initiated*) [126] or an underloaded processor (*receiver-initiated*) [146], or periodically at run-time [147]. The sender and the receiver initiation rules need to distinguish between anomalous states and normal states of a processor. A common policy is to devise an upper threshold for overloaded states and a lower threshold for underloaded states. Eager *et al.* experimented with sender-initiated algorithms that are based on the cpu queue length as a measure, and found the optimal threshold to be not very sensitive to system load [57]. They also compared the sender-initiated algorithm with the receiver-initiated algorithm, both using the same load index, and concluded that the sender-initiated algorithm outperforms the receiver-initiated algorithm in lightly loaded systems, and vice versa in heavily loaded systems [56]. Willebeek-LeMair and Reeves concluded that the receiver-initiated algorithm is a good choice for a broad range of systems supporting a large variety of applications [203].

To take advantage of both initiation policies, symmetrical initiation policies were proposed [43, 175]. They switch between sender and receiver initiation policies at run-time according to the system load state. Since they rely on setting of appropriate upper and lower thresholds, their switch mechanism was very complicated in implementation. A more practical policy is to define overloaded and underloaded states as relative measures. Under this policy, a processor initiates a balancing operation when its load rises or drops by more than a certain percentage since the last operation. This simple rule was successfully implemented in various branch-and-bound computations [131, 191, 217]. An alternative is to define the state of a processor relative to its directly connected neighbors [201]. If its workload is highest among its neighbors, it is overleaded; if its workload is lowest, it is light-loaded.

Periodic initiation policies usually force all processors to participate in load balancing at run-time for the purpose of achieving a global balanced state. We refer to such a load balancing operation as *remapping*. Periodic remapping is a common practice in multiphase data parallel computations [147, 212].

Load Balancing Operation. A load balancing operation is defined by three rules: *location rule, distribution rule* and *selection rule.*

The location rule determines the partners of the balancing operation, *i.e.*, the processors to involve in the balancing operation. We refer to the set of processors that will participate in the operation with respect to some processor as the processor's *balancing domain.* The distribution rule determines how to redistribute workload among processors in the balancing domain. The selection rule selects the most suitable processes for transfer among processors to realize the distribution decision.

By the selection rule, a load balancing operation can be performed either non-preemptively or preemptively. A non-preemptive rule always selects newly created processes, while a preemptive rule may select a running process if needed. Migration of a process preemptively has to first suspend the process and then resume it remotely. The process state needs to be transferred, which is generally more costly than a non-preemptive transfer [115]. In [115], it was shown that non-preemptive transfer is preferred, but preemptive transfer can perform significantly better than non-preemptive transfer in certain cases.

In addition to the transfer overhead, the selection rule also needs to take into account the extra communication overhead that is incurred in the subsequent computation due to process migration. For example, the splitting of tightly coupled processes will generate high communication requirements in the future and consequently may outweigh the benefit of load balancing. In principle, a selection rule should break only loosely coupled processes. Details of the selection rule will be discussed in Chapters 8 and 9 in the context of data parallel applications and branch-and-bound optimizations.

The location and distribution rules together make load balancing decisions. The balancing domain can be characterized as global or local. A global domain allows the balancing operation invoker to find its transfer partners across the whole system, while a local domain restricts the balancing operation to be performed within the set of nearest neighbors. The global and local balancing operations rely on global and local information exchange rules, respectively. We refer to the dynamic load balancing algorithms using local information exchange and local location rules as *nearest-neighbor* algorithms. Nearest-neighbor algorithms are naturally iterative in the sense that they transfer processes successively—that is, from one processor to a neighboring processor at a time—each step according to a local decision made by the sending processor. They are thus also referred to as *iterative* load balancing algorithms [213].

By contrast, dynamic load balancing algorithms that operate on the global domain and are based on global information exchange rules are referred to as *direct* algorithms. A processor executing a direct algorithm would decide on the final destination directly for the processes to be migrated. Suppose there is a heavily loaded processor that wishes to give away a part of its workload to some lightly loaded processor. Using a nearest-neighbor algorithm, this heavily loaded processor (the sender) and all subsequent senders along the way need only to determine the direction of the receiver, rather than to know which processor is the final destination as in direct strategies. Notice that balancing domains with variable sizes and shapes, which are referred to as buddy sets in [172], are possible. Since processors in such a domain may not be directly connected, a load balancing algorithm applied to the domain is still treated as a direct method.

Direct methods, because of their need to match senders and receivers of workloads efficiently, are most appropriate for systems equipped with a broadcast mechanism or a centralized monitor [57, 127, 144, 146, 182]. On the other hand, iterative methods have a less stringent requirement on the spread of local load information around the system than their direct counterparts; this is due to the fact that they migrate processes only to a nearest neighbor in each step. They are therefore suitable for situations in which the locality of communication needs to be maintained. Moreover, iterative algorithms are more effective in multicomputers that are based on a direct network. They are also flexible in allowing the user to control the migrations to achieve a desired degree of balancing, from the weakest degree of load sharing to the strongest degree of global balancing. Since the workload information of a processor is spread out in an iterative fashion, more information can be taken into account in making load balancing decisions by increasing the number of iterative steps. Hence, the number of iterative steps determines the degree of balance that can be achieved. Because of these interesting and practically desirable properties, we pursue after nearest-neighbor methods for the load balancing problem in multicomputers in this work.

Note that nearest-neighbor load balancing algorithms are attractive in communication networks with store-and-forward routing strategies because the communication cost in transferring a message between processors is proportional to its transmission distance. Even in communication networks with pipelined routing strategies (*e.g.*, wormhole [145] and virtual cut-through routing [105]), where the communication cost in transferring a message is much less sensitive to its transmit distance, nearest-neighbor algorithms are still prominent and of practical value because global load balancing algorithms tend to generate a fair amount of communications. In [23], Bokhari showed that global load balancing algorithms on a small fraction of processors can quickly saturate the network, and link contention could turn out to be a serious problem. In [119], Kumar *et al.* compared a nearest-neighbor algorithm with four different global algorithms in the context of the Satisfiability problem and showed that the nearest-neighbor algorithm consistently outperformed the others on a second-generation NCUBE with up to 1024 processors.

1.3 Roadmap for the Book

Combining different approaches that deal with the various issues just discussed yields a large space of dynamic load balancing methods. Our work here represents one case in point. The main distinguishing features of our method are in its load balancing decision-making. The load measurement, initiation, and selection rules are largely application-dependent. Specifically, a nearest-neighbor load balancing algorithm is used, which confines the information exchange rule, and the location and distribution rules of the load balancing operation to a local domain consisting of a processor's direct neighbors. Chapters 3 through 5 are dedicated to the development of two such algorithms, the generalized dimension exchange (GDE) method and the diffusion method. Obviously, the interconnection structure of such a neighborhood has a definite bearing on the characteristics and performance of the nearest-neighboring algorithm in question. When applied to different interconnection structures, these algorithms may require the use of different parameters for their operation so that the best load balancing performance can be achieved. Our analyses provide the optimal parameters to use for a number of popular structures.

To give a flavor of what is involved in the process, Figure 1.2 shows an example of a load balancing scenario involving a 2×3 mesh. The load balancing operation used in this example is based on the GDE method. As will be discussed in greater detail in Chapters 3 and 4, the optimal parameter setting of GDE for this particular mesh is that at every step the load balancing operation would try to "equalize" the workload between two neighbors.[1] The load balancing operation is iterative, comprising a number of steps in which pairs of directly connected nodes execute a load balancing operation. For the purpose of global balancing, all processors need to be involved in load balancing operations. To avoid communication conflicts between pairwise balancing operations, the links of the mesh are labeled with numbers (in parentheses) that enforce an execution order on the pairwise operations.

Figure 1.2(a) represents the load situation of the system at some point in time. A load measurement rule (label **LM** in the figure) is needed to translate the various workloads shown into load indices, as shown in Figure 1.2(b). Based on these indices, an initiation rule then decides whether a load balancing operation is necessary or not. In general, both of these rules are largely application-dependent. In Chapter 8, we consider several data-parallel applications where the computation progresses in phases. A new phase would not begin until the previous phase has completed. This is a "static workload" situation, which will be discussed in full in Chapter 8. The example here can be viewed as what happens between two phases.

[1]The equalization rule here is an approximation to the optimal load division formula to be presented in subsequent chapters.

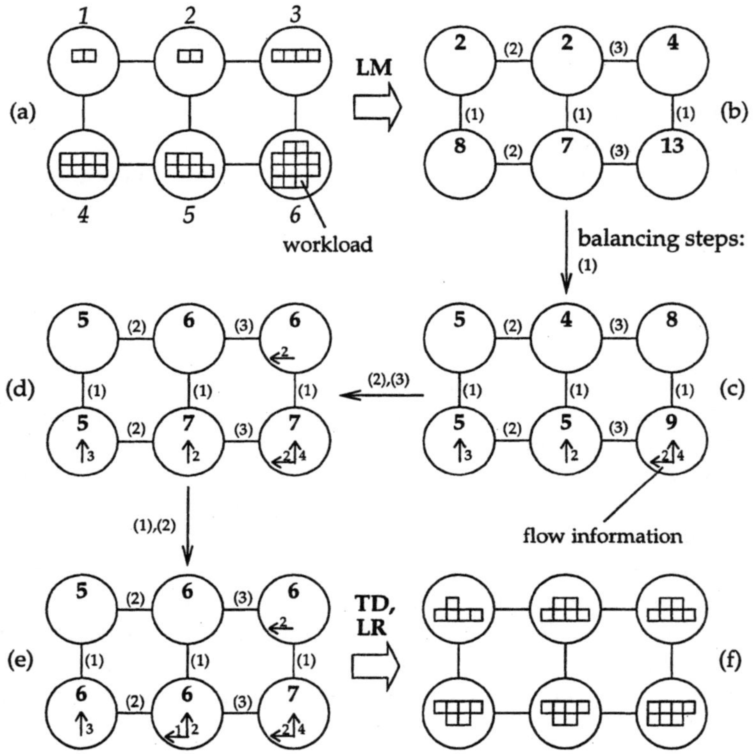

Figure 1.2: An illustration of load balancing algorithms

Figure 1.2(b)–(f) then show the actual operation of the GDE algorithm. For example, from Figure 1.2(a) to the next, all links labeled "(1)" are considered, and the result is that the load indices of each pair of neighbors thus involved are equalized (differ by at most one). For instance, the load indices of nodes 2 and 5 change from (2,7) to (4,5). The amount of load that flows from one node to another is recorded (*e.g.*, a flow of 2 from node 5 to node 2). Then, after several more steps, the overall workload reaches a balanced state. Such a state is detected by a termination detection algorithm (label **TD** in the figure). In Chapter 7, we present such an algorithm which is optimal in terms of efficiency and is fully distributed. Because of the distributed nature of the algorithm, global load difference is not detected. In Figure 1.2(e), which is the balanced state, we see that there is a load difference of 2 between node 1 and node 6. Such differences should not become a serious problem as a perfect load balance is generally not necessary in practice. On the other hand, one can choose finer load indices in order to avoid this problem. Chapter 7 presents the details of how this algorithm is combined with the GDE algorithm in balancing real applications.

Note that in the above only load indices are exchanged and equalized, not the actual workloads. The next and final step (label **LR** in the figure) of the load balancing operation is to redistribute the workload according to the flow information that has been recorded during the preceding operations. The result is shown in Figure 1.2(f).

From the example, it can be seen that the GDE algorithm, which is typical of nearest-neighbor algorithms, possesses the desirable properties of a practical algorithm: it is simple, fully distributed in that it uses only local information for its operation, symmetric, and fast. The last is proven theoretically and through simulation in Chapter 4, and by practical applications in Chapter 8. The algorithm also preserves communication locality. The other algorithm we study in Chapter 6, the diffusion method, shares most of these properties. In Chapter 7, we compare these two algorithms in terms of their performance in various situations.

Nearest-neighbor load balancing algorithms do not always aim for global balanced states. There are situations where the algorithms just need to assure that no idle processors coexist with heavily loaded processors during the execution of a program. In Chapter 9, we apply the GDE and the diffusion algorithms to achieve such a load sharing effect in distributed combinatorial optimizations.

1.4 Models and Performance Metrics

The synopsis just presented is an overview of what is more complicated. The design and analysis of dynamic load balancing algorithms is a complex process because the performance of these algorithms is affected not only by their constituent components, but also by the programs' behaviors and parallel computers' characteristics. This section presents some workload and machine models and defines two major performance metrics. These will serve as the basis for our analyses in subsequent chapters.

1.4.1 The Models

Consider a parallel program running on a parallel computer. The parallel computer is assumed to be composed of N homogeneous processors, labeled from 1 through N. Processors are interconnected by a direct communication network. Processors communicate through message passing. The communication channels are assumed to be full-duplex so that a pair of directly connected processors can send/receive messages simultaneously to/from each other. In addition, we assume that the operations of sending and receiving messages through a channel can take place instantaneously.

The parallel computation comprises a large number of processes, which are the basic units of workload. Processes may be dynamically generated, consumed, and migrated for load balancing as the computation proceeds. We distinguish between the computational operation and the balancing operation. At any time, a processor can perform a computational operation, a balancing operation, or both simultaneously. The concurrent execution of these two operations is possible when processors are capable of multiprogramming or multithreading, or the balancing operation is done in the background by special coprocessors. The total workload of the processors can be either fixed or varying with time during the load balancing operation, which we refer to as the *static* and the *dynamic* workload models, respectively. The simple example shown in the last section is one that assumes a static workload model. The static workload model is valid in situations where the user computation is temporarily suspended for global load balancing (remapping) and resumed afterward. This kind of load balancing has a place in many time-varying data-parallel computations [41, 40, 147, 149]. This dynamic workload model is valid in situations where some processors are performing balancing operations, while the others are performing computational operations. The situation is common in parallel tree-structured computations, such as combinatorial optimizations.

To simplify the theoretical analysis, we further assume that processes are independent, and the total number of processes in a computation is large enough that the workload of a processor is infinitely divisible. These assumptions are for the convenience of the theoretical analyses. The "integer versions" may be more applicable in practice, which can be easily derived from the original versions that are based on infinitely divisible workloads. Processes in tree-structured computations are usually independent or loosely coupled. For example, in game-tree searching, processes searching different branches may need to communicate their final results. There are some other applications, like the N-queens problem and OR-parallel execution of logic programs, where processes are totally independent if all solutions are sought. In data-parallel computations, the model of independent processes can be assumed when the overall computation time of a process in a phase is dominated by its execution time. Even when the communication cost is non-negligible, this assumption can still hold if the balancing operation at run-time preserves the original inter-processor communication relationships. The effectiveness of the model will be demonstrated in data parallel applications in Chapters 8 and 9.

Let t be a time variable, representing global real time. We quantify the workload of a processor i at time t by w_i^t in terms of the number of residing processes. We use integer time to simplify the presentation. The results can be readily expanded to continuous time. Let ϕ_i^{t+1} denote the amount of workload generated or finished between time t and $t+1$. Let $\mathcal{I}(t)$ denote the set of processors performing balancing operations at time t. Then, the change of workload of a processor at time t can be modeled by the following equation in the static workload model

$$w_i^{t+1} = \begin{cases} balance_{j \in \mathcal{A}(i)}(w_i^t,\, w_j^t) & \text{if } i \in \mathcal{I}(t); \\ w_i^t + \phi_i^{t+1} & \text{otherwise} \end{cases} \tag{1.1}$$

and the following equation in the dynamic workload model

$$w_i^{t+1} = \begin{cases} balance_{j \in \mathcal{A}(i)}(w_i^t,\, w_j^t) + \phi_i^{t+1} & \text{if } i \in \mathcal{I}(i); \\ w_i^t + \phi_i^{t+1} & \text{otherwise} \end{cases} \tag{1.2}$$

where $balance()$ is a load balancing operator and $\mathcal{A}(i)$ is a set of processors that are within the load balancing domain of processor i.

This model is generic because the operator $balance()$, the balancing domain $\mathcal{A}()$ of a processor, and the set of processors in load balancing at a certain time t, $\mathcal{I}(t)$, are left unspecified. The operator $balance()$ and the balance domain $\mathcal{A}()$ are set by load balancing operations; the set $\mathcal{I}(t)$ is determined by the initiation rule of the load balancing algorithm. The choice of $\mathcal{I}(t)$ is independent of the load balancing algorithm in that any initiation policy can be used in conjunction with any load balancing operation in implementation. Recall from Section 1.2 that since a load balancing operation incurs non-negligible overheads, different applications may require different invocation policies for a better tradeoff between performance benefits and overheads. For the purpose of global load balancing, all processors need to perform load balancing operations for a short time. That is, $\mathcal{I}(t) = \{1, 2, \ldots, N\}$ for $t \geq t_0$, where t_0 is the instance when the global system state satisfies certain conditions such as those set in [147]. By contrast, load sharing allows processors to invoke a load balancing operation asynchronously at any time according to their own local workload distribution. We thus make a distinction between *synchronous* and *asynchronous* implementations of load balancing operations according to their initiation policies. Figure 1.3 presents one example of these two implementation models in a system of five processors. The dots and triangles represent the computational operations and the load balancing operations, respectively. Chapter 8 considers several practical applications whose computation falls into the category of synchronous implementations, and Chapter 9 presents load distribution strategies for combinatorial optimization problems, which operate in asynchronous fashion.

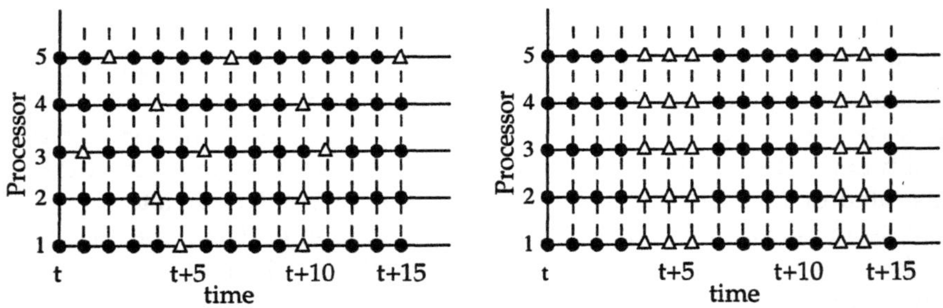

(a) Asynchronous implementation (b) Synchronous implementation

Figure 1.3: An illustration of generic models of load balancing

Note that the load balancing problem in the static workload model resembles another distributed computing problem, the consensus problem, in certain respects. The consensus problem requires the processors of a system to reach an agreement on a common scalar value, such as the average, the maximum, or the minimum, based on their own values [26, 192]. The load balancing problem, however, requires the processors not only to reach a consensus on their average load, but also to adjust their workloads automatically and efficiently. That is, as the load balancing procedure iterates through its course of execution, every node should somehow be instructed to give/take a certain amount of workload to/from each of its nearest neighbors. In practical implementations, these "give/take" decisions could be accumulated until the end of the load balancing procedure, at which time the actual workload migration would then take place. This has been illustrated in the simple example presented in the last section. Examples of how this is done in real implementations will be provided in Chapter 8.

The load balancing problem differs from another distribution problem, the token distribution problem. In the token distribution problem, there is one more assumption about process transfers [98, 156, 158]. That is, a message carries at most one process (token), and the transfer of a process costs one time unit. This assumption confines the problem to the theoretical area because the transfer of larger messages is preferred in practice. In the load balancing problem, we do not impose such a restriction, and that the actual process migrations take place only after the balancing of load indices is complete.

1.4.2 Performance Metrics

In the design and analysis of iterative load balancing algorithms, there are two major performance metrics: *stability* and *efficiency*. The stability measures the ability of an algorithm to coerce any initial workload distribution into an equilibrium state—*i.e.*, the global uniform distribution state in the static workload model and the ability to bound the variance of processors' workloads after performing one or more load balancing operations in the dynamic workload model. The efficiency reflects the time required to either reduce the variance or arrive at the equilibrium state.

Assume $t = 0$ when processors invoke a synchronous or an asynchronous load balancing procedure. Denote the overall workload distribution at certain time t by a vector $\mathbf{W}^t = (w_1^t, w_2^t, \cdots, w_N^t)$. Denote its corresponding equilibrium state by a vector $\overline{\mathbf{W}}^t = (\overline{w}^t, \overline{w}^t, \cdots, \overline{w}^t)$, where $\overline{w}^t = \sum_{i=1}^{N} w_i^t / N$. The workload variance, denoted by ν^t, is defined as the deviation of $\mathbf{W}^t$ from $\overline{\mathbf{W}}^t$; that is,

$$\nu^t = ||\mathbf{W}^t - \overline{\mathbf{W}}^t||^2 = \sum_{i=1}^{N} (w_i^t - \overline{w}^t)^2.$$

Both performance metrics and their relationships were discussed by Stankovic [181] and by Casavant and Kuhl [31, 33] in a more general framework of distributed scheduling. It was shown that the efficiency is an important first-order metric of dynamic scheduling behaviors. It was also suggested that the treatment of the stability should be quite specific to the algorithm and the system environment under consideration and some amount of instability may actually improve efficiency. Load balancing algorithms discussed in this work will be evaluated in terms of these two measures.

2

A SURVEY OF NEAREST-NEIGHBOR LOAD BALANCING ALGORITHMS

Distant water cannot put out a fire close at hand.
—CHINESE PROVERB

Nearest-neighbor load balancing algorithms have emerged as one of the most important techniques for parallel computers based on direct networks. This chapter classifies the nearest-neighbor algorithms by their distribution rules and surveys related works in the literature.

2.1 Classification of Load Balancing Algorithms

Recall from Section 1.2 that every load balancing algorithm has to resolve the issues of workload evaluation, workload information exchange, load balancing operations, and initiation of an operation. Combining different answers to these issues yields a large space of possible designs of load balancing algorithms with widely varying characteristics.

In the literature, there are taxonomies and surveys of load balancing algorithms on LAN-based distributed computing systems [11, 32, 199]. Their classifications are incomplete in the sense they have left out direct-network-based parallel computers. The point-to-point topologies of the communication network render more flexibility in responding to the issues of information exchange, partner location, and workload distributions. The categorization of nearest-neighbor (iterative) and global (direct) algorithms complements these existing taxonomies.

Nearest-neighbor load balancing methods rely on successive approximations to a global optimal workload distribution, and hence at each operation, need only to concern with the direction of workload migration. Some methods would select a single direction (hence one nearest neighbor) while others would consider all directions (hence all the nearest neighbors). These various methods can be further categorized into *deterministic* and *stochastic* methods according to the distribution rule of load balancing operations. Deterministic methods proceed according to certain predefined distribution rules. Which neighbor to transfer extra workload to and how much to transfer depend on certain parameters of these rules such as the states of the nearest-neighbor processors. With stochastic iterative methods, on the other hand, workloads are redistributed in some randomized fashion, subject to the objective of the load balancing.

There are three classes of deterministic methods: *diffusion, dimension exchange,* and the *gradient model.* The diffusion and the dimension exchange methods are closely related; they both examine all the direct neighbors in every load balancing operation. With the diffusion method, a processor balances its workload with all its neighbors. It may "diffuse" fractions of its workload to one or more of its neighbors while simultaneously requesting some workloads from its other neighbors at each operation. By exchanging an appropriate amount of workload with the neighbors, the processor strives to enter a more balanced situation. With the dimension exchange method, a processor goes around the table, balancing workload with its neighbors one at a time; after an operation with a neighbor, it communicates its new workload information to the next neighbor for another operation, and so on. With gradient-based methods, workloads are restricted to being transferred along the direction of the most lightly loaded processor. Load balancing operations with these methods can be successively performed for the purpose of global load balancing.

Stochastic load balancing methods throw dices along the way in an attempt to drive the system into equilibrium state with high probability. The simplest method is *randomized allocation* in which any newly created process is transferred to a (usually neighboring) processor which is randomly selected. This latter processor, upon receiving the process and finding itself to be quite occupied already, can transfer the process to yet another randomly selected processor. Another approach is to use *physical optimization* algorithms that are based on analogies with physical systems. Physical optimization algorithms map the load balancing problem onto some physical systems, and then solve the problem using simulation or techniques from theoretical or experimental physics [67]. Physical optimization algorithms offer a little bit more variety in the control of the randomness in the redistribution of processes. This control mechanism makes the process of load balancing less susceptible to being trapped in local optima and therefore superior to other randomized approaches which could produce locally optimal but not globally optimal results.

Figure 1 summarizes our classification of nearest-neighbor dynamic load balancing strategies in multicomputers.

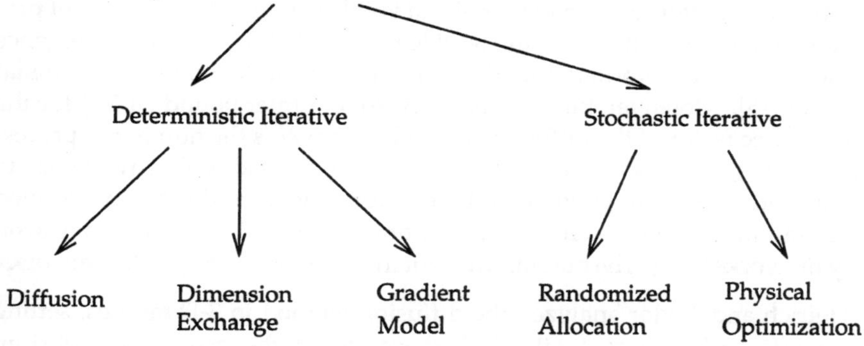

Figure 2.1: A classification of load balancing algorithms

2.2 Deterministic Algorithms

2.2.1 The Diffusion Method

The diffusion method has been around in parallel computing circles for more than a decade. Early experiments with the method can be found in MuNet [74], CHoPP [185], and Roscoe [29]. Casavant and Kuhl gave a formal description of this method using a state transition model—communicating finite automata [33]. They also examined the effects of varying the degree of global workload information on the efficiency of the method and concluded that load balancing based on accurate information about a small subset of the system may be more efficient than using inaccurate information about the whole system [30]. Under the synchronous assumption that a processor would not proceed into the next iteration until all the workload transfers of the current iteration have completed, Cybenko modeled the diffusion method using linear system theories [47]. Specifically, let $W^t = (w_1^t, w_2^t, \ldots, w_n^t)$ denote at time t the workload distribution of the n nodes of the network—*i.e.*, w_i^t is the workload of processor i at time t; and let $\mathcal{A}(i)$ be the set of direct neighbors of processor i. Then the change of workload in processor i from time t to $t+1$ is modeled as

$$w_i^{t+1} = w_i^t + \sum_{j \in \mathcal{A}(i)} \alpha_{i,j}(w_j^t - w_i^t) + \phi_i^{t+1} \qquad 1 \le i \le N \tag{2.1}$$

where $0 < \alpha_{i,j} < 1$ is called the diffusion parameter of i and j, which determines the amount of workload to be exchanged between the two processors; ϕ_i^{t+1} denotes the amounts of workload change from time t to $t+1$. This equation corresponds to one iteration step of the diffusion process. Cybenko showed that the diffusion method is convergent given any initial workload distribution in the static workload model and is able to bound the variance of processors' workload in the dynamic workload model [47]. Similar convergence results in the static workload model were obtained independently by Boillat *et al.* [17, 18]. Moreover, Boillat *et al.* derived an upper bound $O(N^2)$ for the convergence factor of the diffusion method, where N is the number of processors. That is, load balancing with the diffusion method will convergence to an equilibrium state in polynomial time. Subramanian and Scherson derived lower and upper bounds on the running time of the diffusion method in arbitrary networks [184]. The bounds are tight in some common specific networks.

Heirich and Taylor analyzed the diffusion method in 3-D meshes, setting $\alpha_{i,j} = 1/(1+6\beta)$, where β is the desired accuracy in the resulting equilibrium [81]. For the purpose of a global uniform state, β is set to one. They derived the number of operations required to reduce the load imbalance by a factor β. Hong *et al.* [86] and Qiang and Yang [160] also studied the stability of the diffusion method in hypercubes, generalized hypercues, tori, and rings using probabilistic theory. In their work, the diffusion parameters are set as $\alpha_{ij} = 1/(|\mathcal{A}(i)|+1)$ for all i. This choice of the diffusion parameters for the hypercube structure happens to be the optimal choice, in terms of the convergence rate, as proved by Cybenko [47]. Xu and Lau derived the optimal diffusion parameters for the mesh, the torus and the k-ary n-cube networks using circulant matrix theory [211, 214].

On the asynchronous track, the diffusion method was studied theoretically by Bertsekas and Tsitsiklis [16]. In an asynchronous environment, processes at a local processor do not have to wait at predetermined points for predetermined messages from other processors. Because of communication delays, the information maintained in a processor concerning its neighbors' workload could be outdated. Moreover, workloads that are still in transit must be accounted for in the modeling. This makes the theoretical study of the diffusion method in asynchronous systems a difficult one. Using linear system theory, Bertsekas and Tsitsiklis showed that the asynchronous version of the diffusion method is convergent provided that the communication delays are bounded. The result was extended by Song to the case of the total workload being too small to be divided infinitely [180]. Lüling and Monien considered a randomized version of the diffusion method in which a processor in need of load balancing activates an operation among a number of randomly chosen neighbors and showed that the algorithm will keep the workload difference between any two processors bounded [131]. However, the problem of determining its convergence rate or the optimal diffusion parameters remains unsolved.

The theoretical study of the diffusion method revealed its sound mathematical foundation. On the practical side, its effectiveness was demonstrated in applications with various characteristics. Willebeek-LeMair and Reeves [201, 202, 203] and Monien and his associates [130, 191, 217] experimented with the method in the context of distributed computation of branch-and-bound algorithms. Synchronous diffusion method requires a synchronization phase prior to load balancing in order to shift all the processors into load balancing mode for performing local balancing simultaneously. This is a time consuming procedure especially in networks with large diameters. The implementation by Willebeek-LeMair and Reeves [201] reduces this cost by allowing some processors to bypass the load balancing. A processor would participate in the load balancing only when its workload exceeds the average of its direct neighbors including itself by a certain threshold. Experimental results showed that such an asynchronous implementation when applied to the distributed computation of branch-and-bound algorithms performs significantly better especially in heavily loaded situations. Willebeek-LeMair and Reeves also distinguished between sender-initiated and receiver-initiated diffusion methods in their implementations and showed that the latter is better than the former in various respects [203]. Lüling and Monien [130] implemented a similar asynchronous diffusion method and included an extra control mechanism for tuning the threshold using feedbacks from previous load balancing decisions. This adaptive bit was proved to be useful especially for networks with large diameters. In [217], Xu *et al.* implemented a symmetrically-initiated diffusion method and obtained a speedup of 148.5 in the solution of set partition problems on a 256-processor Parsytec GCel.

In branch-and-bound applications, processes are independent of one another, which makes studies of the diffusion method being applied to these applications on multicomputers tractable. For other applications comprising dependent processes, the diffusion method is still effective because it maintains communication locality. Taylor *et al.* [81, 188, 200] applied the diffusion method to two irregular computational fluid dynamics applications: plasma reactor simulations and ion thruster simulations. The applications are parallelized using domain-decomposition approaches. Hence, processes of adjacent regions need to exchange boundary information with each other. For these two simulations, they obtained 88% and 25% improvement, respectively, on a 256-processor Intel Paragon and a 256-processor Cray T3D.

The diffusion method is based on a communication model in which a processor can communicate with all its neighbors simultaneously. This works best therefore on hardware that supports true parallel communications over the set of links of a processor. But even when this is possible, true parallelism is difficult to have as the actions of the local process that carries out the exchanges over the links must execute its steps sequentially. When based instead on a model of serialized communications, the diffusion method, which is patterned after the Jacobi fashion of relaxation, becomes less effective. The alternative is one that is patterned after the Gauss-Seidel fashion of relaxation—the dimension exchange method.

2.2.2 The Dimension Exchange Method

The dimension exchange (DE) method was initially intensively studied in hypercube-structured multicomputers [165, 171]. In an n-dimensional hypercube, each processor compares and equalizes its workload with those of its neighbors one by one. A "sweep" of the iterative process corresponds to going through all the dimensions of the hypercube once. Since the set of neighbors correspond exactly to the dimensions of the hypercube, the processor would have compared and exchanged load with every one of its neighbors after one sweep. Cybenko proved that regardless of the order of stepping through the dimensions, this simple load balancing method yields after one sweep a uniform distribution from any initial workload distribution [47]. He also revealed the superiority of the DE method to the diffusion method on hypercubes in that the former can yield a smaller variance of the workload distribution in dynamic workload models. This theoretical result was supported in part by the experiment carried out by Willebeek-LeMair and Reeves [202, 203]. They used the DE method in distributed computations of branch-and-bound algorithms on an iPSC/2. Prior to load balancing, a global synchronization is required so that all processors become geared up for the execution of the load balancing. Even though the DE method needs a global synchronization beforehand, their experiments showed that the speedup of using the DE method over one with no load balancing is better than the speedup of using the diffusion method because the DE method yields a uniform distribution more quickly. The phenomenon that the benefits of a global load balancing may not be outweighed by its overhead was also observed by Willebeek-LeMair and Reeves [203] and by Shu and Wu [176].

The DE method is not limited to hypercube structures. Using edge-coloring of undirected graphs, Hosseini *et al.* analyzed the method as applied to arbitrary structures [91]. With edge-coloring [65], the edges of a given graph are colored with some minimum number of colors such that no two adjoining edges are of the same color. A "dimension" is then defined to be the collection of all edges of the same color. At each iteration, one particular color/dimension is considered, and only processors on edges with this color execute the DE procedure. Since no two adjoining edges have the same color, each processor needs to deal with at most one neighbor at each iteration—this matches perfectly with an underlying communication mechanism that only supports serialized communications. Figure 2.2(a) shows an example of a 4×4 mesh colored with four colors (minimum)—hence four-dimensional. The four numbers in parentheses correspond to the four colors. Suppose the workload distribution at some time instant is as in Figure 2.2(a), where the number inside a processor represents the workload of the processor. Then, after a sweep of the DE procedure, the workload distribution changes to that in Figure 2.2(b). For an arbitrary structure, it is unlikely that the DE method would yield a uniform workload distribution in a single sweep. Nonetheless, Hosseini *et al.* showed that given any arbitrary structure, the DE method converges eventually to a uniform distribution [91]. Hosseini *et al.*'s results were later on extended to include the average response time as a performance measure as well as to cover a generalization of the binary n-cube, called the Hamming graph [128, 129].

In all the works mentioned above, an exchange over an edge of the network will invariably result in equal workloads in the two processors concerned. This "equal splitting" of workload, although happens to be optimal for hypercubes, is found to be non-optimal for some other structures by Xu and Lau [209, 215]. They generalized the DE method using an exchange parameter λ to control the splitting of workload between a pair of directly connected processors. Consider a k-dimensional color structure, such as the one in Figure 2.2(a). If

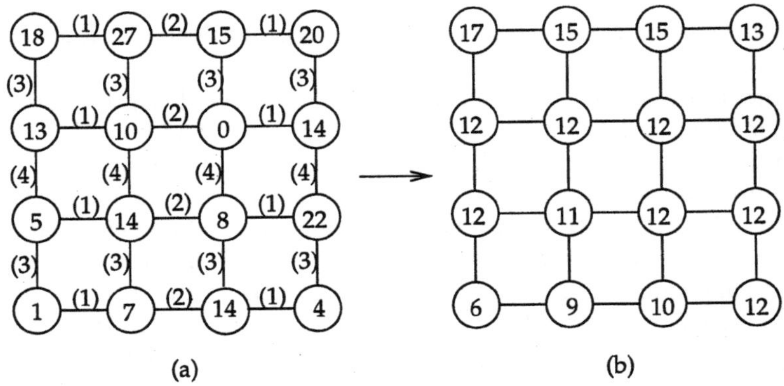

Figure 2.2: Effects of a sweep of the DE algorithm on the workload distribution

processors i and j are direct neighbors, and the edge (i, j) is with color c, $1 \leq c \leq k$, then the change of workload in processor i at time t with $c = (t \bmod k) + 1$ is modeled as

$$w_i^{t+1} = (1 - \lambda)w_i^t + \lambda w_j^t \tag{2.2}$$

where $0 < \lambda < 1$. Note that a single λ is used for the entire network. This generalized DE method reduces to the ordinary dimension exchange method when $\lambda = 1/2$. Xu and Lau found that the optimal exchange parameter for a structure is closely related to its topology and size [209]. For the structures of chain, ring, mesh and torus, they derived the optimal exchange parameters that would lead to the fastest convergence [215]. Boillat presented a version of the dimension exchange method (called Cayley diffusion) in [19], in which he derived the optimal exchange parameters for Cayley graphs.

The DE algorithm discussed above is based on *a priori* edge-coloring of system graphs. The edge-coloring is deterministic in the sense that the colors of incident edges of a node are determined by the system graph. An alternative approach is randomized edge-coloring which colors the edges of the system graph randomly [155]. Ghosh and Muthukrishnan proved that the dimension exchange algorithm based on random matches converges at an asymptotically optimal rate [73]. A match is a set of edges of the same color. A major advantage of the dimension exchange algorithm based on randomized edge-coloring is fault tolerance in the face of link failures.

A variant of the DE method was proposed for the hypercube structure by Hong *et al.* [87], which they called cyclic load balancing. With this method, a processor would equalize its workload with one neighbor of some dimension, return to the execution of the application, and then sometime later equalize its workload again with another neighbor of another dimension, and so on. The length of the time interval between two workload equalizations is adjustable for different desired degrees of balancing. When it is set to zero, the cyclic load balancing method is reduced to the ordinary dimension exchange method.

There have also been studies of the DE method for abstract machine models, such as the work by Plaxton who derived both lower and upper bounds for the time complexity of the method on hypercubes with serialized communications [158]. JáJá and Ryu gave similar results for shuffle-exchange networks, cube-connected cycles and butterfly networks [98], and concluded that the load balancing procedure takes a longer time to complete in these structures than in the hypercube. Both of these studies were targeted at an abstract version of the load balancing problem, the token distribution problem, in which loads are represented by tokens and one message can carry at most one token [156]. These solutions, as well as many others for the problem, however, require some degree of global knowledge (refer to the survey in [9]). A recent algorithm for n-cube networks by Wu and Shu which has a step similar to that of the DE method also relies on global information in order to arrive at a balanced state [208]. Their algorithm is similar to some of the solutions to the token distribution problem.

The DE method in hypercube structures has been thoroughly examined from both theoretical and practical point of view. It outperforms the diffusion method in small- and medium-scale multicomputers in which the cost of the necessary global synchronization phase is not so significant. In large-scale multicomputers, however, its performance is not yet known and requires further work in the future. Hypercubes aside, the DE method on other structures still appears to have been given too little attention—in particular, the problem of calculating the optimal exchange parameters for arbitrary structures.

2.2.3 The Gradient Model

The idea of gradient-based methods is to maintain a contour of the gradients formed by the differences in workloads in the network. Workloads in high points (heavily loaded processors) of the contour would flow naturally, following the gradients, to the lower regions (lightly loaded processors). Two examples of gradient-based methods are the Gradient Model (GM for short) by Lin and Keller [126] and Contracting Within a Neighborhood (CWN for short) by Shu and Kale [175]. The contour in the GM case is called a gradient surface which is in terms of the proximities of heavily or moderately loaded processors to the lightly loaded processors. Since in a distributed environment, maintaining accurate proximity values is very costly, they used an approximation instead, which is called the pressure surface. The pressure surface is simply a collection of propagated pressures of all processors and is maintained dynamically according to the workload distribution. The propagated pressure of a processor i, P_i, is defined as

$$P_i = \begin{cases} 0 & \text{if } P_i \text{ is lightly loaded} \\ 1 + \min\{P_j : P_j \text{ is a neighbor of } P_i\} & \text{otherwise} \end{cases}$$

Figure 2.3 shows an example of a pressure surface which is derived from the workload distribution in Figure 2.2(a). In Figure 2.3, those processors with propagated pressures equal to 0 are lightly loaded; the rest are heavily loaded. Based on the pressure surface, workload in a heavily loaded processor would

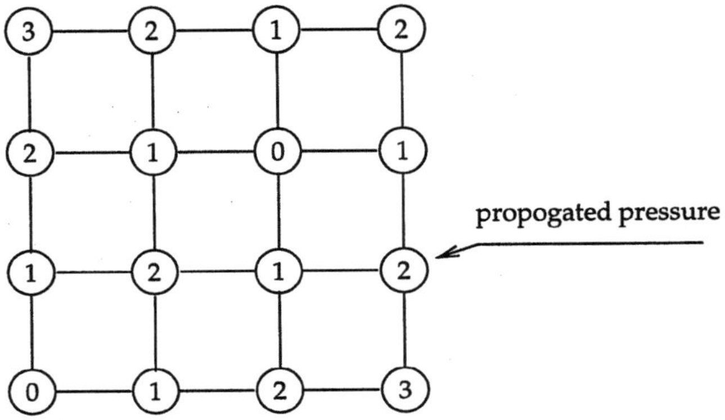

Figure 2.3: An example of the pressure surface defined by the GM algorithm

migrate towards the nearest lightly loaded processor along the steepest gradient. Chowkwanyu and Hwang implemented the GM algorithm in their hybrid load balancer which combined the gradient method with a direct strategy based on the drafting algorithm [43]. Their application of the hybrid load balancer to concurrent Lisp execution on tree and ring structures demonstrated the superiority of the GM algorithm to the drafting algorithm.

In the GM approach, workload migration would only occur between heavily loaded and lightly loaded processors. When there are no lightly loaded processors in the system, no workload migration would take place, or in other words, the algorithm would not try to transfer workload between heavily loaded and *moderately* loaded processors (these moderately loaded processors are also labeled heavily loaded in the GM approach). Therefore, when a large portion of moderately loaded processors suddenly turn lightly loaded, much commotion will result. To remedy, Lüling *et al.* proposed an improved version of the GM algorithm, the Extended Gradient Model (X-GM) [132]. In X-GM, a suction surface is added, which is based on the (estimated) proximities of non-heavily-loaded processors to heavily loaded processors. Then, in addition to workload migration from heavily loaded processors to lightly loaded processors driven by the pressure surface, the suction surface would cause workload migration from heavily loaded processors to nearby local minima which may be moderately loaded processors. Its advantage over the GM algorithm is evident from the results of the simulation experiments carried out by the authors. A related problem of the GM approach is that when there are only a few lightly loaded processors, they may easily get swamped by workloads coming from heavily loaded processors and themselves become heavily loaded. Muniz and Zaluska proposed an Extended Gradient (EG) mechanism that could cure this "overflow" problem [143]. They used a two-phase commit protocol to achieve a more careful placement of newly-created tasks on under-loaded processors. This protocol can also deal with the problem of load information being out-of-date, which happens when messages carrying such information have to travel through many hops.

With the CWN algorithm [175], each processor needs only to maintain the workload indices of its direct neighbors. A processor executing the CWN algorithm would migrate its extra workload (such as a newly created process) to the neighbor with the least workload. A processor that receives the process keeps the process for execution if it is most lightly loaded when compared with all its neighbors; otherwise, it forwards the process to its least loaded neighbor. Thus, a newly created process travels along the steepest load gradient to a local minimum. The analogy is water flowing from the top of a mountain that settles in a nearby basin. To avoid "horizon effect" (water stagnating on a flat surface), the algorithm imposes a minimum distance a process is required to travel. It also imposes a maximum distance a process is allowed to travel in order to cut down on the traveling cost. If we allow these parameters to be tunable at runtime, the algorithm becomes Adaptive Contracting Within a Neighborhood (ACWN for short).

Kale compared ACWN and GM as applied to parallel computations of divide-and-conquer and fibonacci programs through simulation [102], and concluded that ACWN performs better than GM in most cases because of the agility of ACWN in spreading workloads around during load balancing. The same conclusion applies to iterative deepening A* search algorithm which Kale implemented on an iPSC/2. By fixing the values of the minimum and maximum distances a process is allowed to travel at zero and one respectively, Baker and Milner demonstrated on a mesh-connected network of transputers the benefits of CWN over the version with no load balancing [10]. The same restricted version of CWN, coupled with a threshold parameter to classify the states of the processors, has also been used by Su *et al.* in the parallel execution of logic programs [183].

All gradient-based methods can be considered a form of relaxation, in which the single hop migration of workload is a successive approximation towards a global balancing of the system. In the works reviewed above, the issues addressed include which processors to migrate workload to, how far a distance a migrating workload can travel, and of course the correctness (*i.e.*, they indeed can lead to a balanced state), and performance in practical implementations. What seems to be lacking is a more exact characterization and analysis of these algorithms as applied to different structures. For example, the issue of how much to migrate should be but has not been an issue in the above works, which is a very important parameter to consider in the study of the optimality of these and other algorithms based on the gradient idea.

2.3 Stochastic Algorithms

2.3.1 Randomized Allocation

Randomization has long been used as a tool in algorithm design. Stochastic techniques like Monte Carlo and Las Vegas are among the most standard methods for solving certain kinds of problems. The routing chip for the latest generation of transputers (the T9000) [125] has incorporated the randomized routing algorithm by Valiant and Brebner [194]. In randomized load balancing, to migrate some workload, a random choice of a processor is made. There are two issues that need to be resolved: one is whether processes are allowed to be transferred for more than one time, and the other is whether the randomly selected processor is restricted to a nearest neighbor or not. Note that even if a process is allowed to be transferred to a remote processor, the load balancing can still operate in an iterative fashion as it is not necessary that this remote processor be the destination processor for the process.

Eager *et al.* addressed the issue of whether a process should be allowed to be transferred multiple times [56]. They used a parameter, the transfer limit, to control the number of times a process may be transferred. They showed that randomized load balancing algorithms without a transfer limit are unstable in the sense that processors could be devoting all their time to transferring processes and little time to actually executing them. They also demonstrated that setting the transfer limit to one is a satisfactory choice in situations when the system load is high; and it introduces little extra traffic to the system.

Randomized load balancing algorithms with a transfer limit of one randomly assign newly generated processes to processors for execution. To study theoretically the performance of these algorithms, Ben-Asher *et al.* modeled their behavior as the random throwing of a variable number of balls into a fixed number of holes [12]. Each ball is weighted with some value corresponding to the processing requirement of the process modeled by the ball. Under the assumption that the balls' weights are probabilistically distributed with a known expected value as well as minimum and maximum values, they derived an upper bound on the number of balls needed (*i.e.*, number of processes generated at run-time) for the algorithm to achieve optimal or near-optimal load balancing with very high probability.

Lüling *et al.* addressed the issue of whether a process should be migrated only through direct neighbors or not [132]. Algorithms that always pick a random processor among the direct neighbors are called local random algorithms; algorithms that can pick among remote processors are called global random algorithms. They compared local random and global random algorithms through simulation and showed the superiority of global random algorithms. Their global random algorithm was implemented on top of the Chare kernel [102]. Although it was less efficient than the ACWN algorithm of Shu and Kale [175], it performed better than the complicated gradient model in various applications running on an iPSC/2.

Randomized load balancing algorithms, although are rather simple (their analyses are not), can lead to substantial performance improvement over no load balancing [56]. Rabin articulated the benefits of randomization in algorithm design in his classic paper [162], which are yet to be fully seen in future proposals of randomized load balancing algorithms. Ben-Asher *et al.*'s formal analysis of a simple case is an example of theoretical approaches to obtaining a better understanding of the behavior of randomized load balancing algorithms [12]. Similar analyses need to be carried out for other more complicated cases or designs. Examples of using randomized approaches in practical load balancing cases have started to emerge in recent years, such as the work by Chakrabarti *et al.* who successfully applied a randomized strategy to balancing a couple of tree-structured computations (the Gröbner basis problem and the bisection eigenvalue problem) on a CM-5 multiprocessor [34]. The experimental results they obtained are in line with their analysis results that the randomized strategy can lead to parallel running time that is within a constant factor of an inherent lower bound for the application's task graph.

2.3.2 Physical Optimizations

The most common physical optimization algorithm for the load balancing problem is *simulated annealing*. Simulated annealing is a general and powerful technique for combinatorial optimization problems borrowed from crystal annealing in statistical physics [112, 152]. The technique is Monte Carlo in nature, which simulates the random movements of a collection of vibrating atoms in a process of cooling. Atoms are more vibrant at high temperatures than at low temperatures. The objective is to arrive at an optimally low energy configuration of the atoms at some low temperature. At each temperature T, a set of random and permissible proposals of atom configuration are evaluated in terms of the change in energy, δH. A configuration of the atoms is accepted if it represents a decrease in energy (*i.e.*, $\delta H < 0$); otherwise, it is accepted with a conditional probability of $\exp(-\delta H/T)$, which can help to avoid local minima. As the temperature decreases, fewer and fewer increases in energy are accepted and the atoms eventually settle on a low energy configuration that is very close, if not identical, to the optimal. It is conceivable that the slower the annealing process, the more configurations that can be explored at each temperature, and the higher the probability of arriving at an optimal solution at the end.

When applied to load balancing, a configuration corresponds to a state of the system (*i.e.*, global distribution of workload), and the final configuration at some low temperature corresponds to the result—hopefully a balanced state—of the execution of the load balancing procedure. Bollinger and Midkiff applied simulated annealing to static mapping of processes onto processors and improved upon previous results using deterministic methods [24]. Its application to dynamic load balancing was first carried out by researchers at Caltech [69, 205]. Their implementation was a centralized one. During dynamic load balancing, a processor, which has been designated the main balancer, goes through the simulated annealing exercise and arrives at a decision of how the global workload should be redistributed; it then instructs the other processors to implement the decision. This centralized algorithm suffers from a sequential bottleneck due to the main balancer. In fact, simulated annealing, because of its Monte Carlo nature, can be extremely slow, especially in solving a complex problem involving many variables. The current trend is to parallelize the annealing process and execute it on parallel machines [52]. There are even proposals of building parallel machines specifically for simulated annealing, for example, the design by Abramson [1].

To distribute the sequential decision making of simulated annealing among a number of processors so that each processor can offer partial proposals of process redistribution and take part in the evaluation of energy, it is necessary to deal with the problem of "collisions". A collision occurs when the proposed changes made by one processor have conflicts with those made by another processor. Rollback is one technique for solving this problem [68]. With rollback, processors make redistribution decisions in parallel, and then check whether there is any collision. If there is, the processors undo enough of the changes until there is no collision. Fox *et al.* [68] demonstrated this technique in the simulation of fishes and sharks living, moving, breeding, and eating in a two-dimensional ocean (the WaTor problem [51]). However, since it incurred a great deal of overhead in maintaining the history states of the system which were needed for rollbacks, its performance was not satisfactory.

Instead, Williams allowed collisions to occur in his application of the simulated annealing method to the load balancing of unstructured mesh calculations in an NCUBE/10 multicomputer of 16 processors [204]. In his method, collisions occur along boundaries of clusters of mesh nodes. Different clusters during an iteration are handled by different processors, and at the end of each iteration, neighboring processors exchange boundary values to maintain consistency. Note that although allowing collisions to occur did not pose a serious problem in this case, it might lead to incorrect results in other applications. Williams tried various starting temperatures and cooling rates. Despite the possibility of some performance loss due to collisions, the results indicated that with sufficiently slow cooling, the parallel annealing process eventually produced high quality solutions to the load balancing problem. Improvements on the cooling rate will have to rely on successful choices of optimal initial values for the various parameters of the process.

Finally, apart from simulated annealing, two other optimization methods that borrowed ideas from natural sciences have also been adapted to load balancing—genetic algorithms and neural networks. Fox *et al.* have tried out various sequential versions in the context of static load balancing [69, 67, 135]. The performance of parallel versions is still under investigation. Mehra and Wah applied neural networks and AI techniques to automated learning of load balancing strategies and demonstrated their approach can quickly determine the appropriate load balancing parameters [139].

3

THE GDE METHOD

By just exchange one for the other giv'n;
I hold his dear, and mine he cannot miss,
There never was a better bargain driv'n.
—SIR PHILIP SIDNEY

We present in this chapter the generalized dimension exchange (GDE) method for load balancing in multiprocessors. In hypercube-structured multiprocessors, the dimension exchange method works in the way that each processor compares its workload with those of its nearest neighbors one after another. At each of these comparisons, the processor would try to equalize its workload with its neighbor's. To do this systematically, all the processors could follow the order as implied by the dimension indices of the hypercube: equalizing workload with the neighbor along dimension 1, and then along dimension 2, and so on. In arbitrary-structure systems, the dimension can be defined by edge-coloring techniques. With edge-coloring [65], the edges of a given system graph are colored with some minimum number of colors such that no two adjoining edges are of the same color. A "dimension" is then defined to be the collection of all edges of the same color. During each iteration sweep, all colors/dimensions are considered in turn. Since no two adjoining edges have the same color, each node needs to deal with at most one neighbor at each iteration step (each step corresponds to one color; a sweep corresponds to going through all the colors once).

The dimension exchange method is characterized by "equal splitting" of workload between a pair of neighbors at every communication. It has been shown that this simple load balancing method yields a uniform distribution from any given initial workload in a single sweep [47]. For arbitrary networks, it might not be the case. In light of the intuition that nonequal splitting of workload might lead to fewer sweeps necessary for obtaining a uniform distribution in certain networks (think about networks that are not so symmetric), we generalize the dimension exchange method by adding an *exchange parameter* to govern the amount of workload, instead of always half, that is exchanged at every communication. We call this parameterized method the *generalized dimension exchange* (GDE) method [209, 215].

3.1 The GDE Algorithm

Similar to the original dimension exchange method for arbitrary networks [91], the GDE method is based on edge-coloring of the given system graph G. The edges of G are supposed to be colored beforehand with the least number of colors (κ, say), and no two adjoining edges are assigned the same color. We index the colors with integers from 1 to κ, and represent the κ-color graph as G_κ. An edge between vertices i and j with a chromatic index c in G_κ is reresented by a 3-tuple (i, j, c). Let $d(i)$ denote the degree of a node i in G, and $d(G)$ denote the maximum of the degrees of G's nodes. It is known that the minimum number of colors κ is strictly bounded by d, and $d \leq \kappa \leq d+1$ [65]. Figure 3.1 shows examples of colored rings and chains (linear arrays). The integers in parentheses are the assigned chromatic indices.

For a given G_κ, let w_i denote the current local workload of a processor i and λ denote the exchange parameter chosen. Then, the change of w_i in the processor using the GDE method is governed by the following algorithm.

Algorithm: the GDE balancing operator:
    for $(c = 1;\ c \leq \kappa;\ c = c + 1)$ {
        if there exists an edge (i, j) with color c
            $w_i = (1 - \lambda)w_i + \lambda w_j;$
    }

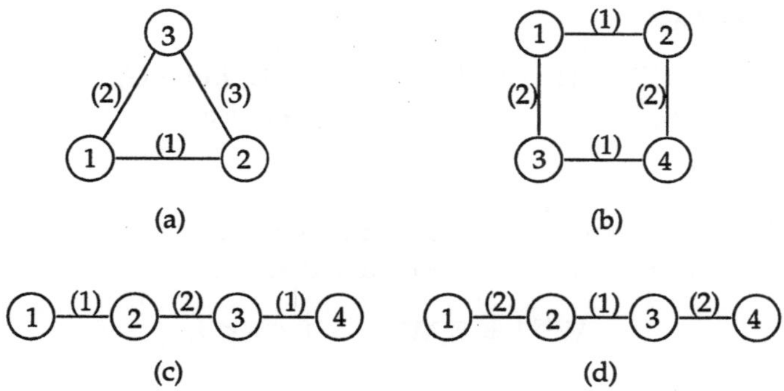

Figure 3.1: Examples of edge-colored graphs

This GDE balancing operator is to be performed in each processor in a fully decentralized manner, and a processor finishes a complete sweep (*i.e.*, one iteration of the while-loop) after κ consecutive exchange operations. As such, the processor interacts with all of its neighbors one at a time in each sweep. In order to guarantee $w_i \geq 0$, the domain of the exchange parameter λ is restricted to [0,1]. By choosing $\lambda = 1/2$, the GDE balancing operation is reduced to a pairwise averaging operation. This special version of the GDE method is referred to as the ADE method.

In the following, we analyze the convergence properties of the GDE algorithm using the matrix iterative approach. The analysis will not only help us understand the dimension exchange policy itself more thoroughly, but also aid in the design of more efficient policies for various structures.

3.2 Convergence Analysis

With the matrix iterative approach, the workload distribution at some time instant is represented by a vector of variables each of which corresponds to the local workload maintained by a processor; and the change to be applied to the distribution according to the balancing policy is represented by a transformation matrix. The whole process of load balancing is then modeled as an iterative process based on the matrix, which is the focus of our analysis.

Let w_i^t $(1 \leq i \leq N)$ denote the local workload of processor i at time t. Then, the workload distribution at time t, denoted by $\mathbf{W}^t$, is a transpose of vector $(w_1^t, w_2^t, \ldots, w_N^t)$. $\mathbf{W}^0$ is the initial workload distribution. Based on the above algorithm, the change of workload in processor i at step t with $c = (t \bmod \kappa)+1$

can be modeled as

$$\begin{array}{ll} w_i^{t+1} = (1-\lambda)w_i^t + \lambda w_j^t & \text{if } \exists_j \ (i,j,c) \in G_\kappa, \\ w_i^{t+1} = w_i^t & \text{otherwise,} \end{array} \tag{3.1}$$

where $0 \leq \lambda \leq 1$.

As a whole, the change of the workload distribution of the entire system at time t with $c = (t \bmod \kappa) + 1$ can be modeled as

$$\mathbf{W}^{t+1} = \mathbf{E}_c \mathbf{W}^t, \qquad 1 \leq c \leq \kappa \tag{3.2}$$

where, for $1 \leq i, j \leq N$ and $i \neq j$, and if $(i,j,c) \in G_\kappa$

$$\begin{array}{lllll} (\mathbf{E}_c)_{i,i} & = & (\mathbf{E}_c)_{j,j} & = & 1-\lambda, \\ (\mathbf{E}_c)_{i,j} & = & (\mathbf{E}_c)_{j,i} & = & \lambda; \end{array}$$

otherwise

$$(\mathbf{E}_c)_{i,i} = 1, \text{ and } (\mathbf{E}_c)_{i,j} = 0.$$

Consequently, the change of the workload distribution of the entire system at time t can be modeled as

$$\mathbf{W}^{t+\kappa} = \mathbf{E}\mathbf{W}^t \tag{3.3}$$

which implies

$$\mathbf{W}^{t\kappa} = \mathbf{E}^t \mathbf{W}^0, \qquad t = 0, 1, 2, \ldots \tag{3.4}$$

where $\mathbf{E} = \mathbf{E}_\kappa \times \mathbf{E}_{\kappa-1} \times \ldots \times \mathbf{E}_1$ is called the *GDE matrix* of the κ-color graph G_κ. Clearly, each element of $\mathbf{E}$ is a polynomial in λ, and by choosing $\lambda = 1/2$, $\mathbf{E}$ reduces to the ADE matrix as given in [91].

With the above formulation, the features of the GDE load balancing method are fully captured by the iterative process governed by $\mathbf{E}$. $\mathbf{E}$ is hence referred to as the characteristic matrix of the dimension exchange algorithm. The stability issue of the algorithm is reduced to the convergence of the sequence $\{\mathbf{E}^t\}$, and the efficiency of the algorithm is reflected by the convergence factor.

We first consider some important properties of the GDE matrix $\mathbf{E}$, which are essential in the ensuing analysis.

Lemma 3.2.1 *Let* $\mathbf{E}$ *be the GDE matrix of* G_κ *of a* κ*-color graph.*

1. *If* $0 \leq \lambda \leq 1$, *then* $\mathbf{E}$ *is nonnegative and doubly stochastic—that is, for all* $1 \leq i, j \leq N$, $(\mathbf{E})_{i,j} \geq 0$, *and* $\sum_{1 \leq j \leq N} (\mathbf{E})_{i,j} = \sum_{1 \leq i \leq N} (\mathbf{E})_{i,j} = 1$.
2. *If* $0 < \lambda < 1$, *then* $\mathbf{E}$ *is primitive—that is, there exists a positive integer* s *such that* $(\mathbf{E}^s)_{i,j} > 0$ *for* $1 \leq i, j \leq N$.

Proof. (1) Suppose $0 \leq \lambda \leq 1$. By definition, $\mathbf{E}_c$ is nonnegative and doubly stochastic for all c, $1 \leq c \leq \kappa$. It is easy to show that their product (of multiplication) preserves the same properties; that is, $\mathbf{E}$ is nonnegative and doubly stochastic [14].

(2) Suppose $0 < \lambda < 1$. Then $(\mathbf{E})_{i,i} > 0$ because $(\mathbf{E}_c)_{i,i} > 0$ for all $1 \leq c \leq \kappa$. Hence, $\mathbf{E}^{N-1} > 0$; and $\mathbf{E}$ is primitive for $0 < \lambda < 1$. □

Because of the nonnegative and doubly stochastic properties, we can analyze the convergence of $\{\mathbf{E}^t\}$ using the theory of nonnegative matrices and finite Markov chain [14]. Let $\mu_j(\mathbf{E})$ $(1 \leq j \leq N)$ be the eigenvalues of $\mathbf{E}$, and $\rho(\mathbf{E})$ be the dominant eigenvalue of $\mathbf{E}$ in modulus, *i.e.*, $\rho(\mathbf{E}) = \max_{1 \leq j \leq N}\{|\mu_j(\mathbf{E})|\}$. We define

$$\gamma(\mathbf{E}) = \max_{1 \leq j \leq N}\{|\mu_j(\mathbf{E})| : \mu_j(\mathbf{E}) \neq 1.\}$$

Then, if $\rho(\mathbf{E}) < 1$, $\gamma(\mathbf{E}) = \rho(\mathbf{E})$; otherwise, $\gamma(\mathbf{E})$ is the sub-dominant eigenvalue of $\mathbf{E}$ in modulus. According to the matrix iterative theory [14], the sequence $\{\mathbf{E}^t\}$ is convergent if and only if $\gamma(\mathbf{E}) < 1$. Along this line, we establish the following convergence theorem.

Theorem 3.2.1 *Let $\mathbf{E}$ be the GDE matrix of a κ-color graph, $\overline{\mathbf{E}}$ a matrix of order N with all elements equal to $1/N$, and $\overline{\mathbf{W}}$ a uniform distribution vector with all elements equal to 1. Then,*

1. $\lim_{t\to\infty} \mathbf{E}^t = \overline{\mathbf{E}}$ *if and only if* $\lambda \in (0,1)$.
2. *For any initial workload distribution $\mathbf{W}^0$, the sequence $\{\mathbf{W}^{t\kappa}\}$ generated by the GDE method converges to $b\overline{\mathbf{W}}$ if $\lambda \in (0,1)$, where $b = \sum_{1\leq i\leq N}(w_i^0)/N$.*

Proof. (1) First, suppose $\lambda \in (0,1)$. Then, from Lemma 3.2.1, $\mathbf{E}$ is nonnegative and primitive. According to the fundamental Perron-Frobenius theorem on nonnegative matrices, we have $\rho(\mathbf{E}) > 0$ and its algebraic multiplicity is equal to 1. Also, since $\mathbf{E}$ is doubly stochastic, $\rho(\mathbf{E}) = 1$. Therefore, $\gamma(\mathbf{E}) < 1$. Hence, $\lim_{t\to\infty} \mathbf{E}^t$ exists, and each column of the limit matrix is a positive eigenvector of $\mathbf{E}$ corresponding to the spectral radius $\rho(\mathbf{E})$. That is, $\lim_{t\to\infty} \mathbf{E}^t = \overline{\mathbf{E}}$. On the other hand, suppose $\lambda = 0$. Then, $\mathbf{E}_c$ is the identity matrix of order n, for all $1 \leq c \leq \kappa$; so is $\mathbf{E}$. Suppose $\lambda = 1$. Then $\mathbf{E}$ is a permutation matrix because for all $1 \leq c \leq \kappa$, $\mathbf{E}_c$ is a permutation matrix. Therefore, $\mathbf{E}$ has the eigenvalue 1 in modulus with multiplicity N when $\lambda = 0$ or 1, and hence $\gamma(\mathbf{E}) = 1$. Thus, $\lim_{t\to\infty} \mathbf{E}^t$ does not exist or if it exists, does not converge to $\overline{\mathbf{E}}$. Consequently, $\lim_{t\to\infty} \mathbf{E}^t = \overline{\mathbf{E}}$ if and only if $\lambda \in (0,1)$.

(2) Since $\lim_{t\to\infty} \mathbf{E}^t = \overline{\mathbf{E}}$, for any initial workload distribution $\mathbf{W}^0$, we have

$$\lim_{t\to\infty} \mathbf{W}^{t\kappa} = \overline{\mathbf{E}}\mathbf{W}^0 = b\overline{\mathbf{W}}$$

where $b = \sum_{1\le i\le N} w_i^0/N$. □

The above theorem tells us that $0 < \lambda < 1$ is a necessary and sufficient condition for the convergence of dynamic load balancing using the GDE method. If $\lambda = 0$, the workload distribution would not change at all after an iteration step, and if $\lambda = 1$, an iteration step would cause a complete swap of the workloads of every pair of vertices and leave the variance of the workload distribution unchanged.

3.3 Convergence Rate Analysis

The introduction of the exchange parameter λ into the dimension exchange method is not for forcing a convergence which is present in the original method but rather accelerating the convergence rate. The problem here is to choose a λ so as to maximize the convergence rate, *i.e.*, minimize the number of iteration sweeps required for reaching a balanced state from any initial workload distribution.

In the static workload model, it is true that $\overline{\mathbf{W}}^t = \overline{\mathbf{W}}^0$ and $\mathbf{E}^t\overline{\mathbf{W}}^t = \overline{\mathbf{W}}^t$. Eq. (3.4) hence yields that

$$\mathbf{W}^t - \overline{\mathbf{W}}^t = \mathbf{E}(\mathbf{W}^{t-1} - \overline{\mathbf{W}}^{t-1}) = \mathbf{E}^t(\mathbf{W}^0 - \overline{\mathbf{W}}^0).$$

Then, by the definition of the workload variance ν^t in Section 1.4 and fundamentals of the matrix iteration theory, we have

$$\nu^t = ||\mathbf{W}^t - \overline{\mathbf{W}}||^2 = ||\mathbf{E}^t(\mathbf{W}^0 - \overline{\mathbf{W}})||^2 \le \gamma^{2t}(\mathbf{E})\nu^0.$$

It says that the workload variance is reduced geometrically and its scale factor is upper bounded by $\gamma(\mathbf{E})$. The bound is tight, and ν^t satisfies[1]

$$\nu^t \simeq \gamma^{2t}(\mathbf{E})\nu^0, \qquad \text{for large } t. \tag{3.5}$$

The sub-dominant eigenvalue in modulus $\gamma(\mathbf{E})$ is thus referred also as the convergence factor of the GDE load balancing algorithm.

Let T be the number of iteration sweeps required to reduce the workload variance of an initial state to some prescribed bound τ. Then, from Eq. (3.5), it follows that

$$T = \frac{\ln\tau - \ln\nu^0}{2\ln\gamma(\mathbf{E})}. \tag{3.6}$$

Hence,

$$T = O(1/\ln\gamma(\mathbf{E})). \tag{3.7}$$

[1]By $g(t) \simeq h(t)$ for large t, we mean that $g(t)/h(t) \longrightarrow 1$ for large t.

That is, the smaller the convergence factor $\gamma(\mathbf{E})$, the higher the efficiency of the GDE load balancing algorithm. Our objective is thus to choose a λ so that $\gamma(\mathbf{E})$ is as close to 0 as possible.

$\gamma(\mathbf{E})$ depends not only on the structure of $\mathbf{E}$, *i.e.*, the arrangement of positive and zero elements in $\mathbf{E}$, but also on the value of each positive element. $(\mathbf{E})_{i,j} > 0, i \neq j$, dictates what fraction of the workload in processor j is to be transferred to processor i in an iteration sweep. For the representation of $(\mathbf{E})_{i,j}$ in closed form, we first define the concept of a *color path* in color graphs. A color path from vertex i to vertex j indicates that processor i will receive some workload from processor j along the path in an iteration sweep.

Definition 3.3.1 *Let G_κ be a κ-color graph of G. A sequence of edges in G_κ of the form*

$$(i = i_0, i_1, c_1), (i_1, i_2, c_2), \ldots, (i_{l-1}, i_l = j, c_l)$$

is called a color path *of length l from vertex i to vertex j if all intermediate vertices i_s $(1 \leq s \leq l-1)$ are distinct and $\kappa \geq c_1 > c_2 > \ldots > c_l \geq 1$. A color path from i to j is closed if $i = j$. Two color paths from i to j in G_κ are said to be distinct if their intermediate vertices do not coincide at all. All the distinct color paths from i to j comprise a set $\mathcal{P}_{i,j}$.*

For example, in the color graph in Figure 3.1(a), there exist from vertex 3 to vertex 2 two distinct color paths, $(3,2,3)$ and $(3,1,2),(1,2,1)$, of length 1 and 2 respectively. The sequence of edges $(2,3,3),(3,1,2),(1,2,1)$ is a closed color path of length 3 incident on node 2. It is clear from the definition that the length of any color path in a κ-color graph cannot be larger than κ.

The following lemma presents the computation formula for the elements of $\mathbf{E}$, which is fundamental to the following analysis. Its proof is based on the concept of color paths and the particular features of each $\mathbf{E}_c$ $(1 \leq c \leq \kappa)$.

Lemma 3.3.1 *Let $\mathbf{E}$ be the GDE matrix of a κ-color graph G_κ. If $0 < \lambda < 1$, then for $1 \leq i, j \leq N, i \neq j$,*

$$\begin{aligned}
(\mathbf{E})_{i,j} &= \sum_{p \in \mathcal{P}_{i,j}} (1-\lambda)^{r_p} \lambda^{l_p} \\
(\mathbf{E})_{i,i} &= (1-\lambda)^{d(i)} + \sum_{p \in \mathcal{P}_{i,i}} (1-\lambda)^{r_p} \lambda^{l_p}
\end{aligned}$$

where l_p is the length of the color path $p \in \mathcal{P}_{i,j}$ of the form

$$(i = i_0, i_1, c_1), (i_1, i_2, c_2), \ldots, (i_{l_p - 1}, i_{l_p} = j; c_{l_p})$$

and $r_p = \sum_{s=0}^{l_p}(n_s)$, *where* n_0 *is the number of incident edges of vertex* i *whose chromatic index is larger than* c_1; n_{l_p} *is the number of incident edge of vertex* j *whose chromatic index is smaller than* c_{l_p}; *and* n_s $(1 \leq s \leq l_p - 1)$ *is the number of incident edges of vertex* i_s *whose chromatic index is larger than* c_{s+1} *and smaller than* c_s.

Proof. Given an ordered pair of vertices $\langle i, j \rangle$ in the color graph G_κ, $i \neq j$, we exhaust the three cases concerning the color paths from vertex i to vertex j.

Case 1: There are no color paths from vertex i to vertex j in G_κ. Then for all $1 \leq c \leq \kappa$, $(\mathbf{E}_c)_{i,j} = 0$. Also, there are $d(i)$ matrices $\mathbf{E}_c$, whose elements in position (i, i) would equal to $1 - \lambda$; elements $(\mathbf{E}_c)_{i,i}$ of other $\kappa - d(i)$ matrices would be 1. From the definition of $\mathbf{E}$,

$$\mathbf{E} = \mathbf{E}_\kappa \times \ldots \times \mathbf{E}_c \times \ldots \times \mathbf{E}_1.$$

It is then clear that $(\mathbf{E})_{i,i} = (1 - \lambda)^{d(i)}$ and $(\mathbf{E})_{i,j} = 0$.

Case 2: There is a single color path of length l from vertex i to vertex j.

1. If $l = 1$, *i.e.*, nodes i and j are adjacent, then

$$\begin{aligned} (\mathbf{E}_c)_{i,j} &= (\mathbf{E}_c)_{i,j} &= \lambda, \\ (\mathbf{E}_c)_{i,i} &= (\mathbf{E}_c)_{j,j} &= 1 - \lambda, \end{aligned}$$

where c is the chromatic index of the edge. Because there are no matrices $\mathbf{E}_h(1 \leq h \leq \kappa$, and $h \neq c)$ in which the elements in positions $(i, j), (j, i), (i, i)$ and (j, j) have the same size as the corresponding elements in $\mathbf{E}_c$, the following statements can be derived according to the definition of $\mathbf{E}$. For all $h, c < h \leq \kappa$, if $(\mathbf{E}_h)_{i,j} = 1$, *i.e.*, vertex i has no incident edges with chromatic index h, then the premultiplication of $\mathbf{E}_c$ by $\mathbf{E}_h$ does not have any effects on the size of the element $(\mathbf{E}_c)_{i,j}$; if $(\mathbf{E}_h)_{i,j} = 1 - \lambda$, *i.e.*, vertex i has an incident edge with chromatic index h, then the premultiplicity of $\mathbf{E}_c$ by $\mathbf{E}_h$ changes the size of the element $(\mathbf{E}_c)_{i,j}$ to $(1-\lambda) \times (\mathbf{E}_c)_{i,j}$. Similarly, for all h, $1 \leq h < c$, the postmultiplicity of $\mathbf{E}_c$ by M_h changes $(\mathbf{E}_c)_{i,j}$ to $(1-\lambda)\mathbf{E}_c$ only when vertex j has an incident edge with chromatic index h.

As a result, we have

$$(\mathbf{E})_{i,j} = (1 - \lambda)^{n_0} \lambda (1 - \lambda)^{n_1} = (1 - \lambda)^{n_0 + n_1} \lambda,$$

where n_0 is the number of incident edges of vertex i whose chromatic index is larger than c and n_1 is the number of incident edges of vertex j whose chromatic index is smaller than c.

2. If $l > 1$, and the color path is of the form

$$(i = i_0, i_1, c_1), (i_1, i_2, c_2), \ldots, (i_{l-1}, i_l = j, c_l)$$

then for all $1 \leq s \leq l$, we have

$$\begin{aligned} (\mathbf{E}_{c_s})_{i,j} &= (\mathbf{E}_{c_s})_{j,i} &= \lambda, \\ (\mathbf{E}_{c_s})_{i,i} &= (\mathbf{E}_{c_s})_{j,j} &= 1 - \lambda. \end{aligned}$$

Generally, $\mathbf{E}$ is of the form

$$\mathbf{E}_{\mathcal{K}} \times \ldots \times \mathbf{E}_{c_1} \times \ldots \times \mathbf{E}_{c_2} \times \ldots \times \mathbf{E}_{c_l} \times \ldots \times \mathbf{E}_1.$$

From the analysis in the case of $l = 1$, it can be deduced that

$$\begin{aligned} (\mathbf{E})_{i,j} &= (1-\lambda)^{n_0}\lambda(1-\lambda)^{n_1}\lambda\cdots(1-\lambda)^{n_{l-1}}\lambda(1-\lambda)^{n_l} \\ &= (1-\lambda)^{n_0+n_1+\ldots+n_l}\lambda^l, \end{aligned}$$

where n_0 is the number of incident edges of vertex i whose chromatic index is larger than c_1, n_l is the number of incident edges of j whose chromatic index is smaller than c_l, and n_s $(1 \leq s \leq l-1)$ is the number of incident edges of vertex i_s whose chromatic index is larger than c_{s+1} and smaller than c_s.

Case 3: There are more than one distinct color path from vertex i to vertex j, all together comprising a set $\mathcal{P}_{i,j}$. Then according to the principle of matrix multiplication, we have

$$(\mathbf{E})_{i,j} = \sum_{p \in \mathcal{P}_{i,j}} ((1-\lambda)^{r_p}\lambda^{l_p}), \qquad 1 \leq i, j \leq N$$

where l_p and r_p are as stated in the lemma.

Hence, the lemma follows. □

As an example, let us examine the GDE matrix of the color graph in Figure 3.1(a).

$$\mathbf{E} = \begin{pmatrix} (1-\lambda)^2 & \lambda(1-\lambda) & \lambda \\ \lambda(1-\lambda) + \lambda^2(1-\lambda) & \lambda^3 + (1-\lambda)^2 & \lambda(1-\lambda) \\ \lambda(1-\lambda)^2 + \lambda^2 & \lambda(1-\lambda) + \lambda^2(1-\lambda) & (1-\lambda)^2 \end{pmatrix}$$

Since there are no closed paths incident on vertices 1 and 2, it follows that

$$(\mathbf{E})_{1,1} = (\mathbf{E})_{3,3} = (1-\lambda)^2.$$

However, $(\mathbf{E})_{2,2}$ equals to $\lambda^3 + (1-\lambda)^2$, the first term of which is due to the closed color path of length 3 incident on vertex 2. Consider the ordered pair of vertices $< 3, 1 >$. There is a color path $(3, 1, 2)$ of length 1 and a color path $(3, 2, 3), (2, 1, 1)$ of length 2 from vertex 3 to vertex 1. They contribute to the first and second terms in $(\mathbf{E})_{2,0}$, respectively.

We next prove, for a given κ-color graph, the existence of an optimal λ that minimize the convergence factor $\gamma(\mathbf{E})$, *i.e.*, maximizes the convergence rate.

Lemma 3.3.2 *Let* $\mathbf{E}$ *be the GDE matrix of a* κ*-color graph. The eigenvalues of* $\mathbf{E}$ *are continuous functions of* λ, $\lambda \in [0, 1]$.

Proof. Because the eigenvalues of $\mathbf{E}$ are just the zeros of its characteristic polynomial, they are continuously dependent on the coefficients of the polynomial according to the fundamental theorem of algebra [89]. Given also the fact that the coefficients of the characteristic polynomial of a square real matrix are continuous functions of the elements of the matrix, it follows that the eigenvalues of $\mathbf{E}$ are continuously dependent on the elements of $\mathbf{E}$. On the other hand, each element of $\mathbf{E}$, which is a polynomial in λ according to the last lemma, continuously depends on λ. Therefore, the eigenvalues of $\mathbf{E}$ continuously depend on λ. □

Theorem 3.3.1 *Let* $\mathbf{E}(\lambda)$ *be the GDE matrix of of a* κ*-color graph. There exists a* $\lambda_{opt} \in (0,1)$ *such that* $\gamma(\mathbf{E}(\lambda_{opt})) \leq \gamma(\mathbf{E}(\lambda))$ *for all* $\lambda \neq \lambda_{opt}$.

Proof. From Lemma 3.3.2, $\gamma(\mathbf{E}(\lambda))$ is continuously dependent on λ, where $\lambda \in [0,1]$. Therefore, there exists a $\lambda_{opt} \in [0,1]$ such that $\gamma(\mathbf{E}(\lambda_{opt})) \leq \gamma(\mathbf{E}(\lambda))$ for all $\lambda \in [0,1]$. In addition, $\gamma(\mathbf{E}(\lambda)) = 1$ if $\lambda = 0$ or 1; otherwise $\gamma(\mathbf{E}(\lambda)) < 1$. Hence, $\lambda_{opt} \in (0, 1)$, and there exists a $\lambda \in (0, 1)$ such that $\gamma(\mathbf{E}(\lambda))$ is smallest. □

Our objective is to determine the optimal λ that minimizes the convergence factor $\gamma(\mathbf{E})$. However, as we found no effective methods available for arbitrary matrices, we limit our scope to particular classes of matrices which correspond to particular kinds of structures. Along this line, we establish below a sufficient condition for a κ-color graph under which $\gamma(\mathbf{E})$ is minimized when $\lambda = 1/2$, and present a number of structures which satisfy the condition. In the next chapter, we derive the optimal exchange parameters for other common structures.

Theorem 3.3.2 *Let* G_κ *be a* κ*-color graph. Assume* G_κ *is regular with* $deg(G_\kappa) = \kappa$, *and* $|\mathcal{P}_{i,j}| = |\mathcal{P}_{i,i}|+1 = |\mathcal{P}_{j,j}|+1$ *for each pair of vertices i and j in* G_κ. *Then* $\lambda = 1/2$ *is the optimal choice in the GDE load balancing.*

Proof. Let $\mathbf{E}$ be the GDE matrix of the color graph G_κ. If G_κ is regular with $d(G_\kappa) = \kappa$, then the incident edges of each vertex have consecutive chromatic indices from 1 to κ. Hence, the computation formula in Lemma 3.3.1 can be simplified as

$$\begin{aligned}(\mathbf{E})_{i,j} &= \sum_{p\in\mathcal{P}_{i,j}}((1-\lambda)^{\kappa-l_p}\lambda^{l_p}),\\ (\mathbf{E})_{i,i} &= (1-\lambda)^{d(i)}+\sum_{p\in\mathcal{P}_{i,i}}((1-\lambda)^{\kappa-l_p}\lambda^{l_p}).\end{aligned}$$

It can be further simplified as

$$\begin{aligned}(\mathbf{E})_{i,j} &= \sum_{p\in\mathcal{P}_{i,j}}(1/2^{\kappa}),\\ (\mathbf{E})_{i,i} &= 1/2^{\kappa}+\sum_{p\in\mathcal{P}_{i,i}}(1/2^{\kappa}).\end{aligned}$$

for $1\le i,j\le N, i\ne j$ when $\lambda=1/2$. Furthermore, if $|\mathcal{P}_{i,j}| = |\mathcal{P}_{i,i}|+1 = |\mathcal{P}_{j,j}|+1$ ($=s$, say), $\mathbf{E}$ is then reduced to a uniform matrix, each element of which is equal to $s/2^{\kappa}$. As a result, the rank of $\mathbf{E}$ equals 1, and all the eigenvalues except $\rho(\mathbf{E})$ are equal to 0. Thus, $\gamma(\mathbf{E})=0$, which maximizes the convergence rate. □

This theorem shows the optimality of the ADE method in a class of interconnection networks. The hypercube is such a structure having the property. Since the hypercube structure is a uniquely colorable graph, *i.e.*, there is only one way of coloring the edges without respect to the permutation of colors; its corresponding color graph is implicit in the following corollary.

Corollary 3.3.1 *With the GDE method, $\lambda = 1/2$ is the optimal choice for load balancing in hypercube structures.*

Proof. It is not hard to verify that an n-dimensional hypercube structure is n-regular and n-colorable. Moreover, for each ordered pair of vertices i,j $(i\ne j)$, there exists a unique color path from vertex i to vertex j, and no closed color paths are incident on any vertex. From the theorem above, the statement holds. □

The ADE method was initially proposed as a heuristic choice for load balancing in hypercube structures [165, 47]. Its optimality is now confirmed by this corollary. In addition to the hypercube, there are other structures that have the same property. The following corollary shows that the product of any two graphs that satisfy the conditions of Theorem 3.3.2 also has the property. The product $P=(V_P,E_P)$ of two graphs $G=(V_G,E_G)$ and $H=(V_H,E_H)$, denoted by $G\times H$, is defined as such so that $((u_1,v),(u_2,v))\in E_P$ if and only if $u_1=u_2$ and v_1 is adjacent to v_2 in H or $v_1=v_2$ and u_1 is adjacent to u_2 in G.

Corollary 3.3.2 *Let G_{κ_1} be a κ_1-color graph of G, and H_{κ_2} be a κ_2-color graph of H. If both G_{κ_1} and H_{κ_2} satisfy the conditions in Theorem 3.3.2, then $\lambda=1/2$ is the optimal choice for GDE balancing applied to the product of G and H.*

Proof. Let $P = G \times H$, with $V_P = \{(i,j) \in V_G \times V_H\}$. Then, it is clear that P is regular and $d(P) = d(G) + d(H) = \kappa_1 + \kappa_2$. Also, P is $(\kappa_1 + \kappa_2)$-colorable by labeling each edge $((i,j_1),(i,j_2))$, $j_1 \neq j_2$, with the same chromatic index as the edge (j_1, j_2) in H, and each edge $((i_1,j),(i_2,j))$, $i_1 \neq i_2$, with the same chromatic index as the edge (i_1,i_2) in G plus κ_2. Clearly, no two adjoining edges of P will be labeled with the same chromatic index in this way.

We then prove $|\mathcal{P}_{(i_1,j_1),(i_2,j_2)}| = |\mathcal{P}_{(i_1,j_1),(i_1,j_1)}| + 1 = |\mathcal{P}_{(i_2,j_2),(i_2,j_2)}| + 1$ for each pair of vertices (i_1, j_1) and (i_2, j_2) in the $(\kappa_1 + \kappa_2)$-color graph of P. For every vertex (i,j) in the color graph, it is clear that any closed color path incident on vertex i (vertex j) in G_{κ_1} (H_{κ_2}) has a corresponding closed color path incident on the vertex (i,j), along which all vertices are with the same fixed second part j (fixed first part i) in their pair of indices. Let $|\mathcal{P}_{i,i}|$ and $|\mathcal{P}_{j,j}|$ denote the number of closed color paths incident on vertex i of G_{κ_1} and on vertex j of H_{κ_2}, respectively. Then,

$$|\mathcal{P}_{(i,j),(i,j)}| = \begin{cases} |\mathcal{P}_{i,i}| + |\mathcal{P}_{j,j}| & \text{if } |\mathcal{P}_{i,i}| = 0 \text{ or } |\mathcal{P}_{j,j}| = 0, \\ |\mathcal{P}_{i,i}| + |\mathcal{P}_{j,j}| + |\mathcal{P}_{i,i}| \times |\mathcal{P}_{j,j}| & \text{if } |\mathcal{P}_{i,i}| \neq 0 \text{ and } |\mathcal{P}_{j,j}| \neq 0. \end{cases}$$

Since G_{κ_1} and H_{κ_2} satisfy the conditions in Theorem 3.3.2, it follows that $|\mathcal{P}_{i,i}|$ is the same for every vertex i in G_{κ_1} and $|\mathcal{P}_{j,j}|$ is the same for every vertex j in H_{κ_2}. Thus, $|\mathcal{P}_{(i,j),(i,j)}|$ is the same for every vertex (i,j) in the edge-colored graph of P.

For any pair of vertices (i_1, j_1) and (i_2, j_2) in the edge-colored graph of P, it follows that

$$\begin{aligned} |\mathcal{P}_{(i_1,j_1),(i_2,j_2)}| &= |\mathcal{P}_{i_1,i_2}| \times |\mathcal{P}_{j_1,j_2}| \\ &= (|\mathcal{P}_{i_1,i_1}| + 1) \times (|\mathcal{P}_{j_1,j_1}| + 1) \\ &= |\mathcal{P}_{i_1,i_1}| + |\mathcal{P}_{j_1,j_1}| + |\mathcal{P}_{i_1,i_1}| \times |\mathcal{P}_{j_1,j_1}| + 1 \\ &= |\mathcal{P}_{(i_1,j_1),(i_1,j_1)}| + 1. \end{aligned}$$

Thus, the product graph P satisfies the conditions in Theorem 3.3.2. The corollary is proved. □

It is known that the chain of 2 nodes satisfies the conditions of Theorem 3.3.2. By the above corollary, its self-products or recursive products, such as the hypercube and the 4-ary n-cube, have the property as well. Another base structure having the property is the complete graph of 4 nodes. Its product with a ring of 4 nodes, as illustrated in Figure 3.2, preserves the optimality of the choice $\lambda = 1/2$ in the GDE load balancing.

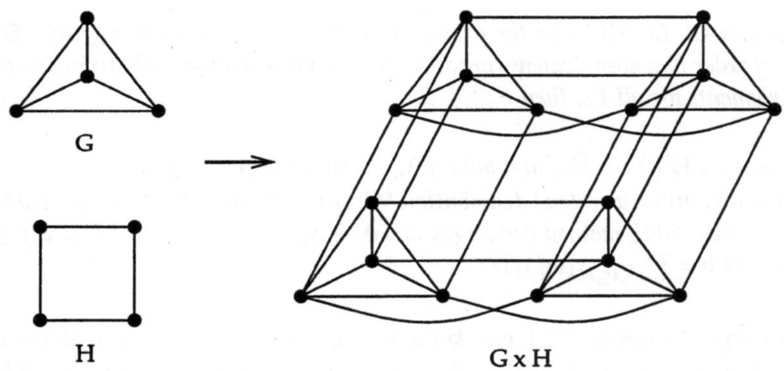

Figure 3.2: An example of graph products that preserve the optimality of the ADE algorithm

3.4 Extension of the GDE Method

We have presented the generalized dimension exchange method with the introduction of an exchange parameter λ which can be tuned to accelerate the convergence rate of load balancing. We conclude this chapter with an extension of the GDE method to further enhance our understanding of the dimension exchange method and its potential. An obvious extension of the method is to relax the restriction of a single value for the exchange parameter and to allow different values of the exchange parameter to be used for different edges.

This extension is easily justified by intuition. For instance, consider a chain. One would tend to think that, for better efficiency, the processors at the two ends should send a major chunk (*i.e.*, a large λ) of its load away during an exchange step, while the processors at the middle should use a more moderate λ. We introduce a set of parameters, $\lambda_{i,j}$, $1 \leq i,j \leq N$ and $\lambda_{i,j} = \lambda_{ji}$, to characterize the set of exchange patterns over all pairs of directly connected processors. Consequently, the basic iterative operation between the two nodes of a colored edge (i,j,c) is modified as

$$w_i = (1-\lambda_{i,j})w_i + \lambda_{i,j}w_j. \tag{3.8}$$

Let Λ denote the set of parameters $\lambda_{i,j}$. Then, by repeating the same matrix modeling technique as in the preceding sections, we obtain an extended GDE matrix $\mathbf{E}(\Lambda)$, each element of which is a polynomial of $\lambda_{i,j}$. It is clear that $\mathbf{E}(\Lambda)$ is nonnegative and doubly stochastic when $0 \leq \lambda_{i,j} \leq 1$, and primitive when $0 < \lambda_{i,j} < 1$ for $1 \leq i,j \leq N$. Similarly to Theorem 3.2.1 we obtain the following convergence theorem.

Theorem 3.4.1 *Let $\mathbf{E}(\Lambda)$ be the extended GDE matrix of a κ-color graph, $\overline{\mathbf{E}}$ be a matrix of order N whose elements are all $1/N$, and $\overline{\mathbf{W}}$ be a uniform distribution vector whose elements are all 1's, then*

1. *$lim_{t\to\infty}\mathbf{E}^t(\Lambda) = \overline{\mathbf{E}}$ if and only if $\lambda_{i,j} \in (0,1)$ for $1 \le i,j \le N$.*
2. *For any initial workload distribution $\mathbf{W}^0$, the sequence $\{\mathbf{W}^{t\kappa}\}$ generated by the extended GDE method converges to $b\overline{\mathbf{W}}$ if $\lambda_{i,j} \in (0,1)$, for all $1 \le i,j \le N$, where $b = \sum_{1\le i\le N}(w_i^0)/N$.*

Similarly, Theorem 3.3.1 can be generalized such that for a given color graph, there exists a vector of $\lambda_{i,j}$ that maximizes the convergence rate of $\mathbf{E}(\Lambda)$. To illustrate the relationship between the convergence rate of $\mathbf{E}(\Lambda)$ and the parameters $\lambda_{i,j}$, we analyze quantitatively the extended GDE matrix on the color chain of order 4 as in Figure 3.1(c). With the extended GDE method, three parameters λ_1, λ_2 and λ_3 are necessary for parameterizing the exchange patterns for edges $(1,2)$, $(2,3)$ and $(2,3)$, respectively. Then, the extended GDE matrix, $\mathbf{E}(\Lambda)$, is

$$\begin{pmatrix} 1-\lambda_1 & \lambda_1 & 0 & 0 \\ \lambda_1(1-\lambda_2) & (1-\lambda_1)(1-\lambda_2) & \lambda_2(1-\lambda_3) & \lambda_2\lambda_3 \\ \lambda_1\lambda_2 & \lambda_2(1-\lambda_1) & (1-\lambda_2)(1-\lambda_3) & \lambda_3(1-\lambda_2) \\ 0 & 0 & \lambda_3 & 1-\lambda_3 \end{pmatrix}.$$

We calculate the subdominant eigenvalue in modulus, $\gamma(\mathbf{E}(\Lambda))$, as λ_i ($i = 1,2,3$) varies from 0.1 to 0.9 in steps of 0.05. It is found that $\gamma(\mathbf{E}(\Lambda))$ equals 0.1, the smallest value in the testing group, when $(\lambda_1,\lambda_2,\lambda_3)$ is equal to $(0.5,0.7,0.6)$ or $(0.6,0.7,0.5)$. Theoretically, the smallest convergence factor $\gamma(\mathbf{E}(\lambda))$ of the chain of 4 nodes, using a single exchange parameter, is equal to 0.172 when $\lambda = 2-\sqrt{2}$. It is known that the smaller the convergence factor, the faster the load balancing arrives at a uniform distribution. Therefore, the extended GDE method using multiple exchange parameters λ_i potentially converges faster than the GDE method with a single, optimal λ.

The dependence of $\gamma(\mathbf{E}(\Lambda))$ on $\lambda_{i,j}$, being an optimization problem with multiple parameters, is somewhat difficult to analyze. In the sequel, we concentrate on the GDE method with a single parameter.

3.5 Concluding Remarks

We have presented in this chapter the generalized dimension exchange method (GDE) for load balancing in distributed memory multiprocessors with point-to-point interconnection networks. It is a fully distributed method and runs in an iterative fashion. It is parameterized by an exchange parameter λ that governs the splitting of load between a pair of nearest neighbor processors during the load balancing process. We have analyzed the convergence and the efficiency properties and presented a necessary and sufficient condition for the convergence of the GDE load balancing with respect to the parameter λ. We have also shown that the ADE method based on pairwise equal splitting of workload achieves optimal efficiency in hypercubes, 4-ary n-cubes, and some special interconnection networks. This however is not always the case in general structures.

The results give us not only a deeper understanding of the dimension exchange method, but also a basis for designing efficient load balancing algorithms in other common networks, such as the mesh, the torus and the k-ary n-cube. That is the theme of Chapter 4.

The dimension exchange algorithm is indeed an elegant load balancing algorithm. There are a number of competitors as has been surveyed in Chapter 2. The diffusion method is one, in which a processor communicates with all of its nearest neighbors simultaneously in a balancing operation, as opposed to one by one as in the dimension exchange method. The diffusion method is the topic of Chapter 5. In the following, we comment on the close relationship between the dimension exchange method and the diffusion method.

By Lemma 3.3.1, $(\mathbf{E})_{i,j} > 0$ if and only if there is a color path from vertex i to j in the edge-colored system graph G. Regard the system graph G as a bi-directional digraph and extend the digraph by adding directional edges $\langle m,n\rangle$ if there exists a color path from vertex n to m. Denote the extended digraph as G'. By Lemma 3.3.1, it follows that $(\mathbf{E})_{i,j}$ if and only if there is a directional edge from vertex i to j in the digraph G'. In other words, the change of workload in processor i in the tth sweep of the pairwise balancing operations is governed by the equation

$$w_i^t = (\mathbf{E})_{i,i}w_i^t + \sum_{j\in\mathcal{A}(i)} (\mathbf{E})_{i,j}w_j^t \tag{3.9}$$

where $\mathcal{A}(i)$ is the set of processors directly connected from processor i in the digraph G'.

Eq. (3.9) is characteristic of diffusive load balancing. Consequently, we draw the conclusion that the dimension exchange load balancing algorithm in a system graph G is equivalent to a diffusive algorithm in an extended structure, G'. Note that G' is denser than G. Therefore, we expect diffusive load balancing in G' to converge faster than it is in G because more processors will be involved in a balancing operation in G'. That is, the dimension exchange method should be more efficient than the diffusion method. Chapter 6 is devoted to a comprehensive and rigorous comparison between these two methods.

4

GDE ON TORI AND MESHES

Nothing in excess.
–ANON. [INSCRIBED ON THE TEMPLE OF APOLLO AT DELPHI]

In the last chapter, we considered the hypercube and some other structures and their optimal pairwise averaging operation in GDE load balancing. One important finding is that the product of any two such structures also has this property. In this chapter, we consider the structures of n-dimensional torus and mesh ($n \geq 1$), and their special cases, the ring, the chain, and the k-ary n-cube. An n-dimensional torus is a variant of the mesh with end-round connections, as illustrated in Figure 4.1 (the end-round connections at the back and bottom are omitted in the figure for clarity). A k-ary n-cube is a network with n dimensions having k nodes in each dimensions [49, 145]. It is a special case of the n-dimensional torus which allows different orders in different dimensions. The order of a dimension refers to the number of nodes in the dimension. The hypercube is a special case of both the n-dimensional mesh and the k-ary n-cube. A hypercube is an n-dimensional mesh with the same

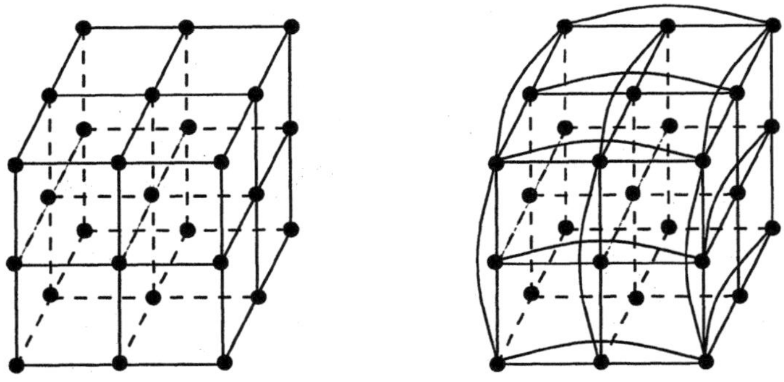

3x3x3 mesh 3x3x3 torus

Figure 4.1: Examples of n-D meshes and tori

order of 2 in each dimension, that is, a 2-ary n-cube. We limit our scope to these structures because they are among the most popular choices of topologies for today's parallel computers [145, 163, 189].

The modeling tool we use for the analysis is a special kind of matrices called *block circulant matrices*. It happens that the GDE matrices of the "even" cases of the above structures—even number of nodes in every dimension—are block circulant matrices. We concentrate on these even cases in the analysis and contend that the results for the even cases should be applicable (approximately) to the non-even cases. We give simulation results and a simple argument in Section 4.3 to support this argument.

For the subsequent analysis, we need to make use of the following two lemmas concerning block circulant matrices and *direct products* of matrices. We omit the proofs which can be easily derived based on the theory of circulant matrices [50].

Let $\mathbf{A}_1, \mathbf{A}_2, \ldots, \mathbf{A}_m$ be square matrices of order r. Then a block circulant matrix is a matrix of the form

$$\Phi_{m,r}(\mathbf{A}_1, \mathbf{A}_2, \ldots, \mathbf{A}_m) = \begin{pmatrix} \mathbf{A}_1 & \mathbf{A}_2 & \cdots & \cdots & \mathbf{A}_m \\ \mathbf{A}_m & \mathbf{A}_1 & \cdots & \cdots & \mathbf{A}_{m-1} \\ & \cdots & & \cdots & \\ \mathbf{A}_2 & \mathbf{A}_3 & \cdots & \cdots & \mathbf{A}_1 \end{pmatrix}$$

If $r = 1$, a block circulant matrix degenerates to a circulant matrix.

Lemma 4.0.1 *Let matrix* $\mathbf{A} = \Phi_{m,r}(\mathbf{A}_1, \mathbf{A}_2, \ldots, \mathbf{A}_m)$. *Then, the eigenvalues of the matrix* $\mathbf{A}$ *are those of matrices* $\mathbf{A}_1 + \omega^j \mathbf{A}_2 + \ldots + \omega^{j(m-1)} \mathbf{A}_m$, $j = 0, 1, \ldots, m-1$, *where* $\omega^j = \cos\frac{2\pi j}{m} + i \sin\frac{2\pi j}{m}, i = \sqrt{-1}$. *In particular, if matrix* $\mathbf{A} = \Phi_{2,r}(\mathbf{A}_1, \mathbf{A}_2)$, *then the eigenvalues of* $\mathbf{A}$ *are those of* $\mathbf{A}_1 + \mathbf{A}_2$, *together with those of* $\mathbf{A}_1 - \mathbf{A}_2$.

Let $\mathbf{A}$ and $\mathbf{B}$ be square matrices of order m and n, respectively. Then the *direct product* of $\mathbf{A}$ and $\mathbf{B}$ is a matrix of order $m \times n$ defined by

$$\mathbf{A} \otimes \mathbf{B} = \begin{pmatrix} a_{0,0}\mathbf{B} & a_{0,1}\mathbf{B} & \dots & a_{0,m-1}\mathbf{B} \\ a_{1,0}\mathbf{B} & a_{1,1}\mathbf{B} & \dots & a_{1,m-1}\mathbf{B} \\ & \dots & & \dots \\ a_{m-1,0}\mathbf{B} & a_{m-1,1}\mathbf{B} & \dots & a_{m-1,m-1}\mathbf{B} \end{pmatrix}$$

Lemma 4.0.2 *Let* $\mathbf{A}, \mathbf{B}$ *be square matrices of order* m *and* n *with eigenvalues* $\mu_i(\mathbf{A})$ *and* $\mu_j(\mathbf{B})$, $i = 1, 2, \dots, m$, $j = 1, 2, \dots, n$. *Then, the eigenvalues of* $\mathbf{A} \otimes \mathbf{B}$ *are* $\mu_i(\mathbf{A}) \times \mu_j(\mathbf{B})$.

For simplicity of notation, we let

$$\mathbf{U} = \begin{pmatrix} \mathbf{U}_1 \\ \mathbf{U}_2 \end{pmatrix} = \begin{pmatrix} \lambda(1-\lambda) & (1-\lambda)^2 \\ \lambda^2 & \lambda(1-\lambda) \end{pmatrix}$$
$$\mathbf{V} = \begin{pmatrix} \mathbf{V}_1 \\ \mathbf{V}_2 \end{pmatrix} = \begin{pmatrix} \lambda(1-\lambda) & \lambda^2 \\ (1-\lambda)^2 & \lambda(1-\lambda) \end{pmatrix}$$
$$\mathbf{Q} = \begin{pmatrix} \mathbf{Q}_1 \\ \mathbf{Q}_2 \end{pmatrix} = \begin{pmatrix} 1-\lambda & \lambda \\ \lambda & 1-\lambda \end{pmatrix}$$

4.1 GDE on n-Dimensional Tori

In this section, we analyze the GDE load balancing algorithm as applied to n-dimensional torus networks. The analysis by induction on the dimension n, $n \geq 1$. We begin with the ring structure and then generalize it to n-dimensional $k_1 \times k_2 \times \cdots \times k_n$ torus.

4.1.1 The Ring

We consider a ring with k vertices labeled 1 through k. Obviously, its edges can be colored with 3 colors if k is odd, and with 2 colors if k is even, as in Figure 3.1. We restrict our attention to even rings whose GDE matrices are in block circulant form; also, even rings can be uniquely colored, *i.e.*, there is only one way of coloring the edges without respect to the permutation of chromatic indices. In Section 4.3. we will show that there is a negligibly small difference between the efficiencies of GDE balancing in non-even and even ring networks in case k is large.

Let $\mathbf{R}_k$ be the GDE matrix of an even color ring with k nodes. It is in a block circulant form, as follows.

Lemma 4.1.1 *The GDE matrix $\mathbf{R}_k$ of a color ring of even order k is a matrix of the form*

$$\begin{pmatrix} \mathbf{V}_2 & & & & \mathbf{U}_2 \\ \mathbf{U} & \mathbf{V} & & & \\ & \mathbf{U} & \mathbf{V} & & \\ & & \ddots & \ddots & \\ & & & \mathbf{U} & \mathbf{V} \\ \mathbf{V}_1 & & & & \mathbf{U}_1 \end{pmatrix}_{k\times k} \tag{4.1}$$

Proof. The proof is by induction on the order of the ring structure. First, it is easy to verify that $\mathbf{R}_4$ is in the form of (4.1). We need to show that if the GDE matrix $\mathbf{R}_{2m}$, $m \geq 2$, is in the form of (4.1), then the GDE matrix $\mathbf{R}_{2m+2}$ is necessarily in that form as well.

Let us view the ring network having $2m+2$ vertices as an expansion of the color ring having $2m$ vertices with two vertices. The vertex labeled $2m-1$ in the original graph is relabeled $2m+2$, and the newly added vertices are labeled $2m$ and $2m+1$, as follows.

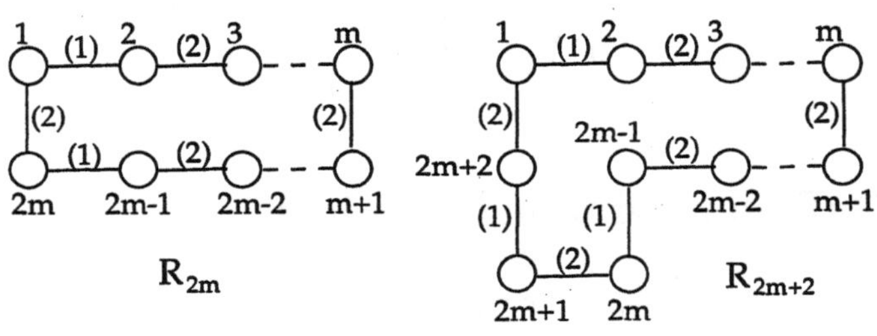

Then, according to the computation formulas in Lemma 3.3.1, we obtain the following.
For $j = 2m+1,\ 2m+2$,

$$\begin{aligned} (\mathbf{R}_{2m+2})_{1,j} &= (\mathbf{R}_{2m})_{1,j-2}, \\ (\mathbf{R}_{2m+2})_{2m+2,j} &= (\mathbf{R}_{2m})_{2m,j-2}, \\ (\mathbf{R}_{2m+2})_{1,j-2} &= 0; \end{aligned}$$

for $j = 1,\ 2$,

$$\begin{aligned} (\mathbf{R}_{2m+2})_{2m+2,j} &= (\mathbf{R}_{2m})_{2m,j}, \\ (\mathbf{R}_{2m+2})_{2m,j} &= 0; \end{aligned}$$

for $i = 2m,\ 2m+1;\ 2m-1 \leq j \leq 2m+2$,

$$(\mathbf{R}_{2m+2})_{i,j} = (\mathbf{R}_{2m})_{i-2,j-2}.$$

Hence, $\mathbf{R}_{2m+2}$, and therefore $\mathbf{R}_k$, are in the form of (4.1). □

As an example, the GDE matrix of the ring of order 6

$$\mathbf{R}_6 = \begin{pmatrix} (1-\lambda)^2 & \lambda(1-\lambda) & 0 & 0 & \lambda^2 & \lambda(1-\lambda) \\ \lambda(1-\lambda) & (1-\lambda)^2 & \lambda(1-\lambda) & \lambda^2 & 0 & 0 \\ \lambda^2 & \lambda(1-\lambda) & (1-\lambda)^2 & \lambda(1-\lambda) & 0 & 0 \\ 0 & 0 & \lambda(1-\lambda) & (1-\lambda)^2 & 0 & 0 \\ 0 & 0 & \lambda^2 & \lambda(1-\lambda) & (1-\lambda)^2 & \lambda(1-\lambda) \\ \lambda(1-\lambda) & \lambda^2 & 0 & 0 & \lambda(1-\lambda) & (1-\lambda)^2 \end{pmatrix}$$

Given this particular structure of the matrix $\mathbf{R}_k$, we can then derive the optimal exchange parameter and explore the effect of the ring order k on the convergence rate.

Theorem 4.1.1 *Let $\mathbf{R}_k(\lambda)$ be the GDE matrix of a color ring of even order k. Then, the optimal exchange parameter $\lambda_{opt}(\mathbf{R}_k)$ is equal to $\frac{1}{1+\sin(2\pi/k)}$. For a given λ, $\gamma(\mathbf{R}_k) \leq \gamma(\mathbf{R}_{k-2})$.*

Proof. Consider the particular form of $\mathbf{R}_k$ as shown in Lemma 4.1.1. Let $k = 2m$. It is easy to see that $\mathbf{R}_k$ can be represented by a block circulant matrix

$$\Phi_{m,k}(\mathbf{A}_1, \mathbf{A}_2, 0, \ldots, 0, \mathbf{A}_m)$$

where

$$\mathbf{A}_1 = \begin{pmatrix} (1-\lambda)^2 & \lambda(1-\lambda) \\ \lambda(1-\lambda) & (1-\lambda)^2 \end{pmatrix} \quad \mathbf{A}_2 = \begin{pmatrix} 0 & 0 \\ \lambda(1-\lambda) & \lambda^2 \end{pmatrix}$$
$$\mathbf{A}_m = \begin{pmatrix} \lambda^2 & \lambda(1-\lambda) \\ 0 & 0 \end{pmatrix}$$

From Lemma 4.0.1, the eigenvalues of the matrix $\mathbf{R}_k$ are those of the matrices, $\mathbf{A}_1 + \omega^j \mathbf{A}_2 + \omega^{j(m-1)} \mathbf{A}_m$, $j = 0, 1, \ldots, m-1$. Since $\omega^{j(m-1)} = \omega^{m-j}$,

$$\mathbf{A}_1 + \omega^j \mathbf{A}_2 + \omega^{j(m-1)} \mathbf{A}_m =$$
$$\begin{pmatrix} (1-\lambda)^2 + \omega^{m-j}\lambda^2 & \lambda(1-\lambda) + \omega^{m-j}\lambda(1-\lambda) \\ \lambda(1-\lambda) + \omega^j\lambda(1-\lambda) & (1-\lambda)^2 + \omega^j\lambda^2 \end{pmatrix}$$

Its eigenvalues are the roots of the characteristic equation

$$\mu^2 - 2\left((1-\lambda)^2 + \lambda^2 \cos(2\pi j/m)\right)\mu + (1-2\lambda)^2 = 0.$$

That is,

$$\begin{aligned} \mu &= (1-\lambda)^2 + \lambda^2 \cos(2\pi j/m) \\ &\quad \pm \lambda\sqrt{(1+\cos(2\pi j/m))((1+\cos(2\pi j/m))\lambda^2 - 4\lambda + 2)}. \end{aligned}$$

where $j = 0, 1, \ldots, m-1$.

Clearly, the dominant eigenvalue of $\mathbf{R}_k$ in modulus, $\rho(\mathbf{R}_k)$, is equal to 1, and when $k \neq 4$, the sub-dominant eigenvalue of $\mathbf{R}_k$ in modulus, $\gamma(\mathbf{R}_k)$, is equal to

$$\begin{cases} (1-\lambda)^2 + \lambda^2 e + \lambda\sqrt{(1+e)((1+e)\lambda^2 - 4\lambda + 2)} & \text{if } 0 < \lambda \leq \frac{2-\sqrt{2(1-e)}}{1+e} \\ 2\lambda - 1 & \text{if } \frac{2-\sqrt{2(1-e)}}{1+e} \leq \lambda < 1 \end{cases}$$

where $e = \cos(2\pi/m)$. Therefore, for a given ring of order $n = 2m$, $n \neq 4$, its optimal exchange parameter

$$\lambda_{opt}(\mathbf{R}_k) = \frac{2 - \sqrt{2(1-\cos(2\pi/m))}}{1+\cos(2\pi/m)} = \frac{1}{1+\sin(2\pi/k)},$$

and

$$\gamma(\mathbf{R}_k) = \frac{1-\sin(2\pi/k)}{1+\sin(2\pi/k)}.$$

When $k = 4$, it is evident by considering the matrix $\mathbf{R}_4$ that $\lambda_{opt}(\mathbf{R}_4) = 1/2$ and $\gamma(\mathbf{R}_4) = 0$, which is reminiscent of the case of the hypercube structure. Moreover, $\gamma(\mathbf{R}_k)$ increases with m for a given λ. That is, for a given λ, $\gamma(\mathbf{R}_k) \geq \gamma(\mathbf{R}_{k-2})$. □

The above theorem says that for a given λ, the more vertices an even ring has, the slower the convergence rate of the GDE balancing process. This is expected because processors located further away from each other need more communication steps for the exchange of their workload information. The theorem also presents the optimal exchange parameter in closed form for any even-order rings. For example, $\lambda_{opt}(\mathbf{R}_{16}) = 2/(2+\sqrt{2-\sqrt{2}}) \approx 0.723$, and $\gamma(\mathbf{R}_{16}) \approx 0.446$ when $\lambda = \lambda_{opt}(\mathbf{R}_{16})$. To verify the analytical results, we plot the convergence factor $\gamma(\mathbf{R}_{16})$ as λ varies from 0.1 to 0.95 in Figure 4.2.

Note that Theorem 4.1.1 is crucial. It serves as a fundamental stone in the following analysis of the GDE balancing in the mesh and the torus. Their optimal exchange parameters and corresponding convergence factors are actually derived from their relationships with those of the ring network.

4.1.2 The n-Dimensional Torus

We first consider the two-dimensional $k_1 \times k_2$ torus with an even number of vertices in both dimensions, It is a product of the ring of order k_1 and the ring of order k_2, and hence the results in the preceding section for the ring can be applied to the analysis here. To handle the degenerate case of k_1 or k_2 equal to

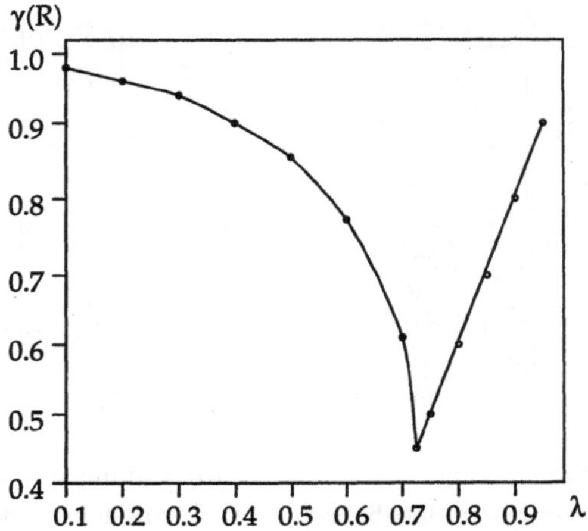

Figure 4.2: The convergence factor, $\gamma(\mathbf{R})$, in a ring as a function of the exchange parameter λ in the GDE method

2, we set $\mathbf{R}_2$ to the GDE matrix for a *chain* of order 2, *i.e.*,

$$\mathbf{R}_2 = \begin{pmatrix} 1-\lambda & \lambda \\ \lambda & 1-\lambda \end{pmatrix}$$

The reason for this is that a ring of two nodes is equivalent to a chain of two nodes as far as the dimensional exchange operator is concerned.

Figure 4.3 shows two common ways of node-labeling an $k_1 \times k_2$ torus: row-major and snake-like row-major. As the spectrum of eigenvalues of the GDE matrix of a network is invariant under any permutation of the node labels, we arbitrarily choose the the snake-like row-major labeling. Similarly, there are two major ways of coloring the edges: row-major and column-major coloring, as shown in the figure. We assume that the torus is colored in the row-major way. Note that, with this coloring, all horizontal edges are smaller than the vertical edges in their chromatic indices. We will soon see that because of the particular structure of the GDE matrix as revealed by the following lemma, these two colorings have the same effect on the convergence rate.

Lemma 4.1.2 *Let $\mathbf{T}_{k_1,k_2}$ be the GDE matrix of a $k_1 \times k_2$ even color torus. Then, $\mathbf{T}_{k_1,k_2} = \mathbf{R}_{k_2} \otimes \mathbf{R}_{k_1}$.*

Proof. Given an ordered pair of vertices $< i, j >$ in the torus,

1. if both i and j are in the same horizontal ring, *i.e.*, $\lfloor i/k_1 \rfloor = \lfloor j/k_1 \rfloor$, then,

$$(\mathbf{T}_{k_1,k_2})_{i,j} = \begin{cases} (1-\lambda)(\mathbf{R}_{k_1})_{i \bmod k_1, j \bmod k_1} & \text{if } k_2 = 2 \\ (1-\lambda)^2(\mathbf{R}_{k_1})_{i \bmod k_1, j \bmod k_1} & \text{otherwise} \end{cases}$$

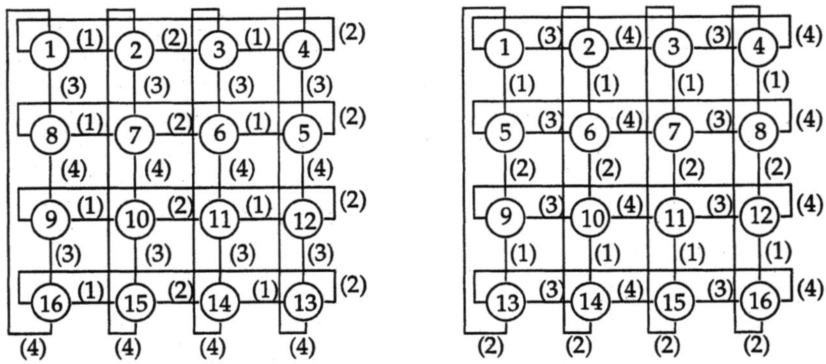

(a) row-major edge-coloring snake-like row-major node-labeling

(b) column-major edge-coloring row-major node-labeling

Figure 4.3: Node-labeling and edge-coloring of the torus

$$= \quad (\mathbf{R}_{n_2})_{\lfloor i/k_1 \rfloor, \lfloor j/k_1 \rfloor} (\mathbf{R}_{k_1})_{i \bmod k_1, j \bmod k_1};$$

It is because the coloring we use ensures that all horizontal edges are smaller than the vertical edges in chromatic indices,

2. if i and j are in different horizontal rings, *i.e.*, $\lfloor i/k_1 \rfloor \neq \lfloor j/k_1 \rfloor$, then there is a color path from i to j, say $p_{i,j}$, if and only if there exists a vertex i_1 such that $i_1 \bmod k_1 = i \bmod k_1$, $\lfloor i_1/k_1 \rfloor = \lfloor j/k_1 \rfloor$, and there exist two color paths $p_{i_1,j}$ and p_{i,i_1} from i_1 to j and from i to i_1, respectively, as in the picture below.

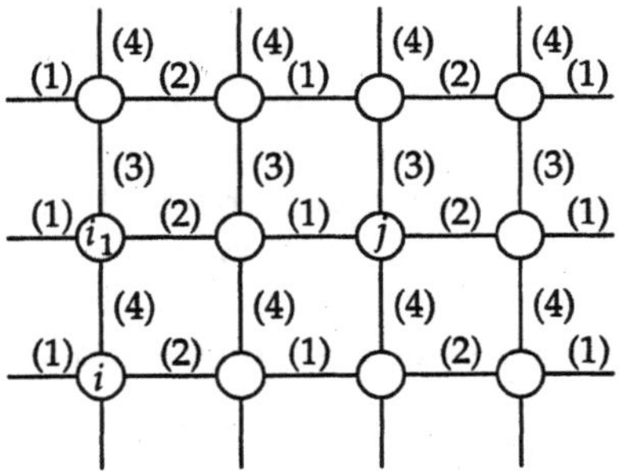

Let l_1 and l_2 be the lengths of $p_{i_1,j}$ and p_{i,i_1}, respectively; r_1 be the sum of (1) the number of incident horizontal edges of i_1 that are between, in color numbers, the incident edges of i_1 along the color path $p_{i,j}$, and (2) the number of incident horizontal edges of i_1 whose color number is less than that of the last edge in $p_{i,j}$; and r_2 be the sum of (1) the number of incident vertical edges of i_1 that are between, in color numbers, the incident edges of i_1 along p_{ij}, and (2) the number of incident vertical edges of i_1 whose color number is larger than that of the first edge in $p_{i,j}$. Then, according to the computation formulas in Lemma 3.3.1, we have

$$\begin{aligned}(\mathbf{T}_{k_1,k_2})_{i,j} &= \lambda^{l_1+l_2}(1-\lambda)^{r_1+r_2} \\ &= \lambda^{l_2}(1-\lambda)^{r_2}\lambda^{l_1}(1-\lambda)^{r_1} \\ &= (\mathbf{R}_{k_2})_{\lfloor i/k_1 \rfloor,\ \lfloor i_1/k_1 \rfloor} \times (\mathbf{R}_{k_1})_{i_1 \bmod k_1, j \bmod k_1} \\ &= (\mathbf{R}_{k_2})_{\lfloor i/k_1 \rfloor, \lfloor j/k_1 \rfloor} \times (\mathbf{R}_{k_1})_{i \bmod k_1, j \bmod k_1}\end{aligned}$$

By referring to the definition of direct product in Lemma 4.0.2, the lemma is proved. □

If instead we use column-major coloring, then all horizontal edges are larger than the vertical edges in chromatic indices. By following the above steps, however, we would find that the resulting GDE matrix is the same as $\mathbf{T}_{k_1,k_2}$. We continue to assume the row-major coloring in the following analysis of the convergence factor.

Theorem 4.1.2 *Let $\mathbf{T}_{k_1,k_2}$ be the GDE matrix of a $k_1 \times k_2$ even color torus. Then, the optimal exchange parameter, $\lambda_{opt}(\mathbf{T}_{k_1,k_2})$, is equal to $\lambda_{opt}(\mathbf{R}_k)$, and for a given λ, $\gamma(\mathbf{T}_{k_1,k_2}) = \gamma(\mathbf{R}_k)$, where $k = \max\{k_1, k_2\}$.*

Proof. From Lemma 4.0.2, it is clear that

$$\gamma(\mathbf{T}_{k_1,k_2}) = \max\{\gamma(\mathbf{R}_{k_1}), \gamma(\mathbf{R}_{k_2})\}$$

because $\rho(\mathbf{R}_{k_1}) = \rho(\mathbf{R}_{k_2}) = 1$. Moreover, from Theorem 4.1.1, $\gamma(\mathbf{R}_{k_1}) \geq \gamma(\mathbf{R}_{k_2})$ if and only if $k_1 \geq k_2$. Hence, $\gamma(\mathbf{T}_{k_1,k_2}) = \gamma(\mathbf{R}_k)$, where $k = \max\{k_1, k_2\}$; and $\gamma(\mathbf{T}_{k_1,k_2})$ is minimized when $\lambda = \lambda_{opt}(\mathbf{R}_k)$. In other words, $\gamma(\mathbf{T}_{k_1,k_2}) = \gamma(\mathbf{R}_k)$ and both $\mathbf{R}_k$ and $\mathbf{T}_{k_1,k_2}$ have the same optimal exchange parameter. □

This theorem shows that the optimal exchange parameter in a $k_1 \times k_2$ torus $\lambda_{opt} = \frac{1}{1+\sin(2\pi/k)}$, where $k = \max\{k_1, k_2\}$. It also reveals an interesting fact that the convergence rate in torus structures is dependent only on the larger dimension order and is insensitive to the smaller one. For example, the $16 \times j$ even tori, $j = 2, 4, \ldots, 16$, all have the same convergence rate for a given λ and share the same optimal exchange parameter

$$\lambda_{opt}(\mathbf{T}_{16,j}) = 2/(2 + \sqrt{2 - \sqrt{2}}) \approx 0.723.$$

An implication of the theorem is that square interconnection network is preferable to the rectangular in terms of the GDE load balancing efficiency.

The results of two-dimensional tori shown above can be generalized to multi-dimensional tori. Consider an $k_1 \times k_2 \times \ldots \times k_n$ even torus and assume that this n-dimensional torus is colored in a way similar to that for the two-dimensional torus. Then, its GDE matrix can be expressed in terms of direct products of color rings.

Lemma 4.1.3 *Let $\mathbf{T}_{k_1,k_2,\ldots,k_n}$ be the GDE matrix of an n-dimensional $k_1 \times k_2 \times \cdots \times k_n$ even color torus. Then,*

$$\mathbf{T}_{k_1,k_2,\ldots,k_n} = \mathbf{R}_{k_1} \otimes \mathbf{R}_{k_2} \otimes \cdots \otimes \mathbf{R}_{k_n}.$$

This lemma can be easily proved by induction on the dimension n. From this lemma, the following result is immediately in order.

Theorem 4.1.3 *Let $\mathbf{T}_{k_1,k_2,\ldots,k_n}$ be the GDE matrix of an n-dimensional $k_1 \times k_2 \times \cdots \times k_n$ even color torus. Then, the optimal exchange parameter, $\lambda_{opt}(\mathbf{T}_{k_1,k_2,\ldots,k_n})$, is equal to $\lambda_{opt}(\mathbf{R}_k)$, $k = \max_{1 \le j \le n}\{k_j\}$; and for a given λ, $\gamma(\mathbf{T}_{k_1,k_2,\ldots,k_n}) = \gamma(\mathbf{R}_k)$.*

Since a k-ary n-cube is a special case of an n-dimensional torus, we have the following corollary.

Corollary 4.1.1 *Let $\mathbf{T}_{k;n}$ be the GDE matrix of a color k-ary n-cube, k is even. Then, the optimal exchange parameter, $\lambda_{opt}(\mathbf{T}_{k;n})$, is equal to $\lambda_{opt}(\mathbf{R}_k)$, and for a given λ, $\gamma(\mathbf{T}_{k;n}) = \gamma(\mathbf{R}_k)$.*

4.2 GDE on n-Dimensional Meshes

In this section, we analyze the GDE load balancing method as applied to n-dimensional meshes which are variants of n-dimensional tori without end-round connections.

4.2.1 The Chain

First consider a chain of with k vertices labeled from 1 to k. Such a chain can be edge-colored in two ways, as in Figure 3.1(c) and (d). Suppose $\mathbf{C}_k^a$, $\mathbf{C}_k^b$ are the GDE matrices of the two color chains of order k. It can be shown that $\mathbf{C}_k^a$ is a transpose of $\mathbf{C}_k^b$ (denoted by $(\mathbf{C}_k^b)^T$). As a matrix and its transpose have the same spectrum of eigenvalues, the two colorings have the same effect on the the convergence rate. Below, we arbitrarily assume the way of coloring edges as in Figure 3.1(c). Similarly to the GDE matrices of color rings, the GDE matrices of color chains can also be represented in a recursive form. Note that we have to consider also the GDE matrices of *odd* chains as they will be needed in the main theorem concerning even chains.

Lemma 4.2.1 *Let $\mathbf{C}_k$ be the GDE matrix of a color chain of order k. Then,*

1. *if k is even, $\mathbf{C}_k$ is a matrix of the form*

$$\begin{pmatrix} \mathbf{Q}_1 & & & & & \\ \mathbf{U} & \mathbf{V} & & & & \\ & \mathbf{U} & \mathbf{V} & & & \\ & & \ddots & \ddots & & \\ & & & \mathbf{U} & \mathbf{V} & \\ & & & & \mathbf{Q}_2 & \end{pmatrix}_{k\times k} \tag{4.2}$$

2. *if k is odd, $\mathbf{C}_k$ is a matrix of the form*

$$\begin{pmatrix} \mathbf{Q}_1 & & & & \\ \mathbf{U} & \mathbf{V} & & & \\ & \ddots & \ddots & & \\ & & \mathbf{U} & \mathbf{V} & \\ & & & \mathbf{U} & \mathbf{Q}_2^T \end{pmatrix}_{k\times k} \tag{4.3}$$

This lemma can be proved in a similar way to the proof of Lemma 4.1.1. Following are two GDE matrices of chains of order 3 and 6, respectively.

$$\mathbf{C}_3 = \begin{pmatrix} 1-\lambda & \lambda & 0 \\ \lambda(1-\lambda) & (1-\lambda)^2 & \lambda \\ \lambda^2 & \lambda(1-\lambda) & 1-\lambda \end{pmatrix}$$

$$\mathbf{C}_6 = \begin{pmatrix} 1-\lambda & \lambda & 0 & 0 & 0 & 0 \\ \lambda(1-\lambda) & (1-\lambda)^2 & \lambda(1-\lambda) & \lambda^2 & 0 & 0 \\ \lambda^2 & \lambda(1-\lambda) & (1-\lambda)^2 & \lambda(1-\lambda) & 0 & 0 \\ 0 & 0 & \lambda(1-\lambda) & (1-\lambda)^2 & \lambda(1-\lambda) & \lambda^2 \\ 0 & 0 & \lambda^2 & \lambda(1-\lambda) & (1-\lambda)^2 & \lambda(1-\lambda) \\ 0 & 0 & 0 & 0 & \lambda & 1-\lambda \end{pmatrix}$$

Having known the particular structure of the GDE matrix, we examine next the convergence rate of the GDE load balancing process in color chains. We first present a lemma concerning the eigenvalues of $\mathbf{C}_k$.

Lemma 4.2.2 *Let $\mathbf{C}_k$ be the GDE matrix of a color chain of order k. Then,*

1. *if k is even ($k = 2m$), the eigenvalues of $\mathbf{C}_k$ are those of $\mathbf{C}_m$, together with those of a matrix of the following form if m is even*

$$\begin{pmatrix} \mathbf{Q}_1 & & & & \\ \mathbf{U} & \mathbf{V} & & & \\ & \ddots & \ddots & & \\ & & \mathbf{U} & \mathbf{V} & \\ & & & & (1-2\lambda)\mathbf{Q}_2 \end{pmatrix}_{m\times m} \tag{4.4}$$

or together with those of a matrix of the following form if m is odd

$$\begin{pmatrix} \mathbf{Q}_1 & & & & \\ \mathbf{U} & \mathbf{V} & & & \\ & \ddots & \ddots & & \\ & & \mathbf{U} & \mathbf{V} & \\ & & & \mathbf{U} & (1-2\lambda)\mathbf{Q}_2^T \end{pmatrix}_{m\times m} \tag{4.5}$$

2. *if k is odd, the eigenvalues of $\mathbf{C}_k$ are those of $\mathbf{R}_{2k}$, excluding those of a matrix of the following form if k is even*

$$\begin{pmatrix} (1-2\lambda)\mathbf{Q}_1 & & & & \\ \mathbf{U} & \mathbf{V} & & & \\ & \ddots & \ddots & & \\ & & \mathbf{U} & \mathbf{V} & \\ & & & & (1-2\lambda)\mathbf{Q}_2 \end{pmatrix}_{k\times k} \tag{4.6}$$

or excluding those of a matrix of the following form if k is odd

$$\begin{pmatrix} (1-2\lambda)\mathbf{Q}_1 & & & & \\ \mathbf{U} & \mathbf{V} & & & \\ & \ddots & \ddots & & \\ & & \mathbf{U} & \mathbf{V} & \\ & & & \mathbf{U} & (1-2\lambda)\mathbf{Q}_2^T \end{pmatrix}_{k\times k} \tag{4.7}$$

Proof. Consider the GDE matrix, $\mathbf{C}_k$, $k = 2m$. According to the permutation

$$\pi_{2m} = \begin{pmatrix} 0 & 1 & \dots & m-1 & m & m+1 & \dots & 2m-1 \\ 0 & 1 & \dots & m-1 & 2m-1 & 2m-2 & \dots & m \end{pmatrix}$$

we rearrange the rows and columns of $\mathbf{C}_k$. This reduces $\mathbf{C}_k$ to a block circulant matrix $\Phi_{2,m}(\mathbf{A}_1, \mathbf{A}_2)$ defined as follows.

1. If m is even,

$$A_1 = \begin{pmatrix} \mathbf{Q}_1 & & & & \\ \mathbf{U} & \mathbf{V} & & & \\ & \ddots & \ddots & & \\ & & \mathbf{U} & \mathbf{U}^T & \\ & & & \mathbf{U}_1 & \end{pmatrix}_{m\times m} \qquad A_2 = \begin{pmatrix} \mathbf{0} & \\ & \mathbf{U}_2 \end{pmatrix}_{m\times m}$$

   It follows that $\mathbf{A}_1 + \mathbf{A}_2 = \mathbf{C}_m$, and $\mathbf{A}_1 - \mathbf{A}_2$ is a matrix of the form of (4.4).

2. If m is odd,

$$\mathbf{A}_1 = \begin{pmatrix} \mathbf{Q}_1 & & & & \\ \mathbf{U} & \mathbf{V} & & & \\ & \ddots & \ddots & & \\ & & \mathbf{U} & \mathbf{U}^T & \\ & & & \mathbf{U} & \mathbf{U}_1^T \end{pmatrix}_{m\times m} \qquad \mathbf{A}_2 = \begin{pmatrix} \mathbf{0} & \\ & \mathbf{U}_2^T \end{pmatrix}_{m\times m}$$

   It follows that $\mathbf{A}_1 + \mathbf{A}_2 = \mathbf{C}_m$, and $\mathbf{A}_1 - \mathbf{A}_2$ is a matrix of the form of (4.5).

From Lemma 4.0.1, part (1) is proved.

The proof of part (2) is similar to that of part (1). Consider the GDE matrix of a color ring of $2k$ nodes, $\mathbf{R}_{2k}$. By rearranging the matrix $\mathbf{R}_{2k}$ as shown in Lemma 4.1.1 according to the permutation π_{2k}, $\mathbf{R}_{2k}$ is reduced to a block circulant matrix $\Phi_{2,k}(\mathbf{A}_1, \mathbf{A}_2)$ defined as follows.

1. If k is even, $\mathbf{A}_1 = \mathbf{R}_k$ and $\mathbf{A}_2 = \begin{pmatrix} \mathbf{V}_1 & & \\ & \mathbf{0} & \\ & & \mathbf{U}_2 \end{pmatrix}_{k\times k}$

2. If k is odd,

$$\mathbf{A}_1 = \begin{pmatrix} \mathbf{V}_2 & & & & \\ \mathbf{U} & \mathbf{V} & & & \\ & \ddots & \ddots & & \\ & & \mathbf{U} & \mathbf{U}^T & \\ & & & \mathbf{U} & \mathbf{U}_1^T \end{pmatrix}_{k\times k} \qquad \mathbf{A}_2 = \begin{pmatrix} \mathbf{V}_1 & & \\ & \mathbf{0} & \\ & & \mathbf{U}_2^T \end{pmatrix}_{k\times k}$$

It happens that $\mathbf{A}_1 + \mathbf{A}_2 = \mathbf{C}_k$ in both cases, and $\mathbf{A}_1 - \mathbf{A}_2$ is a matrix of order k of the form of (4.6) when k is even or of the form of (4.7) when k is odd. Thus, part (2) is proved. □

We are now in the position to derive the optimal exchange parameter of chains and to study the effects of their order on the convergence rate in terms of the relationship between chains and rings.

Theorem 4.2.1 *Let $\mathbf{C}_k$ be the GDE matrix of a color chain of even order k. Then, the optimal exchange parameter, $\lambda_{opt}(\mathbf{C}_k)$, is equal to $\lambda_{opt}(\mathbf{R}_{2k})$. For a given λ, $\gamma(\mathbf{C}_k) = \gamma(\mathbf{R}_{2k})$.*

Proof. Consider the matrix $\mathbf{R}_{2k}$ and suppose $k = 2m$. From Lemma 4.2.2, the eigenvalues of $\mathbf{R}_{2k}$ are those of a matrix of order k in the form of (4.6) (denoted by RC), together with those of the matrix $\mathbf{C}_k$. Clearly, RC can be reduced (by the permutation of π_k as used in the proof of Lemma 4.2.2) to a block circulant matrix $\Phi_{2,m}(\mathbf{A}_1, \mathbf{A}_2)$ defined as follows.

1. If m is even, then

$$\mathbf{A}_1 = \begin{pmatrix} (1-2\lambda)\mathbf{Q}_1 & & & & \\ \mathbf{U} & \mathbf{V} & & & \\ & \ddots & \ddots & & \\ & & \mathbf{U} & \mathbf{V} & \\ & & & & \mathbf{U}_1 \end{pmatrix}_{m\times m} \qquad \mathbf{A}_2 = \begin{pmatrix} \mathbf{0} & \\ & \mathbf{U}_2 \end{pmatrix}_{m\times m}$$

It follows that

$$\mathbf{A}_1 + \mathbf{A}_2 = \begin{pmatrix} (1-2\lambda)\mathbf{Q}_1 & & & & \\ \mathbf{U} & \mathbf{V} & & & \\ & \ddots & \ddots & & \\ & & \mathbf{U} & \mathbf{V} & \\ & & & & \mathbf{Q}_2 \end{pmatrix}_{m\times m} \tag{4.8}$$

$$\mathbf{A}_1 - \mathbf{A}_2 = \begin{pmatrix} (1-2\lambda)\mathbf{Q}_1 & & & & \\ \mathbf{U} & \mathbf{V} & & & \\ & \ddots & \ddots & & \\ & & \mathbf{U} & \mathbf{V} & \\ & & & & (1-2\lambda)\mathbf{Q}_2 \end{pmatrix}_{m\times m} \tag{4.9}$$

2. If m is odd, then

$$\mathbf{A}_1 = \begin{pmatrix} (1-2\lambda)\mathbf{Q}_1 & & & & \\ \mathbf{U} & \mathbf{V} & & & \\ & \ddots & \ddots & & \\ & & \mathbf{U} & \mathbf{V} & \\ & & & \mathbf{U} & \mathbf{U}_1^T \end{pmatrix}_{m\times m} \qquad \mathbf{A}_2 = \begin{pmatrix} \mathbf{0} & \\ & \mathbf{U}_2^T \end{pmatrix}_{m\times m}$$

It follows that

$$\mathbf{A}_1 + \mathbf{A}_2 = \begin{pmatrix} (1-2\lambda)\mathbf{Q}_1 & & & & \\ \mathbf{U} & \mathbf{V} & & & \\ & \ddots & \ddots & & \\ & & \mathbf{U} & \mathbf{V} & \\ & & & \mathbf{U} & \mathbf{Q}_2^T \end{pmatrix}_{m \times m} \tag{4.10}$$

$$\mathbf{A}_1 - \mathbf{A}_2 = \begin{pmatrix} (1-2\lambda)\mathbf{Q}_1 & & & & \\ \mathbf{U} & \mathbf{V} & & & \\ & \ddots & \ddots & & \\ & & \mathbf{U} & \mathbf{V} & \\ & & & \mathbf{U} & (1-2\lambda)\mathbf{Q}_2^T \end{pmatrix}_{m \times m} \tag{4.11}$$

Thus, from Lemma 4.1.1 again, the eigenvalues of $\mathbf{R}_{2k}$ are those of matrices $\mathbf{A}_1 + \mathbf{A}_2$ and $\mathbf{A}_1 - \mathbf{A}_2$, together with those of $\mathbf{C}_k$. Let us then look at the matrices $\mathbf{A}_1 + \mathbf{A}_2$ and $\mathbf{A}_1 - \mathbf{A}_2$. Consider the matrix $\mathbf{A}_1 + \mathbf{A}_2$. It can be shown that after rearrangement according to the permutation $\begin{pmatrix} 0 & 1 & \cdots & m-1 \\ m-1 & m-2 & \cdots & 0 \end{pmatrix}$, the transformed matrix $\mathbf{A}_1 + \mathbf{A}_2$ in the form of (4.8) is equal to a square matrix of order m which is in the form of (4.4), and the transformed matrix $\mathbf{A}_1 + \mathbf{A}_2$, in the form of (4.10), is a transpose of a square matrix of order m which is in the form of (4.5). Hence, from part (1) of Lemma 4.2.2, it follows that the set of eigenvalues of $\mathbf{A}_1 + \mathbf{A}_2$ is included in that of $\mathbf{C}_n$.

Consider the matrix $\mathbf{A}_1 - \mathbf{A}_2$. It is in the form of (4.6) or (4.7). Hence, the eigenvalues of $\mathbf{A}_1 - \mathbf{A}_2$ are those of $\mathbf{R}_n$, excluding those of $\mathbf{C}_m$.

Consequently, $\sigma(\mathbf{R}_{2k}) = \sigma(\mathbf{C}_k) \bigcup \sigma(\mathbf{R}_k)$, where $\sigma(M)$ is the set of all distinct eigenvalues of the matrix M. Hence, from Theorem 4.1.1, it follows that $\gamma(\mathbf{R}_{2k}) = \gamma(\mathbf{C}_k)$. $\gamma(\mathbf{C}_k)$ is minimized when $\lambda = \lambda_{opt}(\mathbf{R}_{2k})$. □

Based on this theorem, the optimal exchange parameters for even color chains can be easily obtained. For example,

$$\lambda_{opt}(\mathbf{C}_8) = \lambda_{opt}(\mathbf{R}_{16}) = \frac{2}{2 + \sqrt{2 - \sqrt{2}}} \approx 0.723.$$

This theorem also says that for a given λ, $\gamma(\mathbf{C}_{k+2}) \geq \gamma(\mathbf{C}_k)$—that is, the more vertices a chain has, the slower its convergence rate.

4.2.2 The n-Dimensional Mesh

Finally, let us look at the GDE load balancing method as applied to even n-dimensional meshes (even number of nodes in both dimensions). Consider a two-dimensional $k_1 \times k_2$ even mesh as in Figure 4.4. Similarly to the case of torus, and without loss of generality, we assume the node-labeling and edge-coloring of Figure 4.4(a). We will show that meshes are related to chains in behavior, just as tori are related to rings.

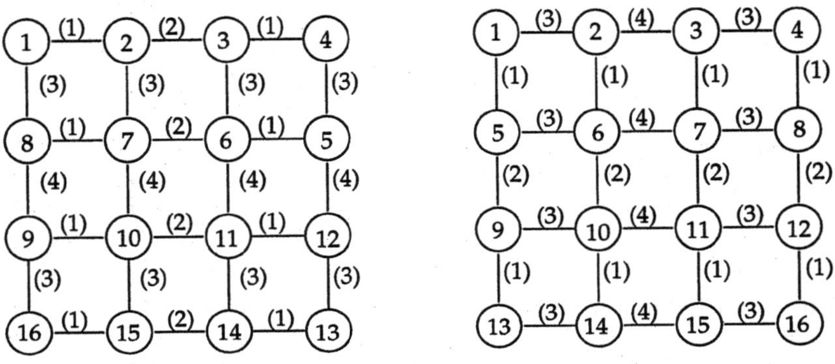

(a) row-major edge-coloring
snake-like row-major node-labeling

(b) column-major edge-coloring
row-major node-labeling

Figure 4.4: Node-labeling and edge-coloring of the mesh

Lemma 4.2.3 *Let $\mathbf{M}_{k_1,k_2}$ be the GDE matrix of a two-dimensional $k_1 \times k_2$ even color mesh. Then, $\mathbf{M}_{k_1,k_2} = \mathbf{C}_{k_2} \otimes \mathbf{C}_{k_1}$.*

This lemma can be proved in a similar way to that of Lemma 4.1.2. This lemma shows the close relationship between the GDE matrices of meshes and chains. For the same reason as given in the case of tori, both ways of coloring, (a) and (b), have the same effect on the convergence rate in meshes. Given this particular form of the matrix $\mathbf{M}_{k_1,k_2}$, we can now study the convergence rate in meshes based on the relationship between meshes and chains.

Theorem 4.2.2 *Let $\mathbf{M}_{k_1,k_2}$ be the GDE matrix of a two-dimensional $k_1 \times k_2$ even color mesh. Then, the optimal exchange parameter, $\lambda_{opt}(\mathbf{M}_{k_1,k_2})$, is equal to $\lambda_{opt}(\mathbf{C}_k)$, where $k = \max\{k_1, k_2\}$; and for a given λ, $\gamma(\mathbf{M}_{k_1,k_2}) = \gamma(\mathbf{C}_k)$.*

Proof. Similarly to the proof of Theorem 4.1.2, we have

$$\gamma(\mathbf{M}_{k_1,k_2}) = \max\{\gamma(\mathbf{C}_{k_1}), \gamma(\mathbf{C}_{k_2})\}$$

Moreover, from the comment that follows the proof of Theorem 4.2.1, we have $\gamma(\mathbf{M}_{k_1,k_2})$ is minimized when $\lambda = \lambda_{opt}(\mathbf{C}_k)$, where $k = \max\{k_1, k_2\}$. □

One can derive the optimal exchange parameter for an even mesh based on the optimal exchange parameter for the corresponding even chain, which is derivable from Theorem 4.2.1. The theorem above says that the convergence rate of a mesh depends only on its larger dimension. For example, the meshes of sizes $8 \times j$, $j = 2, 4, 6, 8$, all have the same convergence rate for a given λ, and the same optimal exchange parameter

$$\lambda_{opt}(\mathbf{M}_{8,j}) = \frac{2}{2 + \sqrt{2 - \sqrt{2}}} \approx 0.723.$$

The results of two-dimensional color meshes can be generalized to multi-dimensional meshes as well, as in the case of torus.

Theorem 4.2.3 *Let $\mathbf{M}_{k_1,k_2,\ldots,k_n}$ be the GDE matrix of a $k_1 \times k_2 \times \ldots \times k_n$ even color mesh. Then, the optimal exchange parameter, $\lambda_{opt}(\mathbf{M}_{k_1,k_2,\ldots,k_n})$, is equal to $\lambda_{opt}(\mathbf{R}_k)$, and for a given λ, $\gamma(\mathbf{M}_{k_1,k_2,\ldots,k_n}) = \gamma(\mathbf{C}_k)$, $k = \max_{1 \leq j \leq n}\{k_j\}$.*

4.3 Simulation

We have derived the optimal exchange parameters which would lead to the fastest convergence rate in n-dimensional tori and meshes. For actual computations, it would be of considerable value to estimate the number of iteration sweeps required for the system to arrive at its load balanced state. From Eq. 3.6, we see that the number of iteration sweep, denoted by T, is dependent upon such factors as the initial workload variance, the the prescribed relative error bound δ, and the convergence factor of the GDE balancing $\gamma(\mathbf{E})$. The term $\gamma(\mathbf{E})$ is in turn determined by the network topology and size and the exchange parameter λ.

4.3.1 Number of Iteration Sweeps

We conducted a statistical simulation experiment on a number of test cases in order to obtain an idea of the number of iteration sweeps necessary for optimal GDE balancing. The simulation results also confirm our theoretical results concerning the equivalence of the various convergence rates and the optimal values for the exchange parameters.

The initial workload distribution $\mathbf{W}^0$ is a random vector, each element w of which is drawn independently from an identical uniform distribution in

$[0, 2b]$, where b is a prescribed bound. The mean workload a processor gets (*i.e.*, the expected workload $\mathcal{E}(w)$) is thus equal to b. The relative error bound τ can be tuned to achieve the desired performance as needed in practice. In our simulation experiments, this value is set to one. That is, the load balancing procedure continues until the Euclidean norm of the error vector is less than one. Figure 4.5 plots the expected numbers of sweeps in the structures of ring 16, chain 8, torus 16×4 and mesh 8×4 in reaching the balanced state from initial workload distributions with a mean of 128 workload units per processor as λ varies from 0.1 to 0.95 in steps of 0.05. Each data point is the average of 100 runs, each using a different random initial load distribution.

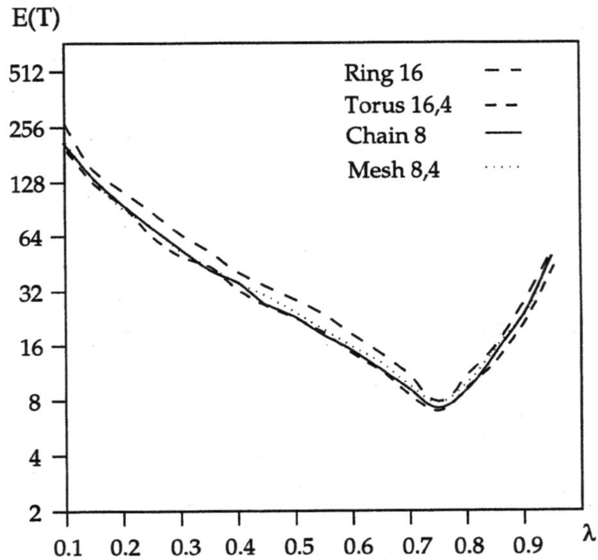

Figure 4.5: Expected number of sweeps necessary for a global balanced state as a function of the exchange parameter λ in various structures

We have learned that these four structures are equivalent in terms of their convergence factors of the GDE method. From the figure, it is clear that the expected number of sweeps in each case for different values of λ rises and drops with the value of $\gamma(\mathbf{E})$ in Figure 4.2, and that the optimal exchange parameter λ_{opt} of each case is not equal to 0.5, but somewhere between 0.7 and 0.8, which is in agreement with the theoretical result of $\lambda_{opt} = 0.723$. In the figure, it also appears that the absolute values of the expected number of sweeps for the various structures are very close to each other, especially near the optimum point, which is in line with the theoretical results on the equivalence of convergence.

Furthermore, it is most encouraging to see that the optimal sweep numbers are rather small—about 8 sweeps (for a chain of 8 nodes, and even for a 16-ary 2-cube). The results for large-scale systems with up to 128 nodes (for chain) are depicted in Figure 4.6. Figure 4.6 also shows that the optimal number of sweeps are linearly proportional to the number of nodes for the chain, and hence to the dimension order k for the k-ary n-cube structure. These really put forth the GDE method as a practical method for load balancing in real multicomputers.

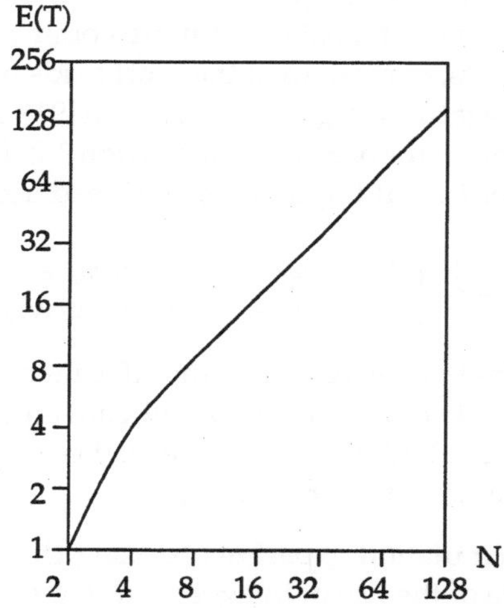

Figure 4.6: Expected number of sweeps necessary for a global balanced state using λ_{opt} for chains of various sizes

Notice that the convergence rates in the theoretical analysis are in terms of sweeps over time. A sweep of the GDE method may involve different numbers of communication steps in various structures. In a k-ary n-cube (k even), a sweep comprises $2n$ communication steps in case $n < 2$ or n steps in case $n = 2$. Thus, for a given number of processors, a higher dimensional k-ary n-cube, even though it takes fewer sweeps to balance the load, requires more communication steps within a sweep in reality. However, in Figure 4.6, we see that the optimal number of sweeps would decrease at a logarithmic rate with the increase of the number of dimensions; this is because the dimension order decreases at the same rate as the increase of the number of dimensions for a given number of nodes. As an example, consider a cluster of 4096 processors, which can be organized as a structure of 64-ary 2-cube, 16-ary 3-cube, 8-ary 4-cube, or 2-ary 12-cube. The optimal sweep numbers for these structures are about 35, 8, 4, and 1 sweep, respectively. Since the number of communication steps within a sweep would only double with every added dimension, it is justified to maintain that in practice the GDE method is most effective in high dimensional k-ary n-cubes (in particular, the binary n-cube and the 4-ary n-cube).

4.3.2 Integer Workload Model

In the theoretical analysis, we represent the workload of a processor by a real number, which is reasonable under the assumption of very fine grain parallelism as exhibited by the computation. To cover medium and large grain parallelisms which are more realistic and more common in practical parallel computing environments, one can treat the workloads of the processors more conveniently as non-negative integers, as is done in [91]. All we need to do is to modify the exchange operator of Eq. (3.1) in Section 3.2. During exchange with a neighbor j, processor i would update its workload according to the revised formula

$$w_i = \begin{cases} \lceil (1-\lambda)w_i + \lambda w_j \rceil & \text{if } w_i \geq w_j \\ \lfloor (1-\lambda)w_i + \lambda w_j \rfloor & \text{otherwise} \end{cases} \tag{4.12}$$

As discussed in [91], the integer version of the ADE method (*i.e.*, $\lambda = 1/2$) is just a perturbation of its real counterpart and will converge to a nearly balanced state. Applying the perturbation theory to the real version of our GDE method verbatim, we can come to a similar conclusion.

We repeated our simulation experiments using the integer version of the GDE method. Because of the use of integer workloads, we allow the load balancing procedure to end with a variance of some threshold value (in workload units) between neighboring processors. This threshold value can be tuned to satisfactory performance of the procedure in practice, as illustrated in [130]. In all our simulation experiments, this value is set to *one* workload unit which is closest to total balancing. Then, it is clear that $0.5 \leq \lambda < 1$ because a pair of neighboring processors with a variance of more than one workload unit would not balance their workloads any more when $\lambda < 0.5$.

Table 4.1 displays the expected numbers of sweeps generated by the experiments for the structures of Ring 16, Chain 8, 16-ary 2-cube (*i.e.*, Torus 16×16), and Mesh 8×4. The initial workload distribution has a mean of 128 units per processor, and λ varies from 0.5 to 0.9 in steps of 0.05. Each data point is the average of 100 runs, each using a different random initial load distribution. The second column in the table shows the convergence factors, $\gamma(\mathbf{E})$, of the GDE matrices of the various cases. From the table, it is clear that the expected number of sweeps in each case for different values of λ rises and drops with the value of $\gamma(\mathbf{E})$, and that the optimal exchange parameter λ_{opt} of each case is not equal to 0.5, but somewhere between 0.7 and 0.8, which is in agreement with the theoretical result of $\lambda_{opt} = 0.723$. It also appears that the absolute values of the expected number of sweeps for the various structures are very close to

Table 4.1: Expected number of sweeps, $\mathcal{E}(T)$, for various structures in the integer workload model

λ	$\gamma(M(\lambda))$	Ring 16	16-ary 2-cube	Chain 8	Mesh 8 × 4
0.50	0.8536	21.33	16.69	19.97	15.78
0.55	0.8206	20.30	16.22	19.08	15.05
0.60	0.7777	16.79	13.91	15.87	12.61
0.65	0.7170	15.17	12.95	14.28	11.37
0.70	0.6112	10.76	9.19	10.22	8.70
0.75	0.5000	8.55	7.69	8.32	7.67
0.80	0.6000	9.68	7.73	9.44	8.27
0.85	0.7000	11.63	9.14	11.54	10.14
0.90	0.8000	15.88	11.72	15.86	13.56
0.95	0.9000	25.42	17.31	25.56	20.80
0.723	0.4465	9.82	8.58	9.19	8.25

each other, especially when near the optimum point, which is in line with our theoretical results on the equivalence of the convergence rates.

4.3.3 The Non-Even Cases

In addition to the even case, we also simulated a few "non-even" cases for which the theoretical analysis has not been able to deal with because of their structural differences from the even cases. We approximated their optimal exchange parameters using the formulas for the even cases. Figure 4.7 plots the simulation results. In line with our remark in the beginning of this chapter, the odd or non-even cases do not behave differently from the even cases in terms of convergence pattern and the optimal exchange parameter. It can be seen by comparing Figure 4.7 with Figure 4.5. Hence, it is reasonable to conclude that the results for the even cases can be applied, as a close approximation, to the non-even cases.

Note that an odd ring has to be colored using three colors, as in Figure 3.1(a). That is, a sweep of the GDE method in an odd ring comprises three communication steps. As only two processors are involved in workload exchange in the third communication step, it seems that much communication bandwidth may be wasted. However, a close examination of the communication pattern of GDE balancing in the odd ring, as shown in Figure 4.8, would reveal that the third chromatic index would account for only a small fraction of the total communication overhead incurred in the balancing process. In the figure, the five big dots in the center represent processors that are connected as a ring. We

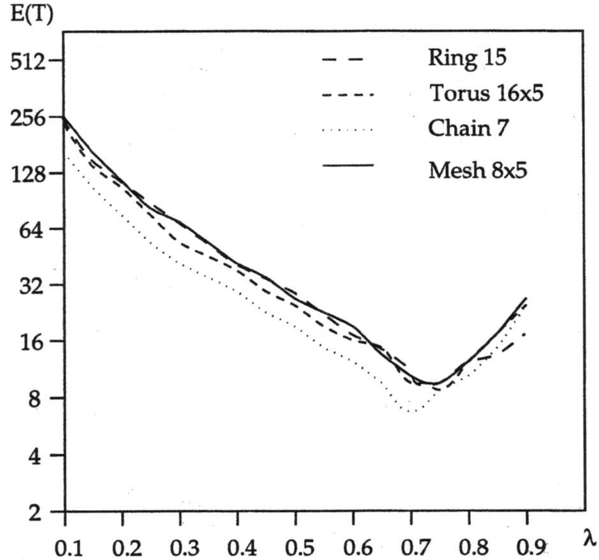

Figure 4.7: Expected number of sweeps necessary for a global balanced state as a function of the exchange parameter λ in various structures of "non-even" cases

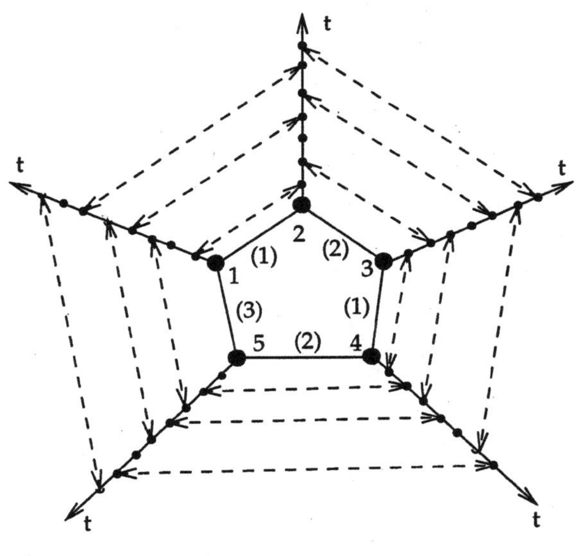

Figure 4.8: A communication pattern of the GDE method in a ring of 5 nodes

attach a time axis t to each processor for easy viewing. Each dotted double-arrow represents a communication step between a pair of nearest neighbors for the exchange of their workloads. At time $t = 1$, all processors except the fifth are involved in communication. Then, the first processor becomes idle at time $t = 2$. While the first and fifth processors are busy executing the third communication step at time $t = 3$, the third and fourth processors are already executing the first communication of the next sweep. At this time, only the second processor is in the idle state. Continue on, we see that the GDE procedure finishes two complete iteration sweeps in five communication steps. In other words, GDE balancing in an odd ring of five nodes costs only one extra communication step more than an even ring of comparable size for two iteration sweeps. This example can be generalized to an odd ring of arbitrary size. In general, the GDE balancing in an odd ring of $2k+1$ nodes costs one communication step more than that in the even ring of $2k$ nodes for k iteration sweeps. Based on the equivalence results between the ring and the other structures in previous sections, we can conclude that there is a negligibly small difference between the efficiencies of optimal GDE balancing in non-even and even cases of these structures when k is large.

4.3.4 Improvements due to the Optimal Parameters

It is clear from the simulation results that the optimal exchange parameter λ_{opt} yields better results than the choice of $\lambda = 1/2$ which is used in the ADE method. To further examine (and quantify) the benefits of our GDE method over the original method, we define a metric for measuring improvements, denoted $\eta_{\lambda_{opt}}$:

$$\eta_{\lambda_{opt}} = \frac{T_h - T_{opt}}{T_h} \times 100\%$$

where T_h and T_{opt} are the expected numbers of sweeps from the choice of $\lambda = 1/2$ and the optimal λ_{opt} respectively. The improvement reflects the superiority of the optimal dimension exchange method over the original one. Figures 4.9-4.12 show the improvements as a function of mean workload per system node for various system sizes.

These curves indicate the significant improvement due to the choice of the optimal exchange parameters. As expected, the larger the system in each class, the better our GDE method with optimal exchange parameters performs. For systems larger than the Ring 32, the Torus 32 × 16, the Chain 16 and the Mesh 16 × 16, the improvement increases to over 80%. That is, the number of sweeps necessary for the GDE balancing is reduced by an order of magnitude due to the use of optimal parameters. These curves also show that the improvement increases as the average workload per processor increases for small-scale systems. For large-scale systems with more than 64 nodes (for ring) or 32 nodes (for chain), the improvement becomes insensitive to the average workload.

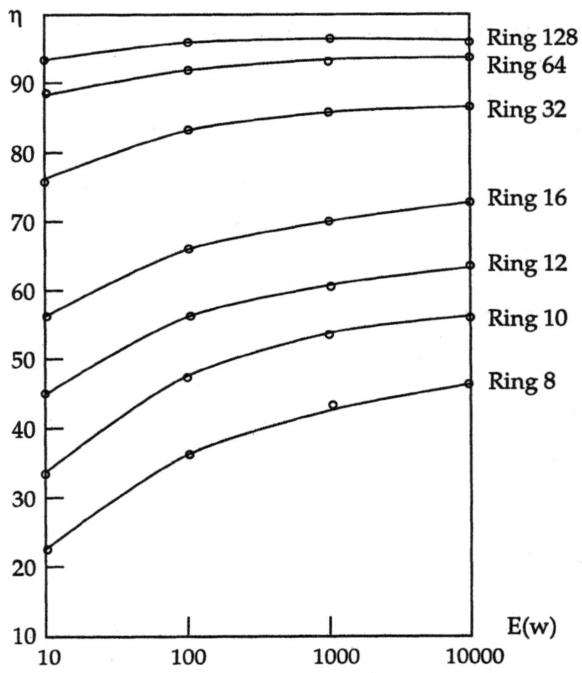

Figure 4.9: Improvements of GDE efficiency due to the optimal exchange parameters on rings of various sizes and workloads

In summary, dynamic load balancing using dimension exchange does benefit significantly from the optimal exchange parameter.

4.4 Concluding Remarks

In this chapter, we have analyzed the GDE method for load balancing as applied to the mesh and the torus, and their special cases: the ring, the torus, the chain, and the k-ary n-cube. We have derived the optimal exchange parameters in closed form, which maximize the efficiency of GDE balancing in these structures. We have revealed a close relationship between their convergence rates and concluded that the GDE method favors high-dimensional k-ary n-cubes for a given number of processors. We have also shown the superiority of the GDE method to the diffusion method when both are applied to these

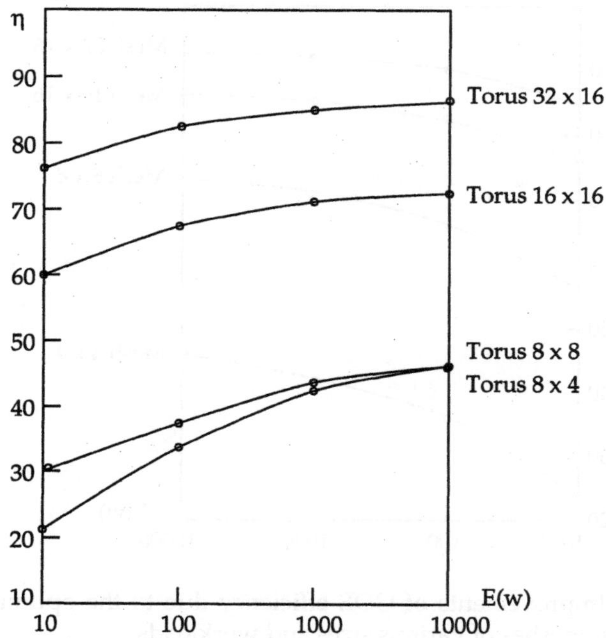

Figure 4.10: Improvements of GDE efficiency due to the optimal exchange parameters on tori of various sizes and workloads

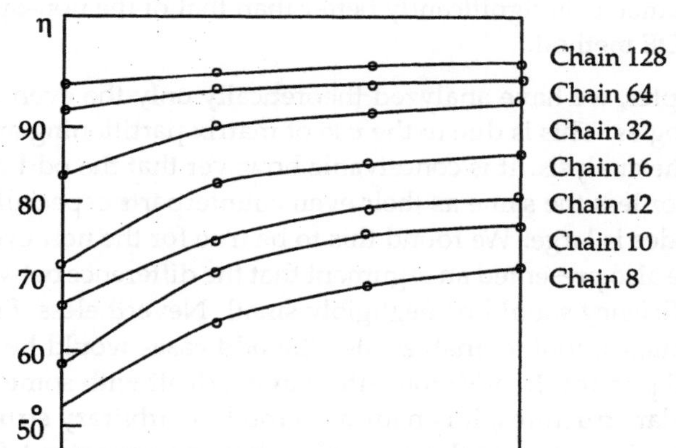

Figure 4.11: Improvements of GDE efficiency due to the optimal exchange parameters on chains of various sizes and workloads

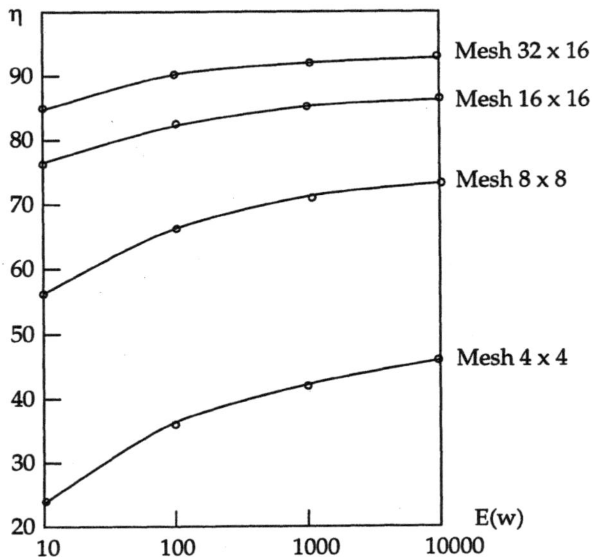

Figure 4.12: Improvements of GDE efficiency due to the optimal exchange parameters on meshes of various sizes and workloads

structures. Through statistical simulation experiments, we can easily see that the efficiency (in terms of number of steps to convergence) of using the optimal exchange parameters is significantly better than that of the non-optimal cases such as the ADE method.

In this chapter, we have analyzed theoretically only the even cases of the various topologies. This is due to the use of matrix partitioning and circulant matrices for the analysis. It is conceivable however that the odd cases would behave more or less the same as their even counterparts especially when the number of nodes is large. We found this to be true for the non-even cases we simulated. We also presented an argument that the difference between the two in terms of efficiency should be negligibly small. Nevertheless, finding a different mathematical tool to analyze also the odd cases would be an interesting theoretical pursuit. In addition, after having dealt with some of the most common regular structures, it is natural to think of arbitrary structures. Unfortunately, the derivation of the optimal exchange parameter λ for arbitrary structures requires a solution to the problem of specifying, in analytical form, the dependence of the subdominant eigenvalue in modulus of a matrix on the matrix elements. This is still open in mathematics [28].

5

THE DIFFUSION METHOD

Fair shares for all, is Labour's call.
—DOUGLAS JAY [SLOGAN FOR BATTERSEA NORTH BY-ELECTION, 1946]

With the diffusion method, each processor would transfer fractions of its workload to some of its neighbors while simultaneously receiving workloads from its other neighbors at each iteration step. In this chapter, we analyze the convergence and the efficiency properties of the diffusive load balancing process. The focus is on the design of efficient diffusion algorithms in the higher-dimensional tori and meshes including their special cases, the ring, the chain, and the k-ary n-cube.

The efficiency of the diffusion method largely depends on how much of the excess workload a processor would transfer to its lightly loaded neighbors in a balancing operation. We use a diffusion parameter α to dictate the size of the workload fraction to be diffused away. We derive the optimal diffusion parameters using circulant matrix theory for the mesh and torus networks. We also show that diffusive load balancing in the torus network converges faster than in the mesh of the same size.

5.1 The Diffusion Method

The execution of the load balancing procedure is divided into a sequence of steps. At each step, a processor would interact and exchange load with all its direct neighbors. Specificall', for a processor i, the change of workload is executed as

$$w_i = w_i + \sum_{j \in \mathcal{A}(i)} \alpha_{i,j} \, (w_j - w_i) \tag{5.1}$$

where w_i and w_j are the current local workloads of processors i and j respectively, $\mathcal{A}(i)$ is the set of nearest neighbors, and $\alpha_{i,j}$ is the *diffusion parameter* which determines the portion of the excess workload to be diffused away between a pair of directly connected processors i and j. Let $d(i) = |\mathcal{A}(i)|$. By choosing $\alpha_{i,j} = 1/(1 + d(i)|)$,

$$w_i = \frac{w_i + \sum_{j \in \mathcal{A}(i)} w_j}{d(i) + 1}$$

That is, the processor takes an average value of its workload plus the total workload of its nearest neighbor processors. We refer to such a special form of the diffusion method as the averaging diffusion (ADF) algorithm.

Let t be the step index, $t = 0, 1, 2, \ldots$, and $w_i^t (1 \leq i \leq N)$ be the local workload of processor i at step t. Then the overall workload distribution at step t, denoted by $\mathbf{W}^t$, is a transpose of the vector $(w_1^t, w_2^t, \ldots, w_N^t)$. $\mathbf{W}^0$ is the initial workload distribution. The change of the workload distribution in the system at step t can be modeled by the equation

$$\mathbf{W}^{t+1} = \mathbf{D}\mathbf{W}^t, \tag{5.2}$$

where $\mathbf{D}$, called a *diffusion matrix*, is given by

$$(\mathbf{D})_{i,j} = \begin{cases} \alpha_{i,j} & \text{if processors } i \text{ and } j \text{ are directly connected,} \\ 1 - \sum_{1 \leq i \leq d(i)} \alpha_{i,j} & \text{if } i = j, \\ 0 & \text{otherwise.} \end{cases}$$

It follows that

$$\mathbf{W}^t = \mathbf{D}^t \mathbf{W}^0, \qquad t = 0, 1, 2, \ldots \tag{5.3}$$

With this formulation, the features of diffusive load balancing are fully captured by the iterative process governed by the diffusion matrix $\mathbf{D}$. $\mathbf{D}$ is hence referred to as the characteristic matrix of the diffusion algorithm. Given the diffusion matrix, two questions are then in order: whether the sequence $\{\mathbf{D}^t\}$ is convergent; if it does, what is the convergence rate of the sequence.

It is easily verified that **D** is a nonnegative, symmetric and doubly stochastic matrix. In light of these properties of **D**, the convergence of diffusive load balancing was proved by Cybenko [47] and Boillat [17] simultaneously. The following theorem is due to Cybenko.

Theorem 5.1.1 *(Cybenko [47]) Given a system graph G and a diffusion matrix D, define an induced graph G' of G by deleting edges (i,j) of G if $\alpha_{i,j} = 0$. The iteration 5.2 always converges to the uniform distribution if and only if the induced graph is connected and either (or both) of the following conditions hold:*

1. *$(1 - \sum_i \alpha_{i,j}) > 0$ for some j;*
2. *the induced graph is not bipartite.*

Regarding the convergence rate, we need to consider the eigenvalue spectrum of **D** as in the analysis of the GDE load balancing method. Let $\mu_j(\mathbf{D})$ $(1 \leq j \leq N)$ be the eigenvalues of **D**, and $\rho(\mathbf{D})$ and $\gamma(\mathbf{D})$ be the dominant and sub-dominant eigenvalues respectively of **D** in modulus. Because of the above properties of **D**, $\rho(\mathbf{D})$ is unique and equal to 1; therefore the convergence rate of the sequence $\{\mathbf{D}^t\}$ is determined by $\gamma(\mathbf{D})$.

Let T be the iteration steps required to drive an initial workload distribution to a balanced state. Similarly to the analysis of the GDE method in Section 3.3, it can be derived that

$$T = O(1/\ln \gamma(\mathbf{D})). \tag{5.4}$$

Our task is then to choose a set of $\alpha_{i,j}$ that would minimize $\gamma(\mathbf{D})$ while preserving the nonnegativity of **D**. We refer to $\gamma(\mathbf{D})$ as the *convergence factor* of the diffusive load balancing method.

Cybenko proved that the ADF policy, in which $\alpha_{i,j} = 1/(n+1)$, is the optimal choice for binary n-cubes in [47]. Boillat showed that the convergence factor of the diffusion method has an upper bound $O(N^2)$, where N is the number of processors [17]. That is, the diffusive load balancing process will converge to an equilibrium state in polynomial time. He also presented the convergence factor of the ADF algorithm when applied to high-dimensional torus networks.

Setting $\alpha_{i,j} = 1/(1 + d(i))$ in the diffusion method is not necessary optimal when applied to networks except the hypercube structure. As in the GDE method, the dependence of $\gamma(\mathbf{D})$ on $\alpha_{i,j}$, being an optimization problem with multiple parameters, is somewhat hard to analyze. In the sequel, we assume a single diffusion parameter α along all communication channels and derive the optimal $\alpha_{opt}(\mathbf{D})$ for the structures of the higher-dimensional torus and mesh, and their special cass, the ring, the chain and the k-ary n-cube. We also examine the relationship between the optimal convergence rates of these structures.

5.2 Diffusion Method on n-Dimensional Tori

We first analyze the diffusion method as applied to n-dimensional torus networks. The analysis by induction on the dimension $n, n \geq 1$. We begin with the ring structure of order k, and then generalize it to the n-dimensional $k_1 \times k_2 \times \ldots \times k_n$ torus. Notice that an even torus (even order in every dimension) is bipartite and therefore, according to Cybenko's theorem, the diagonal elements of the corresponding diffusion matrix must be positive in order that the diffusion process would converge—that is, $\alpha < 1/(2n)$. Our derivation also relies on the theory of circulant matrices because the diffusion matrices of the ring and the torus are, respectively, in circulant and block circulant forms, as defined in Page 54.

5.2.1 The Ring

Let $\mathbf{R}_k$ be the diffusion matrix of a ring structure of order k. By the definition, it can be easily seen that

$$\mathbf{R}_4 = \begin{pmatrix} 1-2\alpha & \alpha & & \alpha \\ \alpha & 1-2\alpha & \alpha & \\ & \alpha & 1-2\alpha & \alpha \\ \alpha & & \alpha & 1-2\alpha \end{pmatrix}$$

Generally, we have the following.

Lemma 5.2.1 $\mathbf{R}_k$ *is a circulant matrix of the form* $\Phi_{k,1}(1-2\alpha, \alpha, 0, \ldots, 0, \alpha)$.

Given this particular structure of the diffusion matrix, we can then derive the optimal diffusion parameter and explore the effect of the ring order k on the convergence factor $\gamma(\mathbf{D})$.

Theorem 5.2.1 *The optimal diffusion parameter for the ring structure of order k, $\alpha_{opt}(\mathbf{R}_k)$, is equal to $1/(3-\cos(2\pi/k))$ if k is even, and $1/(2+\cos(\pi/k)-\cos(2\pi/k))$ otherwise. Moreover, $\gamma(\mathbf{R}_k) < \gamma(\mathbf{R}_{k+2})$.*

Proof. From Lemma 4.0.1, it follows that

$$\mu_j(\mathbf{R}_k) \quad = \quad 1 - 2\alpha + \alpha e^j + \alpha e^{k-j}$$

$$= \quad 1 - 2\alpha + 2\alpha\cos(\frac{2\pi j}{k}),\ j = 0, 1, \ldots, k-1.$$

Note that $e^{k-j} = \cos(\frac{2\pi j}{k}) - \mathbf{i}\sin(\frac{2\pi j}{k})$. We want to determine the value of α such that the sub-dominant eigenvalue in modulus, $\gamma(\mathbf{R}_k)$, is minimized. Since each eigenvalue in modulus μ is linearly dependent on α, it is easy to see that $\gamma(\mathbf{R}_k)$ is minimized at the intersection of the lines P and Q

$$P: \quad \begin{cases} \mu = 4\alpha - 1 & \text{if } k \text{ is even,} \\ \mu = 2\alpha + 2\alpha\cos(\frac{\pi}{k}) - 1 & \text{if } k \text{ is odd,} \end{cases}$$
$$Q: \quad \mu = 1 - 2\alpha + 2\alpha\cos(\tfrac{2\pi}{k},)$$

which are the lines with the steepest and the flattest slopes respectively in the plot of μ versus α, as illustrated in Figure 5.1. It is then clear that the sub-

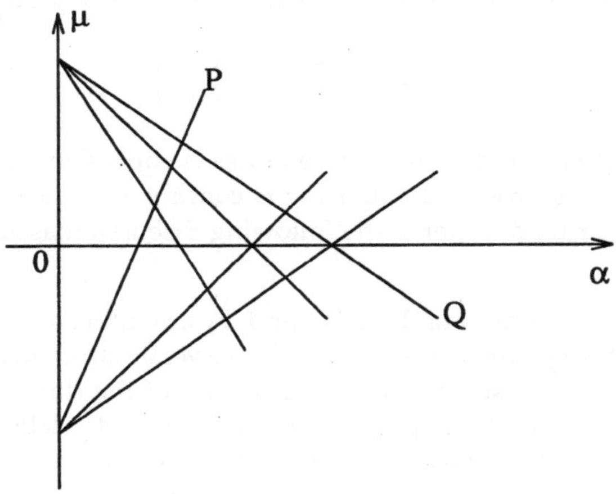

Figure 5.1: The eigenvalues of the diffusion matrix $\mathbf{R}_k$ versus the diffusion parameter

dominant (second largest) eigenvalue in modulus $\gamma(\mathbf{R}_k)$ of $\mathbf{R}_k$ is minimized at the intersection point of lines P and Q whose abscissa corresponds to

$$\alpha = \begin{cases} 1/(3 - \cos(\frac{2\pi}{k})) & \text{if } k \text{ is even,} \\ 1/(2 + \cos(\frac{\pi}{k}) - \cos(\frac{2\pi}{k})) & \text{if } k \text{ is odd.} \end{cases}$$

These values of α preserve the nonnegativity of $\mathbf{R}_k$ because both are less than 1/2. Substituting these values for α in the equation for the eigenvalues yields the optimal diffusion parameter

$$\gamma(\mathbf{R}_k) = \begin{cases} 4/(3 - \cos(\frac{2\pi}{k})) - 1 & \text{if } k \text{ is even,} \\ 2/(3 - 2\cos(\frac{\pi}{k})) - 1 & \text{if } k \text{ is odd.} \end{cases}$$

It follows that $\gamma(\mathbf{R}_{k+2}) > \gamma(\mathbf{R}_k)$. □

By this theorem, $\alpha_{opt}(\mathbf{R}_4) = 1/3$. It implies that the ADF (*i.e.*, taking an average of the total workload) load balancing algorithm performs best in the ring of order 4. However, the optimal diffusion parameter increases with the the increase of the ring order and approaches 0.5 in large-scale systems. This theorem also says that the more nodes the ring has, the slower the convergence of the load balancing procedure, which is not unexpected.[1]

5.2.2 The n-Dimensional Torus

On the basis of the above results for rings, we now consider the diffusive load balancing method in two-dimensional $k_1 \times k_2$ tori ($k_1 \geq 2, k_2 \geq 2$). To handle the degenerate case that k_1 or k_2 equals to 2, we set the diffusion matrix of a ring of order 2 as the diffusion matrix of a chain of order 2. That is,

$$\mathbf{R}_2 = \begin{pmatrix} 1-\alpha & \alpha \\ \alpha & 1-\alpha \end{pmatrix}$$

The reason for this is that a ring of two nodes is equivalent to a chain of two nodes as far as diffusive load balancing is concerned. Since the 2×2 torus degenerates to a ring of order 4, the following discussion assumes k_1 or k_2 is larger than 2.

For simplicity, we assume both k_1 and k_2 are either even or odd. The omitted cases that k_1 even and k_2 odd and vice versa can be analyzed in much the same way. As the spectrum of eigenvalues of the diffusion matrix of a network is invariant under any permutation of the vertex labels, we therefore label the vertices in the "column major" fashion. In the following, $\mathbf{I}_k$ denotes the identity matrix of order k. A two-dimensional torus can be viewed as a stack of rings of order k_1; so we can express its diffusion matrix in terms of the diffusion matrix of the ring, as follows. It can be easily proved by induction on the order of the second dimension k_2.

Lemma 5.2.2 *Let $\mathbf{T}_{k_1,k_2}$ be the diffusion matrix of a two-dimensional $k_1 \times k_2$ torus. Then,* $\mathbf{T}_{k_1,k_2} = \Phi_{k_2,k_1}(\mathbf{R}_{k_1} - 2\alpha\mathbf{I}_{k_1}, \alpha\mathbf{I}_{k_1}, 0, \ldots, 0, \alpha\mathbf{I}_{k_1})$.

As an example, the diffusion matrix of a torus of size 2×4,

$$T_{2,4} = \begin{pmatrix} \mathbf{R}_2 - 2\alpha\mathbf{I}_2 & \alpha\mathbf{I}_2 & & \\ \alpha\mathbf{I}_2 & \mathbf{R}_2 - 2\alpha\mathbf{I}_2 & \alpha\mathbf{I}_2 & \\ & \alpha\mathbf{I}_2 & \mathbf{R}_2 - 2\alpha\mathbf{I}_2 & \alpha\mathbf{I}_2 \\ & & \alpha\mathbf{I}_2 & \mathbf{R}_2 - 2\alpha\mathbf{I}_2 \end{pmatrix}$$

[1]We proved $\gamma(\mathbf{R}_{k+2}) > \gamma(\mathbf{R}_k)$ here; proving $\gamma(\mathbf{R}_{k+1}) > \gamma(\mathbf{R}_k)$ requires solving $1 + \cos^2(\pi/k) - 2\cos(\pi/(k+1)) \leq 0$ for $k \geq 2$.

which is equal to

$$\begin{pmatrix} 1-3\alpha & \alpha & \alpha & & & & \alpha & \\ \alpha & 1-3\alpha & \alpha & \alpha & & & & \alpha \\ \alpha & & 1-3\alpha & \alpha & \alpha & & & \\ & \alpha & \alpha & 1-3\alpha & & \alpha & & \\ & & \alpha & & 1-3\alpha & \alpha & \alpha & \\ & & & \alpha & \alpha & 1-3\alpha & & \alpha \\ \alpha & & & & \alpha & & 1-3\alpha & \alpha \\ & \alpha & & & & \alpha & \alpha & 1-3\alpha \end{pmatrix}$$

Lemma 5.2.2 reveals a close relationship between the diffusion matrices of the torus and the ring. Based on this relationship, we present the optimal parameter for diffusive load balancing in a torus in the following theorem.

Theorem 5.2.2 *The optimal diffusion parameter for the two-dimensional $k_1 \times k_2$ torus, $\alpha_{opt}(\mathbf{T}_{k_1,k_2})$, is equal to*

$$\begin{cases} 1/(5-\cos(2\pi/k)) & \text{if both } k_1 \text{ and } k_2 \text{ are even} \\ 1/(3+\sum_{i=1}^{2}\cos(\pi/k_i)-\cos(2\pi/k)) & \text{if both } k_1 \text{ and } k_2 \text{ are odd} \end{cases}$$

where $k = \max\{k_1, k_2\}$. Moreover, the convergence factor $\gamma(\mathbf{T}_{k_1,k_2})$ is equal to $\gamma(\mathbf{T}_{k,k})$ if both k_1 and k_2 are even.

Proof. From Lemma 4.0.1, the eigenvalues of the block circulant matrix $\mathbf{T}_{k_1,k_2}$ are those of the matrices

$$\begin{aligned} & \mathbf{R}_{k_1} - 2\alpha I_{k_1} + \alpha e^{j_2} I_{k_1} + \alpha e^{k_2-j_2} I_{k_1} \\ = \; & \mathbf{R}_{k_1} - 2\alpha I_{k_1} + 2\alpha\cos(\frac{2\pi j_2}{k_2}) I_{k_1}, \qquad j_2 = 0, 1, \ldots, k_2-1. \end{aligned}$$

Therefore,

$$\begin{aligned} \mu(\mathbf{T}_{k_1,k_2}) &= \mu(\mathbf{R}_{k_1}) - 2\alpha + 2\alpha\cos(\frac{2\pi j_2}{k_2}) \\ &= 1 - 4\alpha + 2\alpha\cos(\frac{2\pi j_1}{k_1}) + 2\alpha\cos(\frac{2\pi j_2}{k_2}), \end{aligned}$$

where $j_1 = 0, 1, \ldots, k_1 - 1$ and $j_2 = 0, 1, \ldots, k_2 - 1$. Then, as illustrated in Figure 5.1, the subdominant eigenvalue in modulus $\gamma(\mathbf{T}_{k_1,k_2})$ is minimized at the intersection point of the lines P and Q

$$\begin{aligned} P: & \begin{cases} \mu = 8\alpha - 1 & \text{if } k_1 \text{ and } k_2 \text{ are even,} \\ \mu = 4\alpha + 2\alpha\cos(\pi/k_1) + 2\alpha\cos(\pi/k_2) - 1 & \text{if } k_1 \text{ and } k_2 \text{ are odd.} \end{cases} \\ Q: & \;\; \mu = 1 - 2\alpha + 2\alpha\cos(2\pi/k), \end{aligned}$$

where $k = \max\{k_1, k_2\}$. The α values corresponding to this intersection point in each case are as that stated in the theorem. Substituting these optimal values for the diffusion parameter in the equation for the eigenvalues yields

$$\gamma(\mathbf{T}_{k_1,k_2}) = \begin{cases} \frac{8}{5-\cos(2\pi/k)} - 1 & \text{if } k_1 \text{ and } k_2 \text{ are even,} \\ \frac{4+2\sum_{i=1}^{2}\cos(\pi/k_i)}{3+\sum_{i=1}^{2}\cos(\pi/k_i)-\cos(2\pi/k)} - 1 & \text{if } k_1 \text{ are } k_2 \text{ are odd.} \end{cases}$$

Clearly, $\gamma(\mathbf{T}_{k_1,k_2}) = \gamma(\mathbf{T}_{k,k})$ in the even case. Hence, the theorem is proved.□

This theorem presents the optimal diffusion parameter in the two-dimension torus network. From this theorem, it can also be seen that the convergence rate of diffusive load balancing in a torus depends only on the larger dimension order when both k_1 and k_2 are even. The smaller dimension order has no effect on the load balancing efficiency. For example, the load balancing in tori of sizes $8 \times j$, $j = 4, 6, 8$, all have the same optimal convergence rate with the optimal diffusion parameter

$$\alpha_{opt} = 2/(10 - \sqrt{2}) \approx 0.11647.$$

The results in two-dimensional tori can be generalized to multi-dimensional tori. Consider an n-dimensional $k_1 \times k_2 \times \ldots \times k_n$ torus. Given any labeling of the nodes, by permutation, we can bring the diffusion matrix into the following iterative form.

$$\mathbf{T}_{k_1,k_2,\ldots,k_n} = \Phi_{k_n,\tilde{N}}(\mathbf{T}_{k_1,k_2,\ldots,k_{n-1}} - 2\alpha I_{\tilde{N}}, \alpha I_{\tilde{N}}, 0, \ldots, 0, \alpha I_{\tilde{N}})$$

where $\tilde{N} = k_1 \times k_2 \times \ldots \times k_{n-1}$. By induction on the number of dimensions n, it follows that

$$\mu(\mathbf{T}_{k_1,k_2,\ldots,k_n}) = 1 - 2n\alpha + 2\alpha \sum_{i=1}^{i=n} \cos(\frac{2\pi j_i}{k_i}), \qquad j_i = 0, 1, \ldots, k_i - 1.$$

Using the technique in the proofs of the above two theorems, we obtain the following result.

Theorem 5.2.3 *The optimal diffusion parameter, $\alpha_{opt}(\mathbf{T}_{k_1,k_2,\ldots,k_n})$, is equal to*

$$\begin{cases} \frac{1}{2n+1-\cos(2\pi/k)} & \text{if } k_i, i = 1, 2, \ldots, n, \text{ are even,} \\ \min\{\frac{1}{2n}, \frac{1}{n+1+\sum_{i=1}^{n}\cos(\pi/k_i)-\cos(2\pi/k)}\} & \text{if } k_i, i = 1, 2, \ldots, n, \text{ are odd,} \end{cases}$$

where $k = \max_{1 \le i \le n}\{k_i\}$. Moreover, the convergence factor $\gamma(\mathbf{T}_{k_1,k_2,\ldots,k_n})$ is equal to $\gamma(\mathbf{T}_{k,k,\ldots,k})$ in the even case.

We omit its proof which is quite similar to those above. Note that the alternative choice of $1/2n$ for $\alpha_{opt}(\mathbf{T}_{k_1,k_2,\ldots,k_n})$ in the odd case is for preserving the nonnegativity of the diffusion matrix.

Since a k-ary n-cube network is a special case of an n-dimensional torus with equivalent order in each dimension, we have the following.

Corollary 5.2.1 *Let $\mathbf{T}_{k;n}$ be the diffusion matrix of a k-ary n-cube network, $k > 2$. Then, its optimal diffusion parameter is*

$$\alpha_{opt}(\mathbf{T}_{k;n}) = \begin{cases} \frac{1}{2n+1-\cos(2\pi/k)} & \text{if } k \text{ is even,} \\ \frac{1}{n+1+n\cos(\pi/k)-\cos(2\pi/k)} & \text{if } k \text{ is odd and } n \le 3, \\ \frac{1}{2n} & \text{if } k \text{ is odd and } n \ge 4. \end{cases}$$

5.3 Diffusion Method on n-Dimensional Meshes

In this section, we consider diffusive load balancing in n-dimensional meshes. Our analysis makes use of the following lemma concerning a *Kronecker sum*: $\mathbf{I}_n \otimes \mathbf{A}_m + \mathbf{B}_n \otimes \mathbf{I}_m$ of an $m \times m$ matrix $\mathbf{A}_m$ and an $n \times n$ matrix $\mathbf{B}_n$ [50]. $\mathbf{I}_n$ ($\mathbf{I}_m$) is the identity matrix of order n (m).

Lemma 5.3.1 *Assume $\mathbf{A}_m$ and $\mathbf{B}_n$ have eigenvalues $\mu_i(\mathbf{A}_m)$ and $\mu_j(\mathbf{B}_n)$, $i = 1, 2, \ldots, m$, $j = 1, 2, \ldots, n$, respectively. Then, the eigenvalues of the matrix $\mathbf{I}_n \otimes \mathbf{A}_m + \mathbf{B}_n \otimes \mathbf{I}_m$ are the $m \times n$ numbers $\mu_i(\mathbf{A}_m) + \mu_j(\mathbf{B}_n)$.*

5.3.1 The Chain

We first consider the chain network of order k, $k > 2$, and present its diffusion matrix in the following form.

Lemma 5.3.2 *Let $\mathbf{C}_k$ be the diffusion matrix of a chain network of order k. Then, $\mathbf{C}_k = (1 - 2\alpha)\mathbf{I}_k + 2\alpha\mathbf{H}_k$, where*

$$\mathbf{H}_k = \begin{pmatrix} 1/2 & 1/2 & & & & \\ 1/2 & 0 & 1/2 & & & \\ & & \ddots & \ddots & & \\ & & & 1/2 & 0 & 1/2 \\ & & & & 1/2 & 1/2 \end{pmatrix}_{k \times k}$$

Note that the matrix $\mathbf{H}_k$ is in the form of a well-studied transition matrix of the k-state elastic random walk with equal transition probabilities (1/2) in a Markov chain [14]. Having known that the diffusion matrix of the chain is in a special form of the transition matrix, we derive next the optimal diffusion parameter.

Theorem 5.3.1 *The optimal diffusion parameter for the chain network, $\alpha_{opt}(\mathbf{C}_k)$, is equal to $1/2$. Moreover, the convergence factor $\gamma(\mathbf{C}_k)$ is proportional to k.*

Proof. From fundamentals of random processes [14], it is known that

$$\mu_j(\mathbf{H}_k) = \cos(\pi j/k), \qquad j = 0, 1, \ldots, k-1.$$

Applying Lemma 5.3.1 and Lemma 5.3.2 to the diffusion matrix $\mathbf{C}_k$ obtains that

$$\begin{aligned} \mu_j(\mathbf{C}_k) &= 1 - 2\alpha + 2\alpha\mu_j(\mathbf{H}_k) \\ &= 1 - 2\alpha + 2\alpha\cos(\pi j/k), \qquad j = 0, 1, \ldots, k-1. \end{aligned}$$

Then, as illustrated in Figure 5.1, the sub-dominant eigenvalue in modulus $\gamma(\mathbf{C}_k)$ is minimized at the intersection point of two lines:

$$\begin{aligned} P: \quad & \mu = 2\alpha + 2\alpha\cos(\pi/k) - 1 \\ Q: \quad & \mu = 1 - 2\alpha + 2\alpha\cos(\pi/k) \end{aligned}$$

It follows that $\alpha_{opt} = 1/2$, and $\gamma(\mathbf{C}_k) = \cos(\pi/k)$. And hence $\gamma(\mathbf{C}_k)$ is proportional to the chain order. □

This theorem shows that the optimal parameter of diffusive load balancing in a chain is fixed at $1/2$ regardless of how long the chain may be. It concludes that the ADF policy would not lead to optimal efficiency of diffusive load balancing in the chain structure.

By comparing the convergence factor $\gamma(\mathbf{C}_k)$ with that of a ring structure $\gamma(\mathbf{R}_k)$, we obtain that

$$\gamma(\mathbf{C}_k) < \gamma(\mathbf{R}_k). \tag{5.5}$$

That is, the diffusive load balancing process in the ring network converges faster than in the chain network of the same order. Expectedly, diffusive load balancing in a chain benefits from an additional end-round connection.

The chain is a special case of the mesh and will serve as a building block for our analysis of diffusive load balancing in the mesh. In the next section, we first study the case of the two-dimensional mesh, and then the n-dimensional mesh by induction on the number of dimensions.

5.3.2 The n-Dimensional Mesh

We consider the two-dimensional $k_1 \times k_2$ mesh, $k_1 > 2$, $k_2 > 2$. Without loss of generality, we assume the nodes are indexed in the "row major" fashion. Let

$\mathbf{M}_{k_1,k_2}$ be its diffusion matrix. Then, by induction on the second dimension k_2, we obtain that $\mathbf{M}_{k_1,k_2}$ is equal to

$$\begin{pmatrix} \mathbf{C}_{k_1} - \alpha\mathbf{I}_{k_1} & \alpha\mathbf{I}_{k_1} & & & & \\ \alpha\mathbf{I}_{k_1} & \mathbf{C}_{k_1} - 2\alpha\mathbf{I}_{k_1} & \alpha\mathbf{I}_{k_1} & & & \\ & & \ddots & \ddots & & \\ & & & \alpha\mathbf{I}_{k_1} & \mathbf{C}_{k_1} - 2\alpha\mathbf{I}_{k_1} & \alpha\mathbf{I}_{k_1} \\ & & & & \alpha\mathbf{I}_{k_1} & \mathbf{C}_{k_1} - \alpha\mathbf{I}_{k_1} \end{pmatrix}$$

This matrix has $k_2 \times k_2$ block elements each of which is a matrix of $k_1 \times k_1$ nonnegative reals. We rewrite it in a more concise form in terms of Kronecker sum of matrices in the following lemma.

Lemma 5.3.3 *Let $\mathbf{C}_k$ be the diffusion matrix of a chain of order k. Then,*

$$\mathbf{M}_{k_1,k_2} = \mathbf{I}_{k_2} \otimes (\mathbf{C}_{k_1} - 2\alpha\mathbf{I}_{k_1}) + \mathbf{H}_{k_2} \otimes 2\alpha\mathbf{I}_{k_1}$$

where $\mathbf{I}_{k_1}$ and $\mathbf{I}_{k_2}$ are identity matrices and $\mathbf{H}_{k_2}$ is defined as in Lemma 5.3.2.

This lemma shows a Kronecker-sum relationship between the diffusion matrices of the mesh and the chain. It serves as the basis for the following theorem concerning the optimal diffusion parameter in the mesh.

Theorem 5.3.2 *The optimal diffusion parameter for the $k_1 \times k_2$ mesh, $\alpha_{opt}(\mathbf{M}_{k_1,k_2})$, is equal to $1/4$. Moreover, the convergence rate $\gamma(\mathbf{M}_{k_1,k_2})$ is equal to $\gamma(\mathbf{M}_{k,k})$, where $k = \max\{k_1, k_2\}$.*

Proof. From Lemma 5.3.1 and Theorem 5.3.1, it follows that

$$\mu(\mathbf{M}_{k_1,k_2}) = 1 - 4\alpha + 2\alpha\cos(\frac{\pi j_1}{k_1}) + 2\alpha\cos(\frac{\pi j_2}{k_2}),$$

where $j_1 = 0, 1, \ldots, k_1 - 1$ and $j_2 = 0, 1, \ldots, k_2 - 1$. Note that the eigenvalues of the matrix $\mathbf{H}_{k_2}$ are available in the proof of Theorem 5.3.1. Without loss of generality, assume $k_1 \geq k_2$. Then, the sub-dominant eigenvalue in modulus, $\gamma(\mathbf{M}_{k_1,k_2})$, is minimized at the intersection point of the lines P and Q:

$$\begin{aligned} P: &\quad \mu = 4\alpha + 2\alpha\cos(\pi/k_1) + 2\alpha\cos(\pi/k_2) - 1 \\ Q: &\quad \mu = 1 - 2\alpha + 2\alpha\cos(\pi/k_1) \end{aligned}$$

These two lines are intersected at the point $\alpha = 1/(3 + \cos(\pi/k_2))$. But this choice of α would lead to a negative element $1 - 4\alpha$ (*i.e.*, a node with four links) in $\mathbf{M}_{k_1,k_2}$. To preserve the nonnegativity of the diffusion matrix, we pick a value of α which is closest to the above α and which would make $1 - 4\alpha$ nonnegative. Hence, $\alpha_{opt} = 1/4$. Substituting this into the equation for $\mu(\mathbf{M}_{k_1,k_2})$ gives $\gamma(\mathbf{M}_{k_1,k_2}) = 1/2 + \cos(\pi/k_1)/2$. Therefore, we have $\gamma(\mathbf{M}_{k_1,k_2}) = \gamma(\mathbf{M}_{k,k})$. □

By comparing the result here with that for the torus in Theorem 5.2.2, we obtain that

$$\gamma(\mathbf{M}_{k_1,k_2}) > \gamma(\mathbf{T}_{k_1,k_2}). \tag{5.6}$$

That is, the diffusive load balancing process in a torus converges faster than that in a mesh of the same dimensions. Again, we see that the end-round connections help.

The above theorem says that the convergence rate of a diffusive load balancing in a mesh depends only on its larger dimension order. It would not be affected by the smaller dimension order. For example, load balancing processes in meshes $\mathbf{M}_{8,j}$, $j = 4, 6, 8$, all have the same convergence rate for the fixed optimal diffusion parameter $\alpha = 1/4$.

These results for two-dimensional meshes can be generalized to n-dimensional $k_1 \times k_2 \times \ldots k_n$ ($k_i > 2, i = 1, 2, \ldots, n$) meshes whose diffusion matrix can be written in the following recursive form.

$$\mathbf{M}_{k_1,k_2,\ldots,k_n} = \mathbf{I}_{k_n} \otimes (\mathbf{M}_{k_1,k_2,\ldots,k_{n-1}} - 2\alpha\mathbf{I}_{\tilde{N}}) + \mathbf{C}_{k_n} \otimes \mathbf{I}_{\tilde{N}}$$

where $\tilde{N} = k_1 \times k_2 \times \ldots \times k_{n-1}$. By induction on the number of dimensions n, it follows that

$$\mu(\mathbf{M}_{k_1,k_2,\ldots,k_n}) = 1 - 2n\alpha + 2\alpha \sum_{i=1}^{i=n} \cos(\frac{\pi j_i}{k_i}), \qquad j_i = 0, 1, \ldots, k_n - 1.$$

Hence, we obtain the following results.

Theorem 5.3.3 *The optimal diffusion parameter* $\alpha_{opt}(\mathbf{M}_{k_1,k_2,\ldots,k_n})$ *is equal to* $1/(2n)$. *Moreover, the convergence rate* $\gamma(\mathbf{M}_{k_1,k_2,\ldots,k_n})$ *is equal to* $\gamma(\mathbf{M}_{k,k,\ldots,k})$, *where* $k = \max\{k_1, k_2, \ldots, k_n\}$.

We can also generalize the comparative results of Inequalities (5.5) and (5.6) in one- and two-dimensional networks to high-dimensional meshes and tori.

Theorem 5.3.4 *The diffusive load balancing process in an n-dimensional torus converges faster than that for an n-dimensional mesh of the same dimensions.*

5.4 Simulation

To obtain an idea of the iteration numbers required by diffusive load balancing for various choices of the diffusion parameters, we simulated a few cases.

For comparison with the GDE method, the simulation is performed on the same initial workload distributions as those used in the simulation of the GDE method. The relative error bound of the simulation is set to 1. Denote the number of iterations by T.

Figures 5.2–5.5 plot the expected iteration numbers in various networks for reaching the balanced state from an initial workload distribution with a workload mean 128 as α varies in steps of 0.05 from 0.10 to the maximum value which preserves the nonnegativity of the corresponding diffusion matrix. The maximum value is 0.5 in the cases of rings and chains, and 0.25 in the cases of two dimensional tori and meshes. Notice that even rings and tori are bipartite graphs, and according to Cybenko's necessary and sufficient conditions for convergence, the value of α should be less than the graph degree. Hence, we set the upper bound of α to 0.49 in even rings and 0.24 in even tori in our experiments. To reduce the effect of the variance of the initial load distribution on the iteration numbers, we take the average of 100 runs for each data point, each run using a different random initial load distribution.

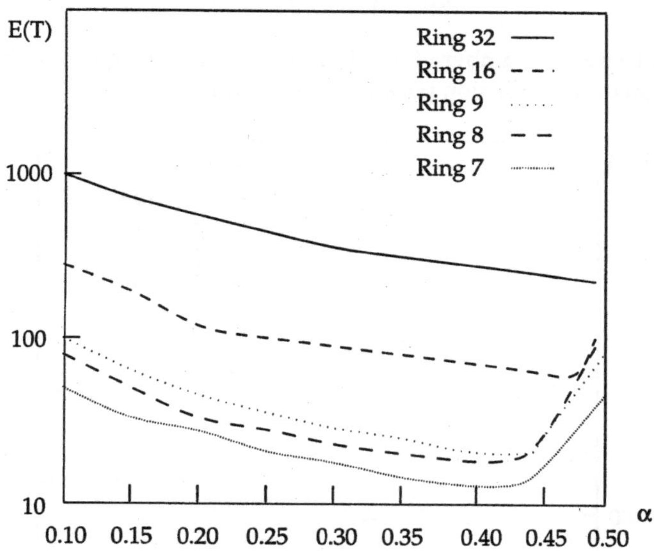

Figure 5.2: Expected number of iterations necessary for a global balanced state as a function of the diffusion parameter α in rings

As can be seen from the figures, the expected number of iterations in each case for different α's varies with the value of $\gamma(\mathbf{D})$. Specifically, the theoretically-proven optimal diffusion parameter of each case yields the best result in terms of the expected number of iterations. Also, the expected number of iterations agrees with $\gamma(\mathbf{D})$ in its dependent relationship with the topolo-

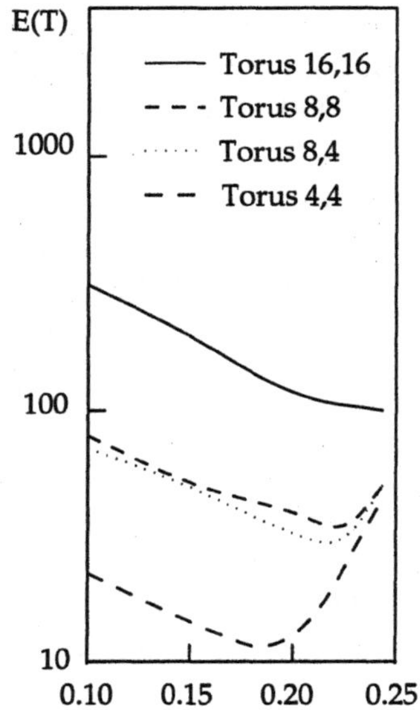

Figure 5.3: Expected number of iterations necessary for a global balanced state as a function of the diffusion parameter α in torus

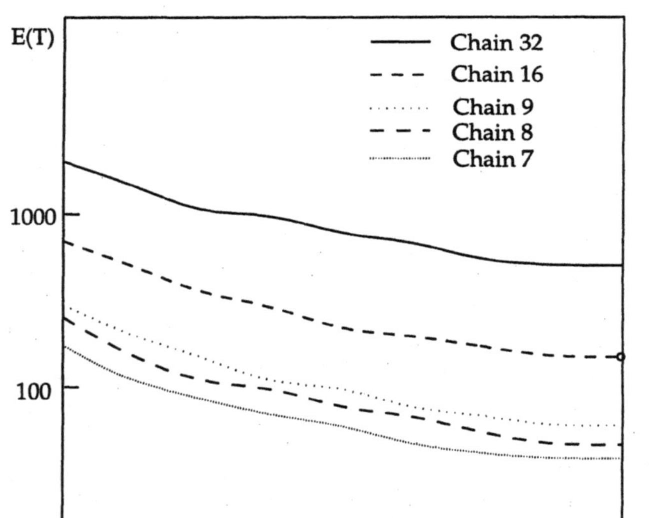

Figure 5.4: Expected number of iterations necessary for a global balanced state as a function of the diffusion parameter α in chains

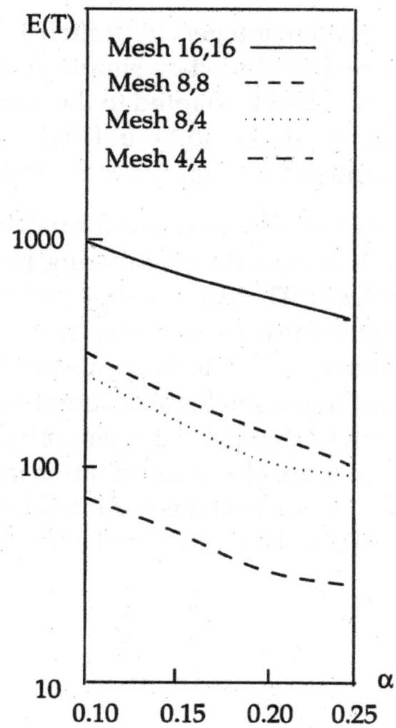

Figure 5.5: Expected number of iterations necessary for a global balanced state as a function of the diffusion parameter α in meshes

gies and sizes of the structures. In particular, from Figure 5.3 and Figure 5.5, it is evident that the expected number of iterations of even tori and meshes is insensitive to their smaller dimensions.

5.5 Concluding Remarks

In this chapter, we have analyzed the diffusion algorithm for load balancing as applied to the mesh and the torus, and their special cases: the ring, the chain, the hypercube, and the k-ary n-cube. We have derived the optimal diffusion parameters for these structures and tight upper bounds on the running time of the algorithm.

The algorithm assumes that workloads are infinitely divisible, and hence represents the workload of a processor by a real number. The assumption is valid in parallel programs that exploit very fine grain parallelism. To cover medium and large grain parallelism, the algorithm must be able to handle indivisible processes. To this end, the algorithm should represent the workload of a processor by a non-negative integer. In Section 4.3.2, we presented an integer version of the GDE method based on simple floor and ceiling functions. The diffusion algorithm can also be adapted to the integer workload model in a similar manner, by touching up Eq. (5.1). In [184], the authors presented an integer version that guarantees convergence to the balanced distribution.

From the simulation, it can be seen that the diffusive load balancing process progressed very slowly. It is because neighboring processors tend to thrash workloads during the process. There are two possible approaches to remedying thrashing and improving the convergence rate. One is to take into account the history information in the current decision-making through employing different values for the diffusion parameter in different iteration steps—that is, to vary the parameter value in the temporal domain. The other is the hierarchical approach that makes use of more global information in making load balancing decisions. Mathematical tools such as the semi-iterative method [195] and the multigrid method [35, 138] could be considered in the analysis of these two approaches.

6

GDE VERSUS DIFFUSION

Let all things be done decently and in order.
—THE BIBLE [I CORINTHIANS]

With the the dimension exchange method, a processor in need of load balancing balances its workload successively with its neighbors one at a time, and each time a new workload index is computed, which will be used in the the subsequent pairwise balancing. By contrast, with the diffusion method, a heavily or lightly loaded processor balances its workload with all of its nearest neighbors simultaneously in a balancing operation. These two methods are closely related, as discussed in Section 3.5. A GDE load balancing process in a network is equivalent to a diffusive balancing process in an extended graph of the network.

The dimension exchange method and the diffusion method lend themselves particularly well to implementation in two basic inter-processor communication models, the *all-port* and the *one-port* model, respectively. The all-port model allows a processor to exchange messages with all its direct neighbors simultaneously in one communication step, while the one-port model restricts a processor to exchange messages with at most one direct neighbor at a time. Both of them were frequently assumed in recent research on communication algorithms [99, 116]. Although the latest designs of message-passing processors tend to support all-port simultaneous communications, the restrictive one-port model is still valid in existing real parallel computer systems. Since the cost in setting up a communication is fixed, the total time spent in sending d messages to d different ports, assuming the best possible overlapping in time, is still largely determined by d unless the messages are rather long.

The all-port and one-port models favor the diffusion and the dimension exchange methods, respectively. In a system that supports all-port communications, a load balancing operation using the diffusion method can be completed in one communication step while that using the dimension exchange method would take a number of steps. It appears that the diffusion method has an advantage over the dimension exchange method as far as exploiting the communication bandwidth is concerned. A natural but interesting question is whether the advantage translates into real performance benefits in load balancing.

Cybenko first compared these two methods when they are applied to hypercube structures [47]. He showed that the dimension exchange method outperforms the diffusion method in terms of their efficiencies and balance qualities in both communication models. On the practical side, Willebeek-LeMair and Reeves implemented these two methods in distributed branch-and-bound computations in a hypercube-structured iPSC/2 system [203]. Their experimental results are in agreement with Cybenko's.

Although the results of both theoretical and experimental study point to the superiority of the dimension exchange method in hypercubes, it might not be the case for other popular networks because the dimension exchange method matches perfectly with the hypercube structure. On the other hand, previous theoretical studies of these two methods were mostly on their synchronous implementations in which all processors participate in load balancing operations simultaneously and each processor cannot proceed into the next step until the workload migrations demanded by the current operation have completed. Although there are a number of work concerning the convergence of diffusive load balancing [16, 131, 180], very few results are available on the efficiency of the diffusion method and the dimension exchange method in asynchronous implementations.

This chapter compares the diffusion and the dimension exchange methods in terms of their efficiency and balancing quality when they are implemented in both one-port and all-port communication models, using synchronous/asynchronous invocation policies, and in static/dynamic workload models. The communication networks to be considered include the structures of n-D tori and meshes, and their special cases: the ring, the chain, the hypercube and the k-ary n-cube. The comparison is under the following assumption.

Assumption 6.0.1 *Initially, processors' workloads, w_i^0, $1 \leq i \leq N$, are N independent and identically distributed (i.i.d.) random variables with expectation μ_0 and variance σ_0^2. At any time t, $t \geq 0$, processors' workload generation/consumption amount, ϕ_i^t, $1 \leq i \leq N$, are zero in the static situation or i.i.d. random variables with expectation μ and variance σ^2 in the dynamic situation.*

As we have illustrated in the preceding chapters, both the dimension exchange and the diffusion methods are parameterized methods. Their performance is largely influenced by the choice of the parameter values. We focus on two choices of the parameter value in each method: the ADE algorithm where $\lambda = 1/2$, the ODE algorithm by setting λ to the optimally-tuned parameter value, the ADF by setting $\alpha = 1/(1+2n)$ and the ODF where α is set to the optimally-tuned diffusion parameter value. The optimality here is in terms of the efficiency in static synchronous implementations among various choices of the dimension exchange and the diffusion parameters. The average versions are the most original versions when the methods were first proposed and are still being employed in real applications today. Our main results are that the dimension exchange method outperforms the diffusion method in the one-port communication model; in particular, the ODE algorithm is found to be best suited for synchronous implementation in the static situation; and that the dimension exchange method is superior in synchronous load balancing even under the all-port communication model; the strength of the diffusion method is in asynchronous implementation under the all-port communication model; the ODF algorithm performs best in this case.

6.1 Synchronous Implementations

In a synchronous implementation of load balancing, all processors perform load balancing operations concurrently and continuously for a time period in order to achieve a global balanced state in the static workload model or to keep the varying system workload variance bounded in the dynamic workload model.

6.1.1 Static Workload Model

In a static synchronous load balancing process, all processors are assumed to perform load balancing operations simultaneously and all computational operations are suspended. This situation is true of periodic load balancing, as experimented in [40, 110, 147, 212]. The efficiency of a load balancing algorithm in this situation is reflected by the number of communication steps required for arriving at a global balanced state from any initial load distribution.

Let **F** be either the dimension exchange matrix **E** or the diffusion matrix **D**. Let T be the number of iteration steps (sweeps) required to reduce the workload variance of an initial state to some prescribed bound. From Eq. (3.4) and (5.3), it follows that

$$T = O(1/\ln \gamma(F)), \tag{6.1}$$

where $\gamma(\mathbf{F})$ is the sub-dominant eigenvalue of **F** in modulus which is also referred to as the convergence factor of a load balancing algorithm.

The convergence factors of the dimension exchange and the diffusion methods when applied to different networks were evaluated in Chapters 4 and 5. We summarize their convergence factors in Table 6.1.

Table 6.1: Convergence factors of the dimension exchange and the diffusion methods, where k is the maximum number of nodes over all dimensions of an n-dimensional network

	Dimension exchange		Diffusion	
	ADE	ODE	ADF	ODF
torus	$\cos^2(2\pi/k)$	$\frac{1-\sin(2\pi/k)}{1+\sin(2\pi/k)}$	$\frac{2n-1+2\cos(2\pi/k)}{2n+1}$	$\frac{2n-1+\cos(2\pi/k)}{2n+1-\cos(2\pi/k)}$
mesh	$\cos^2(\pi/k)$	$\frac{1-\sin(\pi/k)}{1+\sin(\pi/k)}$	$\frac{2n-1+2\cos(\pi/k)}{2n+1}$	$\frac{n-1+\cos(\pi/k)}{n}$

Notice that the convergence factor is in iteration steps (sweeps), each of which is what we called a load balancing operation before. In the one-port communication model, such an operation in both the dimension exchange and the diffusion methods requires $2n$ communication steps in an n-dimensional network. In the all-port communication model, a diffusion load balancing operation requires only one communication step while a dimension exchange operation still requires $2n$ steps. Therefore, Table 6.1 and Eq. (6.1) lead to Table 6.2 which presents the time complexities in communication steps necessary for various load balancing algorithms in both one-port and all-port communication models.

The time complexities given in Table 6.2 are inferred from the convergence factors. For example, the $O(nk)$ estimate for the ODE algorithm follows from

Table 6.2: Time complexities of the dimension exchange and the diffusion methods, where k is the maximum number of nodes over all dimensions in an n-D network

	k-ary n-D Torus		k-ary n-D Mesh	
	1-port	all-port	1-port	all-port
ADE	$O(nk^2)$	$O(nk^2)$	$O(nk^2)$	$O(nk^2)$
ODE	$O(nk)$	$O(nk)$	$O(nk)$	$O(nk)$
ADF	$O(n^2k^2)$	$O(nk^2)$	$O(n^2k^2)$	$O(nk^2)$
ODF	$O(n^2k^2)$	$O(nk^2)$	$O(n^2k^2)$	$O(nk^2)$

the following derivation.

$$\begin{aligned}
\ln(\gamma_{ode}) &= \ln(\frac{1-\sin(2\pi/k)}{1+\sin(2\pi/k)}) \\
&= \ln(1-\frac{2\sin(2\pi/k)}{1+\sin(2\pi/k)}) \\
&\simeq \ln(1-\frac{4\pi}{k+2\pi}) \qquad \text{for large } k \\
&\simeq \frac{4\pi}{k+2\pi}.
\end{aligned}$$

From Eq. (6.1), we have $T_{ode} = O(k)$ in balancing operations. Since an ODE load balancing operation requires $O(n)$ communication steps in both communication models, the estimate $O(nk)$ is thus proved.

The entries of the table can be summarized as follows.

Theorem 6.1.1 *Suppose processors are running synchronous load balancing processes in the static workload model. Then, both the ADE and the ODE algorithms converge asymptotically faster than the diffusion method in the one-port communication model. In the all-port communication model, the ODE algorithm converges also faster than the other three algorithms by a factor of k.*

6.1.2 Dynamic Workload Model

In dynamic synchronous implementations, all processors are performing the balancing and the computational operations concurrently. Load balancing in this situation aims at keeping the variance of processors' workloads bounded as tightly as possible. The performance of the synchronous implementation of the diffusion method in the dynamic situation has been evaluated in [47, 86, 160]. In [47], Cybenko showed that the diffusion method keeps the asymptotic variance bounded. He also proved that the asymptotic variance from the diffusion method is larger than the variance from the ADE algorithm when both are applied to the hypercube network. Given this, we are still unable to draw a conclusion regarding the superiority of the ADE algorithm in terms of their stabilities. In [86], Hong, Tan and Chen reported a constant bound for the workload variance when the ADF algorithm runs in the hypercube network. This result was extended later by Qian and Yang to generalized hypercubes and mesh structures [160]. Although the bounds they derived are independent of time, they are too loose to be used for the comparison of balance qualities during load balancing. Also, the approaches used in [86, 160] are unsuitable for the analysis of the dimension exchange method because of their different operational behaviors.

In this subsection, we develop a new approach for analyzing the balance qualities of different algorithms. We present a closed form of the workload variance when a load balancing process runs in the torus and the hypercube networks. Our analytical approach takes advantage of the fact that each processor in an n torus has $2n$ nearest neighbors. The approach is not applicable to the case of the mesh networks as they are not regular networks. Nevertheless, since an n-D mesh has only a fraction of its processors whose degree is smaller than $2n$, our results as a reasonable approximation can be applied to the mesh structure as well; this is supported by our simulation results to be presented in Section 6.3. For simplicity in presentation, let d denote the degree of a torus throughout this chapter. That is, $d = 2n$ for a n-dimensional torus.

Our analysis is based on a lemma concerning the sample variance of a combination of random variables in a sample set. Let $\mathcal{E}(\cdot)$ be the expected value of a random variable. We present the lemma without proof because it can be easily shown using fundamental statistical theories.

Lemma 6.1.1 *Suppose that $\zeta_1, \zeta_2, \ldots, \zeta_N$ are N i.i.d. random variables with variance σ^2, and $\overline{\zeta} = \sum_{i=1}^{N} \zeta_i$. Then,*

1. *for any k, $1 \le k \le N$,*

$$\mathcal{E}(|\sum_{i=1}^{k} a_i \zeta_i - \overline{\zeta}|^2) = (\sum_{1=1}^{k} a_i^2 - \frac{1}{N})\sigma^2, \tag{6.2}$$

where $0 < a_i < 1$ satisfies $\sum_{i=1}^{k} a_i = 1$; and the variance is minimized at $a_i = 1/k$ for a given k.

2. *for any* k_1 *and* k_2 *and* $1 \leq k_1 \leq k_2 \leq N$,

$$\mathcal{E}(|\sum_{i=1}^{k_1} a_i\zeta_i - \overline{\zeta}|^2) \geq \mathcal{E}(|\sum_{j=1}^{k_2} b_j\zeta_j - \overline{\zeta}|^2) \tag{6.3}$$

where $0 < a_i < 1$ *satisfies* $\sum_{i=1}^{k_1} a_i = 1$ *and* $0 < b_j < 1$ *satisfies* $\sum_{j=1}^{k_2} b_j = 1$.

Dimension exchange method. First, we consider synchronous load balancing with the dimension exchange method. We present a closed form of the workload variance when the dimension exchange method runs in the torus in Theorem 6.1.2.

Theorem 6.1.2 *Suppose processors are running a synchronous load balancing process with the dimension exchange method under Assumption 6.0.1, except that a processor* i *generates/consumes* ϕ_i *workload at a pairwise balancing operation. Then,* $\mathcal{E}(\mathbf{W}^t)$ *is a uniform distribution at any time t, and*

$$\mathcal{E}[\nu_{de}^t] = (sb^{dt+d}\sigma_0^2 + s\frac{1-b^{dt+d}}{1-b^d}\sigma^2)N - (t+1)d\sigma^2 - \sigma_0^2, \tag{6.4}$$

where $b = (1-\lambda)^2 + \lambda^2$ *and* $s = 1 + b + b^2 + \cdots + b^{d-1}$.

Proof. A load balancing operation in an n-dimensional torus comprises $2n$ pairwise balancing steps. Recall that t is the index of load balancing operations in the GDE method. To examine closely the dynamic behavior of the GDE algorithm in the level of pairwise operations, we introduce one more variable t' to denote the index of pairwise steps such that $t = 0$ if and only if $t' = 0$, and t indexes the time instances t' that are integer multiplies of d. Let $\mathbf{E}$ be the GDE matrix of a color torus. Then, from Eq. (3.1) to Eq. (3.4) in Section 3.2. we have that at time t', $t' = dt$,

$$\begin{aligned}
\mathbf{W}^{t'} &= \mathbf{E}_d\mathbf{W}^{t'-1} + \mathbf{\Phi}^{t'} \\
&= \mathbf{E}_d\mathbf{E}_{d-1}\mathbf{W}^{t'-2} + \mathbf{E}_d\mathbf{\Phi}^{t'-1} + \mathbf{\Phi}^{t'} \\
&= \Pi_{c=d}^{1}\mathbf{E}_c\mathbf{W}^{t'-d} + \Pi_{c=d}^{2}\mathbf{E}_c\mathbf{\Phi}^{t'-d+1} + \cdots + \mathbf{E}_d\mathbf{\Phi}^{t'-1} + \mathbf{\Phi}^{t'} \\
&= \mathbf{E}\mathbf{W}^{t'-d} + \sum_{c=1}^{d}(\Pi_{j=d}^{c+1}\mathbf{E}_j\mathbf{\Phi}^{t'-d+c}),
\end{aligned} \tag{6.5}$$

where $\Pi_{j=d}^{c}\mathbf{E}_j = \mathbf{E}_d \times \mathbf{E}_{d-1} \times \cdots \times \mathbf{E}_c$, and $\Pi_{j=d}^{d+1}\mathbf{E}_j = 1$.

Let $\Psi^t = \sum_{c=1}^{d}(\Pi_{j=d}^{c+1}\mathbf{E}_j\mathbf{\Phi}^{t'-d+c})$ be the distribution of workloads which are generated/consumed from time $t' - d$ to t', *i.e.*, the tth balancing operation.

Using index t instead of t', Eq. (6.5) leads to

$$\begin{aligned}\mathbf{W}^t &= \mathbf{E}\mathbf{W}^{t-1} + \Psi^t \\ &= \mathbf{E}^t\mathbf{W}^0 + \sum_{j=1}^{t} \mathbf{E}^{t-j}\Psi^j.\end{aligned} \tag{6.6}$$

Applying the expectation operator, $\mathcal{E}$, to Eq. (6.6), we obtain that

$$\begin{aligned}\mathcal{E}(\mathbf{W}^t) &= \mathcal{E}(\mathbf{E}^t\mathbf{W}^0 + \sum_{j=1}^{t} \mathbf{E}^{t-j}\Psi^j) \\ &= \mathbf{E}^t\mathcal{E}(\mathbf{W}^0) + \sum_{j=1}^{t} \mathbf{E}^{t-j}\mathcal{E}(\Psi^j) \\ &= \mu_0\mathbf{u} + dt\mu\mathbf{u},\end{aligned}$$

where $\mathbf{u}$ is a unitary vector of size N. It is a uniform distribution. The first part of the lemma is thus proved.

Next, we consider the workload variance at time t, $\mathcal{E}(\nu_{de}^t)$. Let $\overline{\Psi}^t$ be the uniform distribution of workloads that are generated/consumed in the round t. Then, $\overline{\Psi}^t = \sum_{c=1}^{d} \overline{\Phi}^{t'-d+c}$, and $\overline{\mathbf{W}}^t = \overline{\mathbf{W}}^{t-1} + \overline{\Psi}^t$. By the definition of workload variance in Section 1.4.2, we have

$$\begin{aligned}\mathcal{E}(\nu_{de}^t) &= \mathcal{E}(||\mathbf{W}^t - \overline{\mathbf{W}}^t||^2) \\ &= \mathcal{E}(||\mathbf{E}\mathbf{W}^{t-1} - \overline{\mathbf{W}}^{t-1}||^2) + \mathcal{E}(||\Psi^t - \overline{\Psi}^t||^2) \\ &= \mathcal{E}(||\mathbf{E}^{t+1}\mathbf{W}^0 - \overline{\mathbf{W}}^0||^2) + \textstyle\sum_{i=0}^{t} \mathcal{E}(||\mathbf{E}^i\Psi^{t+1-i} - \overline{\Psi}^{t+1-i}||^2).\end{aligned} \tag{6.7}$$

To prove the theorem concerning $\mathcal{E}(\nu_{de}^t)$, it suffices to show that

$$\mathcal{E}(||\mathbf{E}^i\Psi^{t+1-i} - \overline{\Psi}^{t+1-i}||^2) = b^{id}sN\sigma^2 - d\sigma^2, \qquad \text{for } 0 \le i \le t. \tag{6.8}$$

It can be shown by induction. We first consider $\mathcal{E}(||\Psi - \overline{\Psi}||^2)$. It is the workload variance augmented in a sweep of pairwise balancing operations. By the definition of Φ, we have

$$\begin{aligned}\mathcal{E}(||\Psi^t - \overline{\Psi}^t||^2) &= \mathcal{E}(||\sum_{c=1}^{d}(\Pi_{j=d}^{c+1}\mathbf{E}_j\Phi^{t'-d+c} - \overline{\Phi}^{t'-d+c})||^2) \\ &= \sum_{c=1}^{d}\mathcal{E}(||\Pi_{j=d}^{c+1}\mathbf{E}_j\Phi^{t'-d+c} - \overline{\Phi}^{t'-d+c}||^2) \\ &= \sum_{c=1}^{d-1}(b^cN-1)\sigma^2 + (N-1)\sigma^2 \\ &= sN\sigma^2 - d\sigma^2,\end{aligned} \tag{6.9}$$

where the second step is due to the fact that $\Pi_{j=d}^{c+1}\mathbf{E}_j\Phi^{t'-d+c} - \overline{\Phi}^{t'-d+c}$ are zero mean independent random variables for $1 \leq c \leq d$, and the third step is due to the following reasons. Each component of the vector $\Pi_{j=d}^{c}\mathbf{E}_j\Phi$ for any c, $1 \leq c < d$, is a linear combination of two components of the vector $\Pi_{j=d}^{c+1}\mathbf{E}_j\Phi$ with coefficients $1-\lambda$ and λ. It can thus be inferred that a component of $\Pi_{j=d}^{c}\mathbf{E}_j\Phi$ is a linear combination of 2^{d-c+1} components of Φ. Their coefficients are presented in the middle column of Table 6.3. Let a_i, $i = 1, 2^{d-c+1}$, denote the coefficients. It is clear that $\sum_{i=1}^{2^{d-c+1}} a_i = 1$, as shown in the third column of the table. From Lemma 6.1.1, we thus have

$$\mathcal{E}(||\Pi_{j=d}^{c}\mathbf{E}_j\Phi - \overline{\Phi}||^2) = Nb^{d-c+1}\sigma^2 - \sigma^2.$$

The third step of Eq. (6.9) therefore holds.

Table 6.3: Coefficients of a linear combination of 2^{d-c+1} components; each component of vector $\Pi_{j=d}^{c+1}\mathbf{E}_j\Phi$ is a linear combination of 2^{d-c+1} components of Φ with the coefficients; let $\overline{\lambda} = 1 - \lambda$.

c	Coefficients a_i, $i = 1,\ 2^{d-c+1}$								$\sum a_i^2$
d				$\overline{\lambda}$	λ				b
$d-1$			$\overline{\lambda}^2$	$\lambda\overline{\lambda}$	$\lambda\overline{\lambda}$	λ^2			b^2
$d-2$	$\overline{\lambda}^3$	$\lambda\overline{\lambda}^2$	$\lambda\overline{\lambda}^2$	$\lambda^2\overline{\lambda}$	$\overline{\lambda}^2\lambda$	$\lambda^2\overline{\lambda}$	$\lambda^2\overline{\lambda}$	λ^3	b^3
$\cdots$				$\cdots$					$\cdots$
1	$\overline{\lambda}^d$	$\lambda\overline{\lambda}^{d-1}$	$\lambda^2\overline{\lambda}^{d-2}$	$\cdots$		$\lambda^{d-2}\overline{\lambda}^2$	$\lambda^{d-1}\overline{\lambda}$	λ^{d-1}	b^d

We proceed to prove Eq. (6.8) by induction on i. Assume

$$\mathcal{E}(||\mathbf{E}^i\Psi^{t+1-i} - \overline{\Psi}^{t+1-i}||^2) = b^{id}sN\sigma^2 - d\sigma^2.$$

We then consider $\mathcal{E}(||\mathbf{E}^{i+1}\Psi^{t-i} - \overline{\Psi}^{t-i}||^2)$. Since ϕ_i^t is assumed to be independent of time t, Φ^t is independent of t as well. Then,

$$\mathcal{E}(||\mathbf{E}^{i+1}\Psi^{t-i} - \overline{\Psi}^{t-i}||^2) = \mathcal{E}(||(\Pi_{j=d}^{1}\mathbf{E}_j)\mathbf{E}^i\Psi^{t-i+1} - \overline{\Psi}^{t-i+1}||^2).$$

From the explanation of Eq. (6.9), it is known that a sequence of suffix operators $\Pi_{j=d}^{1}\mathbf{E}_j$ changes the vector $\mathbf{E}^i\Psi$ in such a way that each of its new components becomes a combination of its 2^d original components with 2^d coefficients defined in the last row of Table 6.3. Consequently

$$\mathcal{E}(||\mathbf{E}^{i+1}\Psi^{t-i} - \overline{\Psi}^{t-i}||^2) = b^d b^{di}sN\sigma^2 - d\sigma^2 = b^{di+d}sN\sigma^2 - d\sigma^2,$$

which concludes the induction and proves the second part of the lemma. □

From the lemma, it is evident that $\mathcal{E}(\nu_{de}^t)$ is minimized at $\lambda = 1/2$ over all possible choices of the dimension exchange parameter. Thus, we have

$$\mathcal{E}(\nu_{ade}^t) \leq \mathcal{E}(\nu_{ode}^t). \tag{6.10}$$

Diffusion method. Next, we consider synchronous implementations of the diffusion method. We present a companion to Theorem 6.1.2.

Theorem 6.1.3 *Suppose processors are running a synchronous diffusion load balancing process under Assumption 6.0.1. Then, $\mathcal{E}(\mathbf{W}^t)$ is a uniform distribution at any time t and*

$$\mathcal{E}(\nu_{df}^t) = (a^{t+1}\sigma_0^2 + \frac{1-a^{t+1}}{1-a}\sigma^2)N - (t+1)\sigma^2 - \sigma_0^2, \tag{6.11}$$

where $a = (1-d\alpha)^2 + d\alpha^2$.

Proof. The uniform distribution of $\mathcal{E}(\mathbf{W}^t)$ resulting from the diffusion method can be easily shown. We omit its proof because it is also available as a special case in the proof of the uniform distribution of $\mathcal{E}(\mathbf{W}^t)$ resulting from the dimension exchange method.

Consider the expected workload variance $\mathcal{E}[\nu_{df}^t]$. By its definition and Assumption 6.0.1, we have

$$\begin{aligned}
\mathcal{E}(\nu_{df}^t) &= \mathcal{E}(||\mathbf{W}^t - \overline{\mathbf{W}}^t||^2) \\
&= \mathcal{E}(||\mathbf{D}\mathbf{W}^{t-1} - \overline{\mathbf{W}}^{t-1}||^2) + \mathcal{E}(||\Phi^t - \overline{\Phi}^t||^2) \\
&= \mathcal{E}(||\mathbf{D}^{t+1}\mathbf{W}^0 - \overline{\mathbf{W}}^0||^2 + \sum_{i=0}^{t}\mathcal{E}(||\mathbf{D}^i\Phi^{t+1-i} - \overline{\Phi}^{t+1-i}||^2) \\
&= N(a^{t+1} - \frac{1}{N})\sigma_0^2 + \sum_{i=0}^{t}(a^i - \frac{1}{N})\sigma^2 \\
&= (a^{t+1}\sigma_0^2 + \frac{1-a^{t+1}}{1-a}\sigma^2)N - (t+1)\sigma^2 - \sigma_0^2,
\end{aligned}$$

where the fourth step is based on the following observations. An operation $\mathbf{D}$ on the workload distribution Φ changes each of its components to become a linear combination of the component's $d+1$ sub-components with coefficients $1-d\alpha, \alpha, \alpha, \ldots, \alpha$; and a sequence of operation $\mathbf{D}^t$ changes each component of Φ to become a linear combination of its $(d+1)^t$ sub-components. From Lemma 6.1.1, it is known that the variance of a combination of random variables is determined only by their combinatorial coefficients. Therefore, we have

$$\mathcal{E}(||\mathbf{D}\Phi - \overline{\Phi}^{t+1-i}||^2) = N(a - 1/N)\sigma^2,$$

and

$$\mathcal{E}(||\mathbf{D}^t\Phi - \overline{\Phi}||^2) = N(a^t - 1/N)\sigma^2,$$

where $a = (1 - d\alpha)^2 + d\alpha^2$. □

Consider the term $a = (1 - d\alpha)^2 + d\alpha^2$ in Theorem 6.1.3. It is minimized at $\alpha = 1/(d + 1)$ over all possible choices of the parameter α, which happens to be the choice of the ADF algorithm in n-dimensional meshes and tori. Immediately, we obtain

$$\mathcal{E}(\nu^t_{adf}) \leq \mathcal{E}(\nu^t_{odf}). \tag{6.12}$$

We further compare $\mathcal{E}(\nu^t_{ade})$ with $\mathcal{E}(\nu^t_{adf})$ in both one-port and all-port communication models. Notice that Theorem 6.1.2 holds under the assumption that the workload generation/consumption ratios ϕ^t_i in each pairwise balancing step of a round of dimension exchange operation has the same statistical characteristics as those in a diffusion operation. It is therefore fair to compare $\mathcal{E}(\nu^t_{df})$ of Eq. (6.11) with $\mathcal{E}(\nu^t_{de})$ of Eq. (6.4). Consider the all-port communication model. Substituting $1/d + 1$ for α in $\mathcal{E}(\nu^t_{df})$ and $1/2$ for λ in $\mathcal{E}(\nu^t_{de})$, we obtain $\mathcal{E}[\nu^t_{adf}] = A_1\sigma^2 + A_2\sigma_0^2$, where

$$\begin{aligned} A_1 &= \frac{d+1}{d}[1 - (\frac{d}{d+1})^{t+1}]N - (t+1), \\ A_2 &= \frac{1}{(d+1)^{t+1}} - 1; \end{aligned}$$

and $\mathcal{E}[\nu^t_{ade}] = B_1\sigma^2 + b_2\sigma_0^2$, where

$$\begin{aligned} B_1 &= (2 - \frac{1}{2^{d-1}})\frac{1 - 1/2^{t+1}}{1 - 1/2^d}N - (t+1)d, \\ B_2 &= (2 - \frac{1}{2^{d-1}})\frac{1}{2^{dt+d}} - 1. \end{aligned}$$

It can be easily verified that $A_1 > B_1$ and $A_2 > B_2$. Hence,

$$\mathcal{E}(\nu^t_{ade}) \leq \mathcal{E}(\nu^t_{adf}), \qquad \text{for } t \leq N/d.$$

Since $N \gg d$ in the mesh and the torus, the above relationship holds for any time instant of interest in practice.

In the case of the one-port communication model, the workload generated/consumed by a processor in a single diffusion operation is expected to be $d\mu$ with variance $d\sigma^2$. Then, $\mathcal{E}(\nu^t_{df})$ of Eq. (6.11) becomes

$$(a^{t+1}\sigma_0^2 + \frac{1 - a^{t+1}}{1 - a}d\sigma^2)N - (t+1)d\sigma^2 - \sigma_0^2.$$

Again, $\mathcal{E}(\nu^t_{ade}) \leq \mathcal{E}(\nu^t_{adf})$ at any time t.

Conclusively, we obtain the following theorem concerning the balance quality of different load balancing algorithms.

Theorem 6.1.4 *Suppose processors are running synchronous dimension exchange and diffusion load balancing processes under Assumption 6.0.1 Then,*

$$\mathcal{E}(\nu^t_{ade}) \le \mathcal{E}(\nu^t_{ode}),\ \mathcal{E}(\nu^t_{adf}) \le \mathcal{E}(\nu^t_{odf}),\ \textit{and}\ \ \mathcal{E}(\nu^t_{ade}) \le \mathcal{E}(\nu^t_{adf})$$

in both one-port and all-port communication models.

First of all, the theorem shows that the dimension exchange method ensures higher balancing quality than the diffusion method in both one-port and all-port communication models in the mesh and the tours. The theorem also indicates that both the ADE and ADF outperform the ODE and ODF in the dynamic workload model, respectively, even though the optimally-tuned algorithms improve the efficiency significantly in the static workload model.

6.2 Asynchronous Implementations

In an asynchronous implementation of load balancing, processors perform balancing operations discretely based on their own local workload distributions and invocation policies. Load balancing algorithms are orthogonal to invocation policies. A balancing operator can be used together with any invocation policy in a processor. Also, different load balancing algorithms can be used by the processor at different invocation instances during the execution of programs. In order to isolate the effects of a balancing operator on the workload variance from the effect of an invocation policy, we consider load balancing algorithms in a single time step. We focus on the static situation of load balancing in which the underlying computation in a processor is suspended while the processor is performing load balancing operations. The dynamic situation presents only a few relatively minor differences to the analysis of the effects of load balancing.

Let ν^0 be the original system workload variance when $t = 0$, and ν be the system workload variance when $t = 1$. Our comparison will be made between ν_{ade}, ν_{ode}, ν_{adf}, and ν_{odf} which are the results from various load balancing operations.

We summarize our comparative results in the following theorem. It says that the dimension exchange and the diffusion methods are suitable for the one-port and the all-port communication models, respectively. In addition, it reveals that the ODF algorithm outperforms the ADF algorithm in higher dimensional meshes and tori although the ODF was originally proposed for use in synchronous global balancing.

Theorem 6.2.1 *Suppose processors are running an asynchronous load balancing process under Assumption 6.0.1. Then,*

1. *For the one-port communication model,* $\mathcal{E}(\nu_{ade}) \leq \mathcal{E}(\nu_{df})$*, but for the all-port model,* $\mathcal{E}(\nu_{df}) \leq \mathcal{E}(\nu_{ade})$.
2. *For two- or higher-dimensional meshes or tori,* $\mathcal{E}(\nu_{odf}) \leq \mathcal{E}(\nu_{adf})$*, but for chain and ring networks,* $\mathcal{E}(\nu_{adf}) \leq \mathcal{E}(\nu_{odf})$.
3. *For the all-port communication model,* $\mathcal{E}(\nu_{ude}) \leq \mathcal{E}(\nu_{ode})$.

Proof. The theorem is proved through the derivation of the closed form of each variance $\mathcal{E}(\nu)$. The calculation of $\mathcal{E}(\nu)$ is based on Lemma 6.1.1 concerning the sample variance of a combination of random variables in a sample set. At certain time in an asynchronous load balancing process, there might be more than one processor that are invoking load balancing within their neighborhoods simultaneously. Let $\widetilde{\mathcal{A}}(i) = \{i\} \cup \mathcal{A}(i)$ denote the balancing domain of an invoker processor i. The balancing domains of concurrent invokers may overlap or may be separated from each other. As a whole, those processors that are running load balancing processes are partitioned into a number of separated spheres, some of which are singular balancing domains and some are unions of overlapping domains. Processors in different spheres perform load balancing operations independently, while processors in the same sphere perform load balancing in a synchronous manner.

Suppose initially there are m independent balancing spheres in the system, denoted by $\mathcal{B}_1, \mathcal{B}_2, \cdots, \mathcal{B}_m$. Then, by the definition of the workload variance ν and Assumption 6.0.1, we have

$$\begin{aligned}
\mathcal{E}(\nu) &= \mathcal{E}(\sum_{i=1}^{N} |w_i^1 - \overline{w}^1|^2) \\
&= \sum_{i=1}^{N} \mathcal{E}(|w_i^1 - \overline{w}^1|^2) \\
&= \sum_{j=1}^{m} \sum_{i \in \mathcal{B}_i} \mathcal{E}(|w_i^1 - \overline{w}^1|^2) + \sum_{i \notin \cup_{j=1}^{m} \mathcal{B}_j} \mathcal{E}(|w_i^1 - \overline{w}^1|^2) \\
&= \sum_{j=1}^{m} \sum_{i \in \mathcal{B}_j} \mathcal{E}(|w_i^1 - \overline{w}^1|^2) + (N - N')(1 - \frac{1}{N})(\sigma_0^2 + \sigma^2), \quad (6.13)
\end{aligned}$$

where $N' = |\cup_{i=1}^{m} \mathcal{B}_i|$ is the number of processors involved in load balancing. The last term of (6.13) is due to the underlying computational operations. It is a constant for a given N' and independent of the topological relationships among the N' processors. The first term of (6.13) is due to load balancing operations in all separated balancing spheres. It is a simple arithmetic sum of workload variances of each sphere, $\sum_{i \in \mathcal{B}_j} \mathcal{E}(|w_i^1 - \overline{w}^1|^2)$. As a whole, Eq. (6.13) implies that the expected value of the system workload variance is influenced independently by load balancing operations within different balancing spheres.

Therefore, it suffices to compare the effects of load balancing algorithms within different spheres using Lemma 6.1.1

6.2.1 Load Balancing in a Singular Balancing Domain

We first consider load balancing in spheres of singular balancing domains. Suppose $\mathcal{B}_1$ is such a sphere, and without loss of generality, $\mathcal{B}_1 = \widetilde{\mathcal{A}}(1) = \{1, 2, 3, \cdots, d+1\}$. That is, processor 1 invokes a load balancing operation within its d neighbors which are labeled from 2 to $d+1$. Let $X = \sum_{i=1}^{d+1} \mathcal{E}(|w_i^1 - \overline{w}^1|^2)$, denoting the expected value of workload variance of sphere $\mathcal{B}_1$.

Diffusion. With the diffusion algorithm, the workloads of processors at the end of a diffusion operation are given, according to Eq. (5.1), by

$$w_i^1 = \begin{cases} (1-d\alpha)w_1^0 + \alpha \sum_{j=2}^{d+1} w_i^0 & \text{if } i = 1 \\ \alpha w_1^0 + (1-\alpha)w_i^0 & \text{if } 2 \le i \le d+1 \end{cases} \tag{6.14}$$

Invoking Lemma 6.1.1 on each component w_i^1, we have

$$\begin{aligned} X_{df} &= \sum_{i=1}^{d+1} \mathcal{E}(|w_i^1 - \overline{w}^1|^2) \\ &= \mathcal{E}\left(|(1-d\alpha)w_1^0 + \alpha \sum_{i=2}^{d+1} w_i^0 - \overline{w}^0|^2\right) \\ &= (d^2\alpha^2 + 3d\alpha^2 - 4d\alpha + d + 1 - \frac{d+1}{N})\sigma_0^2. \end{aligned} \tag{6.15}$$

X_{df} is a convex function of α. It is is minimized at $\alpha = 2/(3+d)$. Let $\alpha_{min} = 2/(3+d)$. We replace α by α_{min} in the expression of X_{df}, and obtain

$$X_{df}(\alpha_{min}) = (\frac{d^2+3}{d+3} - \frac{d+1}{N})\sigma_0^2. \tag{6.16}$$

Recall that $\alpha_{adf} = 1/(d+1)$, and that $\alpha_{odf} = 1/d$ in a mesh and $\alpha_{odf} = 1/(d+1-\cos(2\pi/k))$ in a torus, where k is the maximum dimensional order of the torus. It follows that

i) in the case of a chain of any order or the case of a ring of order k, $k \ge 12$, $\alpha_{adf} < \alpha_{min} < \alpha_{odf}$ and $|\alpha_{adf} - \alpha_{min}| < |\alpha_{odf} - \alpha_{min}|$;
ii) in the case of higher dimensional meshes and tori, $\alpha_{adf} < \alpha_{odf} < \alpha_{min}$.

Consequently, with the diffusion method, we have

$$\begin{cases} X_{df}(\alpha_{min}) \le X_{adf} \le X_{odf} & \text{if } n = 1 \text{ and } k \ge 12, \\ X_{df}(\alpha_{min}) \le X_{odf} \le X_{adf} & \text{if } n \ge 2 \end{cases} \tag{6.17}$$

Dimension exchange. With the dimension exchange method, processor 1 is assumed to perform pairwise load balancing with processors $2, 3, \ldots, d+1$ in turn in a dimension exchange load balancing operation. Assume the underlying system is in the one-port communication model. Then, the workload generation/consumption ratio in a round of pairwise balancing steps has the same statistical characteristics as those in a diffusion operation. Consequently, according to Eq. (3.1) in Section 3.2, the processors' workloads at the end of a dimension exchange operation become

$$w_i^1 = \begin{cases} (1-\lambda)^d w_1^0 + \lambda \sum_{j=0}^{d-1} (1-\lambda)^j w_{d-j+1}^0 & \text{if } i = 1; \\ (1-\lambda) w_2^0 + \lambda w_1^0 & \text{if } i = 2; \\ (1-\lambda) w_i^0 + \lambda (1-\lambda)^{i-2} w_1^0 + \lambda^2 \sum_{j=0}^{i-3} (1-\lambda)^j w_{i-1-j}^0 & \text{if } 3 \le i \le d+1. \end{cases} \tag{6.18}$$

In particular, the processors' workloads at the end of an ADE operation are

$$w_i^1 = \begin{cases} \frac{w_1^0}{2^d} + \lambda \sum_{j=0}^{d-1} \frac{w_{d-j+1}^0}{2^j} & \text{if } i = 1; \\ \frac{w_2^0 + w_1^0}{2} & \text{if } i = 2; \\ \frac{w_i^0}{2} + \frac{w_1^0}{2^{i-1}} + \frac{1}{4} \sum_{j=0}^{i-3} \frac{w_{i-1-j}^0}{2^j} & \text{if } 3 \le i \le d+1. \end{cases} \tag{6.19}$$

Invoking Lemma 6.1.1 on each component w_i^1, we have

$$X_{ade} = \left(\frac{3d + 5 + 2^{2-2d}}{9} - \frac{d+1}{N} \right) \sigma_0^2. \tag{6.20}$$

From (6.16) and (6.20), it is known that $X_{ade} \le X_{df}(\alpha_{min})$. It is thus proved that in the one-port communication model,

$$\mathcal{E}(\nu_{ade}) \le \mathcal{E}(\nu_{df}). \tag{6.21}$$

In the all-port communication model, a dimension exchange pairwise balancing step takes as much time as a diffusion load balancing operation. That is, in a time step of the diffusion method, a processor balances with only one of its neighbors with the dimension exchange method. Hence,

$$X_{ade} = (1 - \frac{2}{N})\sigma_0^2 + (d-1)(1 - \frac{1}{N})\sigma_0^2.$$

Clearly, $X_{df} \le X_{ade} \le X_{ode}$. Consequently,

$$\mathcal{E}(\nu_{df}) \le \mathcal{E}(\nu_{ade}) \le \mathcal{E}(\nu_{ode}). \tag{6.22}$$

6.2.2 Load Balancing in a Union of Overlapping Domains

We now consider load balancing in spheres which are unions of overlapping balancing domains. A balancing sphere can be a union of any number of overlapping domains. In consideration of the likelihood that few processors will be invoking load balancing simultaneously in asynchronous implementations, we focus on the union of two balancing domains only. Figure 6.1 illustrates three topological relationships between a pair of processors which have overlapping balancing domains in 2-D meshes and tori. The triangles are invokers of load balancing processes and the dots are processors being involved in load balancing.

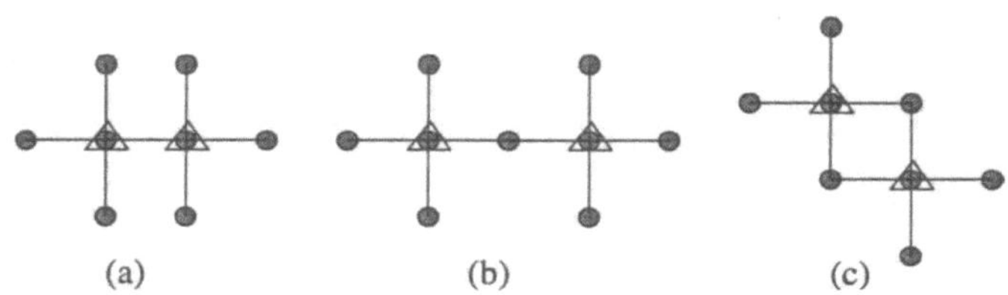

Figure 6.1: Asynchronous load balancing in overlapping balancing domains

Assume $\mathcal{B}_2$ is a union of balancing domains of processors j_1 and j_2. That is, $\mathcal{B}_2 = \widetilde{\mathcal{A}}(j_1) \cup \widetilde{\mathcal{A}}(j_2)$. Let Y denote the expected value of the workload variance of $\mathcal{B}_2$, i.e., $Y = \sum_{i \in \mathcal{B}_2} \mathcal{E}(|w_i^1 - \overline{w}^1|^2)$. Suppose processors j_1 and j_2 have the same number of direct neighbors.

j_1 and j_2 directly connected. First we consider the case that processors j_1 and j_2 are directly connected, as in Figure 6.1(a). With the diffusion method, it is known that each processor in $\widetilde{\mathcal{A}}(j_1)\backslash\{j_2\}$ (or $\widetilde{\mathcal{A}}(j_2)\backslash\{j_1\}$) changes its workload in the same way as in load balancing within a singular balancing domain $\widetilde{\mathcal{A}}(j_1)$ (or $\widetilde{\mathcal{A}}(j_2)$). Therefore,

$$Y_{df} = 2X_{df} - 2\left[(1-\alpha)^2 + \alpha^2 - \frac{1}{N}\right]\sigma_0^2. \tag{6.23}$$

It can be easily verified that Y_{df} is minimized at $\alpha_{min} = (2d-1)/(d^2+3d-2)$. And,

$$Y_{df}(\alpha_{min}) = d - \frac{4d^2 - 4d + 1}{d^2 + 3d - 2}. \tag{6.24}$$

As in the case of singular balancing domain, it can be shown that

i) in the case of a chain of any order or a ring having more than 5 nodes, $\alpha_{adf} < \alpha_{min} < \alpha_{odf}$ and $|\alpha_{adf} - \alpha_{min}| < |\alpha_{odf} - \alpha_{min}|$;

ii) in the case of higher dimensional meshes and tori, $\alpha_{adf} < \alpha_{odf} < \alpha_{min}$.

Consequently, with the diffusion method, we have

$$\begin{cases} Y_{df}(\alpha_{min}) \leq Y_{adf} \leq Y_{odf} & \text{if } d = 2 \text{ (i.e., chains and rings),} \\ Y_{df}(\alpha_{min}) \leq Y_{odf} \leq Y_{adf} & \text{if } d \geq 2 \text{ (i.e., meshes and tori).} \end{cases} \tag{6.25}$$

With the dimension exchange method, both processors j_1 and j_2 perform pairwise balancing operations with their neighbors in turn according to the order which is preset through edge-coloring of the system graph. The change of the workload distribution in $\mathcal{B}_2$ is thus influenced by the execution order across the communication channels. Suppose the channel (j_1, j_2) is indexed as c^{th}. Without loss of generality, we relabel the processor j_1 as 1, processor j_2 as $c+1$, and others in $\mathcal{A}(j_1)$ as 2 to $d+1$ (excluding $c+1$). Then, it is clear that w_i^1, $(2 \leq i \leq c)$, is equivalent to that in Eq. (6.18) w_i^1, $(i > c)$, differs from that in Eq. (6.18) because w_{c+1}^1 may be different from w_{c+1}^0 at the time processor 1 communicates processor $c+1$. From Lemma 6.1.1(2), it is also known that

$$\mathcal{E}(|w_{d+1}^1 - \overline{w}^1|^2) \leq \mathcal{E}(|w_i^1 - \overline{w}^1|^2), \qquad \text{for } i \geq 2.$$

Thus, we obtain

$$\begin{aligned} Y_{ade} &\leq 2X_{ade} - 2\mathcal{E}(|w_{d+1}^1 - \overline{w}^1|^2) \\ &\leq 2X_{ade} - 2(\frac{1}{3} + \frac{2}{3 \times 2^{2d}} - \frac{1}{N})\sigma_0^2. \end{aligned} \tag{6.26}$$

The comparison between Y_{ade} of Eq. (6.26) and $Y_{df}(\alpha_{min})$ of Eq. (6.24) yields $Y_{ade} \leq Y_{df}(\alpha_{min})$. Consequently, we obtain the following results in the case that processors j_1 and j_2 are adjacent:

$$\mathcal{E}(\nu_{ade}) \leq \begin{cases} \mathcal{E}(\nu_{adf}) \leq \mathcal{E}(\nu_{odf}) & \text{if } d = 2 \text{ (chains and rings);} \\ \mathcal{E}(\nu_{odf}) \leq \mathcal{E}(\nu_{adf}) & \text{if } d > 2 \text{ (meshes and tori).} \end{cases} \tag{6.27}$$

j_1 and j_2 non-adjacent. In the cases that processors j_1 and j_2 are non-adjacent, as illustrated in Figures 6.1(b) and 6.1(c), there are at most two processors in the intersection of their balancing domains in the mesh and torus networks. Let b be the cardinality of the intersection $\widetilde{\mathcal{A}}(j_1) \cap \widetilde{\mathcal{A}}(j_2)$, $b = 1$ or 2. Then, with the diffusion method,

$$\begin{aligned} Y_{df} &= 2X_{df} - 2b[(1-\alpha)^2 + \alpha^2 - \frac{1}{N}]\sigma_0^2 + b[(1-2\alpha)^2 + 2\alpha^2 - \frac{1}{N}]\sigma_0^2 \\ &= 2X_{df} - s[(1-2\alpha^2) - \frac{1}{N}]\sigma_0^2; \end{aligned} \tag{6.28}$$

and with the ADE algorithm,

$$Y_{ade} \leq 2X_{ade} - b\left[\frac{1}{3} + \frac{2}{3 \times 2^{2d}} - \frac{1}{N}\right]\sigma_0^2. \tag{6.29}$$

Similarly to the case that processors j_1 and j_2 are directly connected, we obtain $Y_{ade} \leq Y_{df}, Y_{adf} \leq Y_{odf}$ in case $d = 2$, and $Y_{odf} \leq Y_{adf}$ in case $d > 2$. Evidently, Eq. (6.27) still holds.

Notice that the preceding analysis of the dimension exchange method is implicitly based on the assumption of one-port communication model. In the all-port communication model, a dimension exchange pairwise balancing step corresponds to a diffusion balancing operation. Because two pairwise balancing operations in a union of two balancing domains can be performed concurrently, we thus have

$$Y_{de} = 4[(1-\lambda)^2 + \lambda^2 - \frac{1}{N}]\sigma_0^2 + (2d - 4 - b)(1 - \frac{1}{N})\sigma_0^2, \tag{6.30}$$

where $b = 1$ or 2. Obviously, $Y_{df} \leq Y_{ade} \leq Y_{ode}$. That is

$$\mathcal{E}(\nu_{df}) \leq \mathcal{E}(\nu_{ade}) \leq \mathcal{E}(\nu_{ode}). \tag{6.31}$$

The theorem is then proved. □

Note that the proof of the theorem assumes the static workload model in which processors suspend their computational operations during the execution of balancing operations. The theorem still holds in the dynamic situation. Consider processors in balancing sphere $\mathcal{B}$. Since the workloads generated/consumed from time 0 to time 1 in any processor i, $i \in \mathcal{B}$, will not be considered in its load balancing operation at time step 1, the operation in the dynamic situation then results in a workload variance of $\mathcal{E}(|w_i^1 - \overline{w}^1|^2) + \sigma^2$, where $\mathcal{E}(|w_i^1 - \overline{w}^1|^2)$ is the processor's workload variance in the static situation. As a whole, the accumulative workload variance of processors in balancing sphere $\mathcal{B}$ in the dynamic situation is $\sum_{i \in \mathcal{B}} \mathcal{E}(w_i^1 - \overline{w}^1|^2) + N'\sigma^2$, where $N' = |\mathcal{B}|$. The added term is a constant for a given N' and independent of the load balancing algorithm used. Hence, the arguments in the proof of the theorem are valid in the dynamic situation.

To conclude this section, we remark that a diffusion load balancing operation averages the workload of a processor, say processor 1, and its surrounding d processors, labeled from 2 to $d+1$, in a simple way that processor 1 gives $\alpha(w_1 - w_i)$ loads to processor i, in the case of $w_1 > w_i$, and takes $\alpha(w_i - w_1)$ load from processor i, otherwise ($2 \leq i \leq d+1$). In a singular balancing domain, there might be a variant of the ADF algorithm which strives for local load balancing. Specifically, processor 1 calculates the local average $\overline{w}_1$ as

$$\overline{w}_1 = \frac{w_1 + \sum_{2 \leq i \leq d+1} w_i}{1 + d},$$

and then gives or takes $|w_i - \overline{w}_1|$ loads to or from processor i according to whether processor i is deficient or not. After such an operation, each processor $i, 2 \leq i \leq d+1$ ends up with the same workload as processor 1. Consequently, the expected workload variance of the domain $\sum_{i=1}^{d+1} \mathcal{E}(|w_i^1 - \overline{w}^1|^2)$ becomes

$$\left(1 - \frac{d+1}{N}\right) \sigma_0^2,$$

which is obviously smaller than that of the ADE method even in the one-port communication model. Although it incurs more overheads than an ODF or ADF operation, such a variant of diffusion operation is preferred in singular balancing domains. However, it may not be effective in balancing spheres where a number of balancing domains overlap with each other because processors in such a sphere are unable to balance their workloads with all the processors in such an operation.

6.3 Simulations

In the preceding two sections, we explored a number of relationships between the dimension exchange and the diffusion methods with respect to their efficiencies and balancing qualities. In order to obtain an idea of the magnitude of their differences, we conducted a statistical simulation of these load balancing algorithms on various topologies and sizes of communication networks and using synthetic workload distributions. The experimental results also serve to verify the theoretical results.

The experiment includes three parts. They are a simulation of synchronous load balancing in a static workload situation, a simulation of asynchronous load balancing in the dynamic situation, and a simulation of synchronous load balancing in the dynamic situation. In each simulation, the initial workload distribution $\mathbf{W}$ is assumed to be a random vector, each element w of which is drawn independently from an identical uniform distribution in $[0, 1000]$. Each data point obtained in the experiment is the average of 20 runs, using different random initial workload distributions and different workload generation ratios. We also assume that the underlying system implements the all-port communication model so that a dimension exchange balancing operation takes $2n$ diffusion operations in an n-D mesh or torus. A diffusion operation is taken as a basic time step in a load balancing process.

6.3.1 Static Workload Model

The simulation of static synchronous load balancing processes is similar to those conducted in Sections 4.3 and 5.4. We measure the number of communication steps, denoted by T, necessary for arriving at a global balanced state. In the simulation, we define the global balanced state to be the state in which the system workload variance is less than or equal to one. Figure 6.2 and Figure 6.3 plot the simulation results from different load balancing algorithms executed in the ring of sizes (N) varying from 2 to 128 nodes and in the 2-D mesh of sizes varying from 2×2 to 32×32, respectively. These two figures clearly indicate

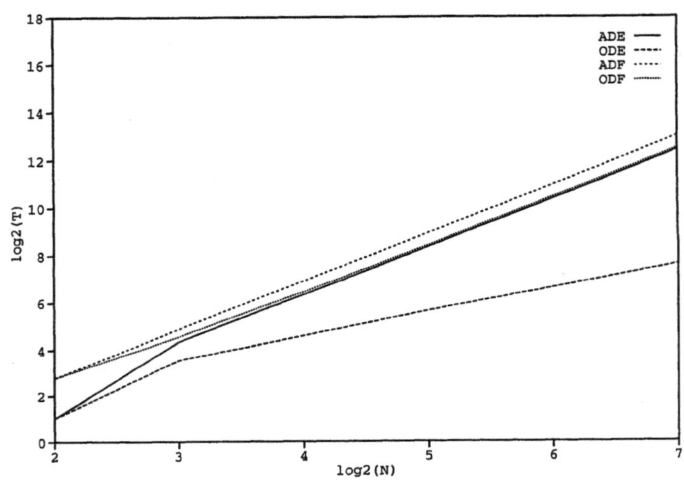

Figure 6.2: The number of communication steps necessary for reaching a global balanced state in a static synchronous load balancing process in rings of sizes varying from 4 to 128 nodes

that the dimension exchange method outperforms the diffusion method even in the all-port communication model. In particular, we see that the ODE algorithm does accelerate the dimension exchange load balancing process significantly. In the ring of 64 nodes, for example, $T_{ode} = 98$ with the ODE algorithm while $T_{ade} \simeq T_{odf} = 1305$ and $T_{adf} = 1684$ with the others. Its improvement over the ADE algorithm reaches as high as 92.5%. In Figure 6.3, we also see that the number of communication steps T in a 2-D mesh is dependent only on the size of its larger dimension and is insensitive to the size of its smaller dimension. This observation was proved to be true in both the mesh and the torus in [215]. Thus, an ODE load balancing process in a 64-ary 2-cube only requires about 196 communication steps for arriving at a global balanced state. It

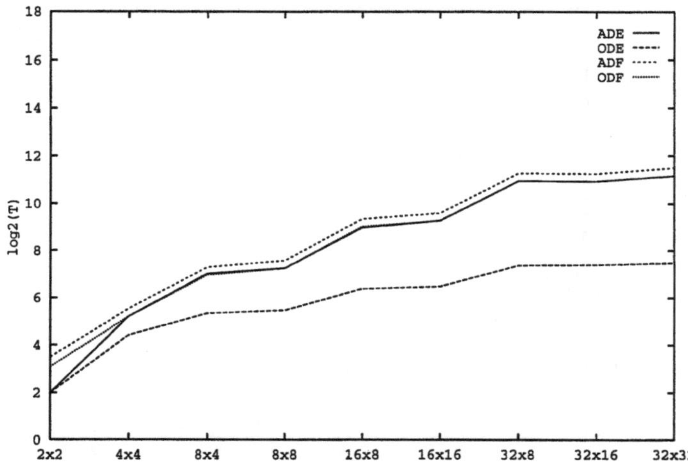

Figure 6.3: The number of communication steps necessary for reaching a global balanced state in a static synchronous load balancing process in 2-D meshes of sizes varying from 2×2 to 32×32

really puts forth the ODE algorithm as a practical method for dynamic global balancing in real multicomputers.

Furthermore, in order to examine the effects of a single load balancing operation, we plot in Figure 6.4 the system workload variance in the first 100 steps of various load balancing processes in the ring of 32 nodes. The figure illustrates that the ODE algorithm suppresses the system workload variance substantially although its initial reduction ratio seems to be not as satisfactory as that of the ADE algorithm. The ODF and the ADF algorithms have the same relationship in their reduction ratios. This says that both the ODE and the ODF algorithms may not outperform their local average balancing counterparts in the short term.

6.3.2 Dynamic Workload Model

In the dynamic situation, we assume that the expected workload generation ratio of a processor at each time step is 100 with the variance of 30 and the consumption ratio is a constant 100. In the simulation of asynchronous load balancing, we use a simple invocation policy such that once a processor's workload drops or rises beyond a pair of preset bounds, $w_{underload}$ and $w_{overload}$, the processor would activate a load balancing operation. Evidently, the pair of

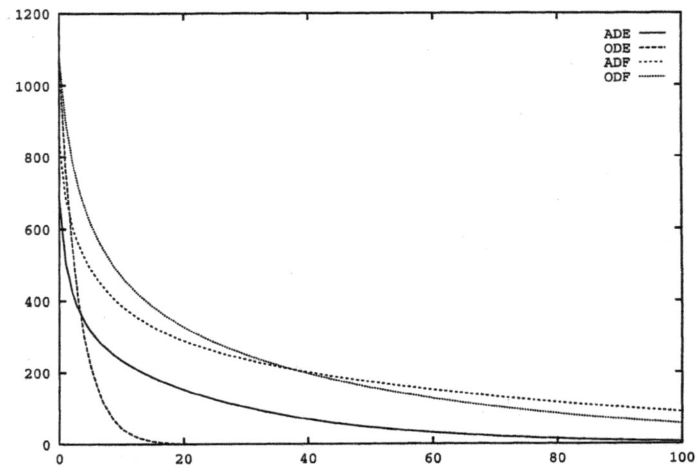

Figure 6.4: Reduction of the workload variance of a static synchronous load balancing process in a ring of 32 nodes

thresholds determine the degree of asynchronism of a load balancing process. Suppose $w_{underload}$ and $w_{overload}$ are symmetric with respect to the expected workload of a processor $\mathcal{E}(w)$. We then measure the range between $w_{underload}$ and $w_{overload}$ by an index *range*. Since $\mathcal{E}(w) = 500$ at any time, it follows that $w_{underload} = 500 - range/2$ and $w_{overload} = 500 + range/2$. Figures 6.5 and 6.6 plot the system workload variances resulting from different load balancing algorithms in a ring of 64 nodes and a mesh of size 16×16 for the case of $range = 600$.

From these two figures, it can be seen that the ADE algorithm reduces the initial system workload variance more rapidly than the diffusion method and keeps it bounded at a much lower level. It can also be observed that both the ODE and the ODF algorithms, the optimally-tuned algorithms for global synchronous load balancing, do not gain significant benefits in asynchronous implementations.

Synchronous implementations of load balancing are special cases of asynchronous implementations in which *range* is set to zero so that all processors participate in load balancing simultaneously. The simulation of synchronous implementations in the static situation was conducted in the first experiment, and its results in a ring of 32 nodes are reported in Figure 6.4. Figures 6.7 and 6.8 present the simulation results of dynamic synchronous implementations in the 16×16 torus and the 16×16 mesh. In agreement with the findings from

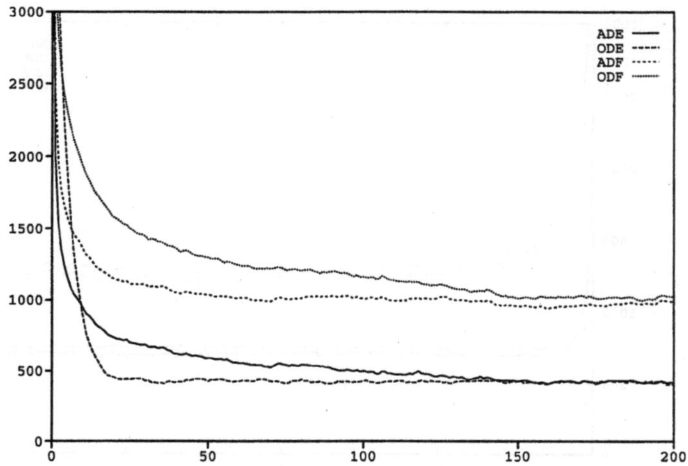

Figure 6.5: Change of the workload variance of a dynamic asynchronous load balancing process in a ring of size 64

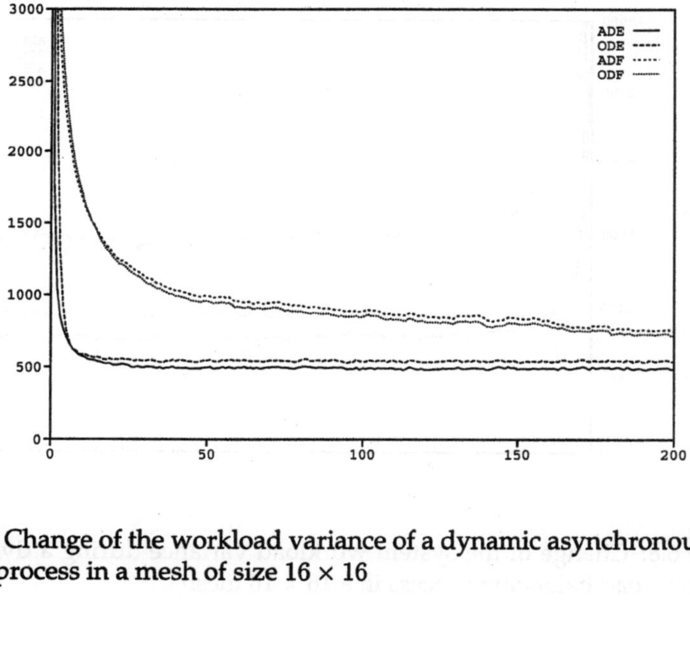

Figure 6.6: Change of the workload variance of a dynamic asynchronous load balancing process in a mesh of size 16×16

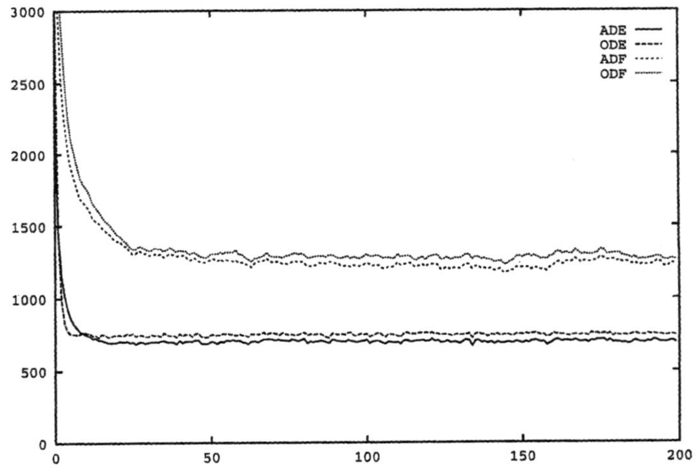

Figure 6.7: Change of the workload variance of a dynamic synchronous load balancing process in a 16 × 16 torus

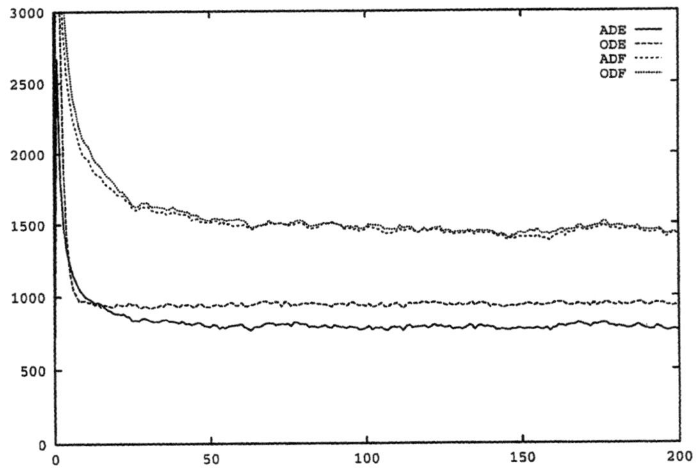

Figure 6.8: Change of the system workload variance during a dynamic synchronous load balancing process in a 16 × 16 mesh

Figure 6.4, Figures 6.7 and 6.8 show that the superiority of the dimension exchange method over the diffusion method holds under the synchronous invocation policies as well, and that the ADE algorithm has an advantage over the diffusion method in both short and long terms.

6.4 Concluding Remarks

We have compared the dimension exchange (DE) and the diffusion (DF) methods with respect to their efficiency in driving any initial workload distribution to a uniform distribution and their ability in controlling the growth of the variance among the processors' workloads. We focused on their four instances, the ADE, the ODE, the ADF and the ODF, which are the most common versions in practice. The comparison was made comprehensively in both one-port and all-port communication models with consideration of various implementation strategies: synchronous/asynchronous invocation policies and static/dynamic random workload behaviors.

Let "$a \succ b$" denote the relationship that a outperforms b, and "$a \sim b$" the relationship that a is approximately equivalent to b in performance. Then, our comparative results can be summarized as in Tables 6.4 and 6.5.

Table 6.4: Comparative results between the GDE and the diffusion methods in the one-port communication model

	Static load balancing	Dynamic load balancing
Synchronous	$ODE \succ ADE \succ ODF \sim ADF$	$ADE \succ ADF$ $ADE \succ ODE$ $ADF \succ ODF$
Asynchronous	$ADE \succ \{ADF, ODF\}$ $ADF \succ ODF$ in case $n = 1$ $ODF \succ ADF$ in case $n \geq 2$	same as left

Specifically, the dimension exchange method outperforms the diffusion method in the one-port communication model. The ODE algorithm lends itself best to synchronous implementation in the static situation. We also revealed the superiority of the dimension exchange method in synchronous load balancing even in the all-port communication model. The strength of the diffusion method is in asynchronous implementation in the all-port communication model. The ODF algorithm performs best in that case.

This comparative study not only provides an insight into nearest-neighbor

Table 6.5: Comparative results between the GDE and the diffusion methods in the all-port communication model

	Static load balancing	Dynamic load balancing
Synchronous	$ODE \succ ADE \sim ODF \sim ADF$	$ADE \succ ADF$ $ADE \succ ODE$ $ADF \succ ODF$
Asynchronous	$\{ADF, ODF\} \succ ADE \succ ODE$ $ADF \succ ODF$ in case $n = 1$ $ODF \succ ADF$ in case $n \geq 2$	same as left

load balancing algorithms, but also offers practical guidelines to system developers in designing load balancing architectures for various parallel computation paradigms. In Chapter 8, we evaluate the synchronous performance of the GDE method in mapping and remapping of data parallel computations. We also apply both the diffusion and the dimension exchange methods to distributed branch-and-bound computations, which is also meant to verify our comparative results regarding the two methods in asynchronous situations.

7

TERMINATION DETECTION OF LOAD BALANCING

"Begin at the beginning," the King said, gravely, "and go till you come to the end; then stop."
—LEWIS CARROLL [ALICE'S ADVENTURES IN WONDERLAND]

We have considered so far the GDE method and the diffusion method for load balancing in distributed memory multiprocessors. The focus has been on their convergence and rates of convergence. What is left to be addressed is the applicability of these methods in practice. For this purpose, this chapter is devoted to a fundamental problem—termination detection—which arises in the implementation of iterative load balancing algorithms. Other issues like load measurements and invocation policies will be examined in Chapters 8 and 9 when the algorithms are implemented in real applications.

With iterative load balancing algorithms, the load balancing procedure is considered terminated when the variance of the global workload distribution across the processors becomes less than a certain prescribed bound. From the practical point of view, the detection of the global termination is by no means a trivial problem because there is a lack of consistent knowledge in every processor about the whole workload distribution as the load balancing progresses. In order to assist the processors in inferring global termination of the load balancing procedure from local workload information, it is necessary to superimpose a distributed termination detection mechanism on the load balancing procedure.

7.1 The Termination Detection Problem

The problem of termination detection is one of the most heavily studied problems in distributed computing since its early discussion in [70]. A general scenario in which termination detection for a distributed computation would operate is as follows. The distributed computation is in terms of a collection of disjoint processes, which cooperate and communicate with one another by message-passing. Each processes switches between busy and idle states in an unpredictable manner. Only busy processes are allowed to send messages to other processes; an idle process would turn busy upon receipt of a message from a busy process; busy processes can become idle at any time. The computation is terminated if and only if all processes become idle and no messages are in transit. The problem of termination detection is to devise an algorithm that can detect global termination of the underlying computation, should it occur. A brief survey of the most well-known algorithms with various characteristics can be found in [136, 137, 117].

In this study, we are interested in termination detection for iterative load balancing algorithms, in which a processor modeled by a process balances its workload in phases by iteratively exchanging load information with the neighboring processors. Termination detection is therefore needed at the end of each phase. We characterize the behavior of termination detection for iterative procedures in Figure 7.1. At the point of termination evaluation, we distinguish between busy and idle states of a processor. A processor is in idle state when it is locally balanced; busy otherwise. An idle state is one in which the workload remains unchanged after an iteration phase. A busy processor would communicate its newly computed result in a data message to its dependent processors and an idle processor would wait for data messages from its busy neighbors in the iteration. A busy processor can become idle for the next iteration, and an idle processor may return to busy on receipt of a data message from a busy processor during the communication phase. Global termination occurs when all processors become idle. Apart from these data

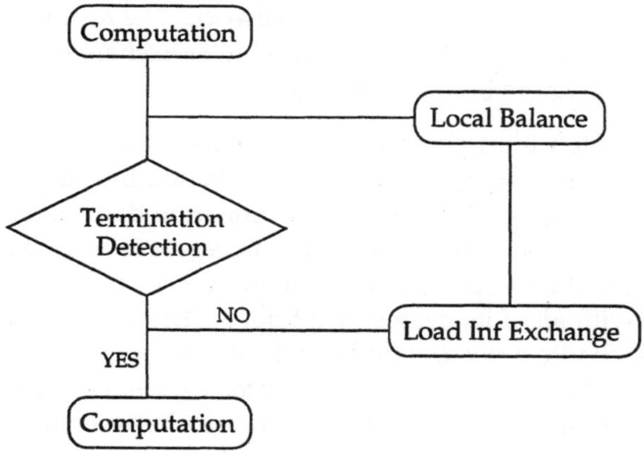

Figure 7.1: Termination detection for iterative load balancing algorithms

messages of the load balancing algorithm, control messages are used to pass information about termination around, which can emanate from both busy and idle processors. Processors would not change their states on receipt of control messages. The difference between the time when global termination occurs and the time when it is detected by processors is called the *termination delay* associated with a detection algorithm. Our principal objective is to minimize the delay for termination detection.

As the processors are synchronized by their exchanging newly computed values, the load balancing procedure can be viewed as having a global virtual time which is advanced by the execution of the iteration steps. Therefore, termination detection algorithms making use of global virtual time such as [79, 164] seem most applicable to this particular computation model. However, because of the requirement in these algorithms that control information for termination detection must be propagated along a Hamiltonion circuit, at least $N - 1$ iteration steps are necessary for detecting a termination, where N is the number of processors. If the detection is done by one particular processor, which is the case in many of the existing algorithms, additional steps would be needed to notify the other processors.

There are other algorithms such as [58, 169, 186] that allow control information to propagate along any existing communication channels. They share the idea of keeping a counter in every processor to tell how far the farthest busy processor might be. They are all fully distributed and symmetric in that all processors execute the same syntactically identical code and detect global termination simultaneously. In particular, the algorithm proposed by Szymanski, Shi and Prywes (SSP algorithm for short) has the minimum delay of $D + 1$ [186] when applied to our computation model of iterative load balancing algorithms, where D is the diameter of the network. The result is optimal in the case that a processor is allowed to broadcast to or exchange information with all of its direct neighbors in one time step.

With the SSP algorithm, the control information for termination detection is abstracted as a local integer counter S maintained in every processor. This counter's value changes as the iterative termination detection algorithm proceeds. S is equal to zero if and only if the processor is in an busy state. During the communication step of an iteration phase, each processor exchanges its counter value with all of its nearest neighbors. Then in the computation step of the phase, each idle processor updates its counter to be $1 + \min\{S, InputS\}$, where $InputS$ is the set of all received counter values. Evidently, the counter in a processor actually corresponds to the distance between this processor and the nearest busy processor, and since the control information of a busy processor can propagate over at most one edge in an iteration phase, a processor that just turned idle requires at least $D+1$ steps to confirm global termination. Hence, the delay for termination detection using the SSP algorithm is equal to $D + 1$. The requirement of one more step than diameter D is due to the fact the farthest busy processor in a globally terminated state must be at a distance greater than the network diameter.

Notice that the change of the counter values in the SSP algorithm behaves consistently with the diffusion load balancing: in the communication step of an iteration, a processor updates its counter only after having collected all the counter values of the neighboring processors. This is particularly desirable for the implementation of the diffusion method because the control messages for termination detection can be piggybacked on the data messages of diffusive load balancing, in which case the communication overhead for termination detection is almost negligible.

7.2 An Efficient Algorithm Based on Edge-Coloring

Recall that in multiprocessors, the communication model can be serial which restricts a processor to communicating with at most one nearest neighbor at a time. If we adopt the serial model, one step in the SSP algorithm must now be counted as d communication operations, where d is the degree of the network. Referring to the D lower bound, this makes the SSP algorithm far from optimal. In the ensuing sections, we present an algorithm which has a much better performance in the serial model [210, 216]; its delay is $\widetilde{D} + 1$ *iteration sweeps*, where $\widetilde{D}$ is called the *color-diameter* of the network and an iteration sweep comprises approximately d communication operations between processors. For some regular topologies, an iteration sweep equals exactly d communication operations, and $\widetilde{D} = D/d$, and hence the delay is $D + d$ communication operations which is optimal for reasonably large networks or networks with a small degree. For other common topologies, it is near optimal. What is more important, our algorithm's behavior is consistent with load balancing based on the dimension exchange method, and hence is most suitable for the implementation of the GDE method.

7.2.1 The Algorithm

Our algorithm bears certain resemblance to the SSP algorithm, but its updating of the counter S follows a different protocol. We serialize the communication step of an iteration phase into a number of consecutive exchange operations based on edge-coloring of the system graph, as illustrated in Chapter 2. Given a κ-color graph G_κ, of which each edge is labeled by a chromatic index c, $1 \leq c \leq \kappa$. Then, a communication step is serialized into κ operations, one for each index c. An exchange operation for color c causes two neighboring processors connected by an edge of color c to exchange their counter values. After each of these little exchanges with a neighbor, a processor would update its counter immediately with the value received from the other processor if the latter is smaller than this processor' current counter value. And at the end of each iteration step, the processor sets the counter to 0 if the processor is still busy with its local balancing; otherwise, it increments the counter value by 1. When S reaches a predefined value, the processor stops with the sure knowledge that the load balancing has reached global termination.

The algorithm follows. The variable *InputS* temporarily stores the neighboring counter value received in the current exchange operation.

```
Algorithm for Processor i (1 ≤ i ≤ N):
    S = 0;
    while (S < PredefinedValue) {
        for (c = 1; c ≤ κ; c = c + 1)
            if (an incident edge colored c exists) {
                InputS = Exchange(c);
                S = min{S, InputS};
            }
        if (LocalTerminated)
            S = S + 1;
        else
            S = 0;
    }
```

For each color (each iteration of the for-loop), the procedure *Exchange*(c) is executed which causes the counter values of the this processor and a neighboring processor connected by the edge colored c to exchange their counter values, where c is the current color (loop index). If the processor has no incident edge colored c, it skips this one and goes on to the next color. Note that unlike the SSP algorithm in which the counter is not updated until all the neighboring counter values are received, our algorithm compares the local counter with a neighbor's counter value as soon as the latter comes in through the exchange.

This algorithm is fully distributed and each processor runs the syntactically identical code. It is also fully symmetric in that all processor will detect global termination simultaneously. Below, we give an example to illustrate how the counter S gets updated as load balancing proceeds.

Let $S_i^c(t)$ denote the counter value of processor i after the exchange (after line 7) over the edge colored c (if there is one) has taken place within iteration step t, $S_i^-(t)$ the counter value of processor i at the end of the for loop (after line 8 before line 9), and $S_i(t)$ the counter value at the end of the iteration step t (after line 12). Clearly, $S_i^-(t) \leq S_i^c(t)$ for all c. Table 7.1 gives a partial trace of the counter distribution when we apply the algorithm to the 2×4 mesh network of Figure 7.2. The counter distribution is assumed to be

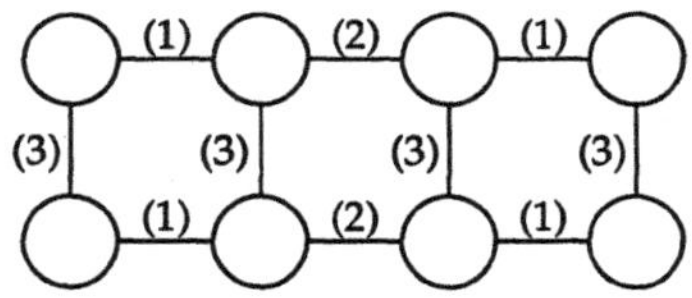

Figure 7.2: A color mesh of 2×4

$(0, 1, 1, 1, 1, 1, 1, 1)$ at t_0, the instant at which our tracing begins; processor 1 becomes idle at step t_0+2; processor 2 returns to busy at step t_0+2 and becomes idle again at t_0+4; processor 3 returns to busy at t_0+4 and becomes idle again at t_0+5, and global termination occurs at this point since all eight processors are idle. All the counter values reach 3 at t_0+7, which is the (earliest) point at which every processor is sure of the global termination—the detection delay is three iteration steps. This implies that *PredefinedValue* has been set to 3 in the algorithm. The following analysis on the global termination condition tells us how this number comes about.

7.2.2 Determination of Termination Delay

Before proceeding, we introduce here some concepts which will be used for the determination and analysis of the termination delay $PredefineValue$. Recall that in Chapter 3 a *color path* is defined to be a sequence of edges whose chromatic indices are in descending order. Based on this concept, we introduce the concepts of *color-distance* and *color-diameter* as follows.

Table 7.1: A trace of the counter distribution of processors in a 4 × 2 mesh structure; the numbers in parentheses are the counter values received in the current exchange

Processor	1	2	3	4	5	6	7	8
$S_i(t_0)$	**0**	1	1	1	1	1	1	1
$S_i^1(t_0+1)$	0(1)	0(0)	1(1)	1(1)	1(1)	1(1)	1(1)	1(1)
$S_i^2(t_0+1)$	0	0(1)	0(0)	1	1	1(1)	1(1)	1
$S_i^3(t_0+1)$	0(1)	0(1)	0(1)	1(1)	1(1)	0(0)	0(0)	0(0)
$S_i(t_0+1)$	**0**	1	1	2	2	1	1	1
$S_i^1(t_0+2)$	0(1)	0(0)	1(2)	1(1)	1(1)	1(2)	1(1)	1(1)
$S_i^2(t_0+2)$	0	0(2)	0(0)	1	1	1(1)	1(1)	1
$S_i^3(t_0+2)$	0(1)	0(1)	0(1)	1(1)	1(1)	0(0)	0(0)	0(0)
$S_i(t_0+2)$	1	**0**	1	2	2	1	1	1
$S_i^1(t_0+3)$	0(0)	0(0)	1(2)	1(1)	1(1)	1(2)	1(1)	1(1)
$S_i^2(t_0+3)$	0	0(1)	0(0)	1	1	1(1)	1(1)	1
$S_i^3(t_0+3)$	0(1)	0(1)	0(1)	1(1)	1(1)	0(0)	0(0)	0(0)
$S_i(t_0+3)$	1	**0**	1	2	2	1	1	1
$S_i^1(t_0+4)$	0(0)	0(1)	1(2)	1(1)	1(1)	1(2)	1(1)	1(1)
$S_i^2(t_0+4)$	0	0(1)	0(0)	1	1	1(1)	1(1)	1
$S_i^3(t_0+4)$	0(1)	0(1)	0(1)	1(1)	1(1)	0(0)	0(0)	0(0)
$S_i(t_0+4)$	1	1	**0**	2	2	1	1	1
$S_i(t_0+5)$	2	1	1	1	1	1	1	2
$S_i(t_0+6)$	2	2	2	2	2	2	2	2
$S_i(t_0+7)$	3	3	3	3	3	3	3	3

Definition 7.2.1 *In the κ-color graph G_κ, a processor j is said to be reachable from processor i in one trip if there exists a color path from i to j. The* color-distance *from processor i to processor j, denoted by $\widetilde{D}(i,j)$, is the minimum number of trips required for going from i to j. The greatest color-distance among the color-distances of all the processor pairs in G_κ is called the* color-diameter *of G_κ, denoted by $\widetilde{D}(G_\kappa)$.*

As an example, let us examine the color graph of 2×4 mesh in Figure 7.2. It is clear that processor 7 is reachable from 1 in one trip because of the color path $(1,8,3)$, $(8,7,1)$, and that processor 5 is reachable from 2 in one trip because of the color path $(2,7,3)$, $(7,6,2)$, $(6,5,1)$. Hence, $\widetilde{D}(1,7) = \widetilde{D}(2,5) = 1$; Similarly, we have $\widetilde{D}(1,5) = \widetilde{D}(1,6) = 2$, Thus, $\widetilde{D}(G_\kappa) = 2$.

The color-distance from processor i to j tells how many sweeps are required for the processor j to detect any state change of i. The color-diameter of the graph reveals the maximum propagation delay in terms of sweeps for a processor to get to know other processors' states. The following analysis shows that the value of the $\widetilde{D}(G_\kappa)$ is also the lower bound of the delay for termination detection, and all the counters of the processors reach the bound simultaneously. That is, $PredefinedValue = \widetilde{D}(G_\kappa)$.

The presentation of the analysis is similar to that in [186]. First, we derive a recursive expression of S from the above algorithm.

Proposition 7.2.1 *For any processor i, $1 \le i \le N$,*

$$S_i(t+1) = \begin{cases} 0 & \textit{if processor } i \textit{ is not terminated} \\ \min_{j \in I^+(i)}(S_j(t)) + 1 & \textit{otherwise} \end{cases}$$

where $I^+(i) = I(i) \bigcup \{i\}$, and $I(i)$ is the set of processors that i can reach in one trip.

Proof. If $j \in I(i)$, then there exists a color path from i to j. Suppose this color path has the form $(i, i_1, c_1), (i_1, i_2, c_2), \ldots, (i_{l-1}, j, c_l)$, where $c_1 > c_2 > \ldots > c_l$. Then, it is clear that $S_i^{c_1}(t+1) \le S_i^{c_2}(t+1) \le \cdots \le S_{j_1}^{c_l}(t+1) \le S_j(t)$. Since $S_i(t+1) \le S_i^{c_1}(t+1)$, it follows that $S_i(t+1) \le S_j(t)$. In addition, if there exists a processor $j \notin I(i)$ and $j \neq i$, $S_i(t+1)$ will not be influenced by $S_j(t)$. Thus, the proposition is proved. □

The above proposition reveals that a non-zero counter value of a processor contains more information than just its own current state (which is *idle*). The historical states of processors that processor i can reach may be deduced from S_i. In the most trivial case, if the counter value of a processor i equals 1, then the processor can infer that there exists at least one unstable processor within $I^+(i)$ in the last iteration sweep. Generally, if $S_i(t) = a > 0$, then the following properties concerning historical state information can be derived.

Proposition 7.2.2 *Suppose at some iteration sweep t, there is a stable processor i with $S_i(t) = a > 0$. Then*

1. *there exists a processor j satisfying $\widetilde{D}(i,j) \le a$, $S_j(t-a) = 0$*
2. *for any processor j satisfying $\widetilde{D}(i,j) < a$, $S_j(t-t') > 0$, where $\widetilde{D}(i,j) \le t' < a$*

Proof. Part (1) can be proved by induction on the integer a. The statement trivially holds for $S_i(t) = a = 1$. Now suppose it holds for $S_i(t) = a = b > 1$. If $S_i(t) = b+1$, then according to Proposition 1, there exists at least one processor $j \in I^+(i)$ with counter value $S_j(t-1) = b$. From the hypothesis, there exists a processor k satisfying $\widetilde{D}(j,k) < b$ with the counter value $S_k(t-b-1) = 0$. Since the processor k also satisfies $\widetilde{D}(i,k) < b+1$, Part (1) is proved. The proof of Part (2) proceeds in a similar way. □

Part 1 of the proposition says that if an idle processor finds its counter value to be $r > 0$ at the end of some iteration step, then there exists a processor which is at most r color paths away from this processor and whose state was busy r iterations ago. That is, the counter value (= 0) of this busy processor got propagated to the idle processor within r iterations; while on the way, this value got incremented by one at each iteration. Part 2 says that if this value did get propagated all the way to the idle processor in question, then there must not have been any busy processors that were within r color paths from this processor during the period of the propagation.

On the basis of the properties of S, we are now in the position to establish the condition for global termination in terms of S.

Theorem 7.2.1 *For any processor i in the κ-color graph G_κ, it detects global termination when $S_i = \widetilde{D}(G_\kappa) + 1$.*

Proof. In order to be certain about global termination when a processor satisfies this condition $S_i(t) = \widetilde{D}(G_\kappa) + 1$, it suffices to show that at time t, all other processors $j, j \neq i$, have the same counter value, *i.e.*, $S_j(t) = \widetilde{D}(G_\kappa) + 1$. Suppose at time t, $S_i(t) = \widetilde{D}(G_\kappa) + 1$, but there exists a processor j such that $S_j(t) = a < \widetilde{D}(G_\kappa) + 1$. According to Part (1) of Proposition 2, there exists a processor, say k, with $S_k(t - a) = 0$. On the other hand, from Part (2) of Proposition 2, all the counter values at time $t - a$ must be positive. We conclude from the contradiction that $S_i(t) = \widetilde{D}(G_\kappa) + 1$ if and only if $S_j(t) = \widetilde{D}(G_\kappa) + 1$. Thus, the theorem is proved. □

In summary, for any given processor structure, the global termination condition is dependent on a single value—the structure's color-diameter, $\widetilde{D}(G_\kappa)$. The processors exit the iteration loop simultaneously with the same counter value $\widetilde{D}(G) + 1$. Hence, the constant $PredefinedValue$ in the algorithm should be set to $\widetilde{D}(G_\kappa) + 1$. The delay of the algorithm is $\widetilde{D}(G_\kappa) + 1$ iteration sweeps which is measured from the instant the last busy processor turns idle.

7.3 Optimality Analysis of the Algorithm

We have shown that for a given system structure G, the termination delay of the algorithm is equal to its color diameter $\widetilde{D}(G_\kappa) + 1$ which is in terms of number of iteration sweeps. Referring to the termination detection code in the algorithm, we note that one iterative sweep comprises κ communication operations, κ being the number of colors. Hence, the termination delay in communication operations is equal to $\kappa(\widetilde{D}(G_\kappa) + 1)$. Since the edges of a graph G can usually be colored in more than one way, and that different ways of coloring may result in different color diameters, and hence different termination delays, we would like to determine the best coloring scheme for a given structure G so that the minimum termination delay can be achieved.

7.3.1 Lower Bound of Termination Delay

The termination delay of the algorithm, as we have defined before, is the time period from the occurrence of a global termination till the termination is detected by each processor. Clearly, the lower bound of the termination delay (in communication steps) should be the minimum time required by each processor to learn the state information of every other processors. It is the lower bound of the time for *gossiping* [80] in the given graph.

The gossiping problem has been studied by a number of researchers under various communication models. Under the same serial communication model (1-port, full-duplex, but with no coloring or whatsoever to schedule the exchanges over the edges[1]), Farley and Proskurowski analyzed the problem for the ring, the mesh, and the torus [61]. Their results, which can serve as the lower bounds of the termination delay, are summarized in Table 7.2.

Table 7.2: Lower bounds of gossiping time in various structures

Chain of size k	$k-1$ if k is even; k otherwise
Ring of size k	$k/2$ if k is even; $\lceil k/2 \rceil + 1$ otherwise
Mesh of size $k_1 \times k_2$	$k_1 + k_2 - 2$ if $k_1 \neq 3$ or $k_2 \neq 3$
Torus of size $k_1 \times k_2$	$\lfloor k_1/2 \rfloor + \lfloor k_2/2 \rfloor$ if k_1 and k_2 are even

7.3.2 Termination Delay in Meshes and Tori

We now present the optimality analysis of the termination delay of applying the algorithm to the the structures of n-dimensional torus and mesh ($n \geq 1$), and their special cases, the ring, the chain, and the k-ary n-cube. Instead of directly working out the appropriate coloring schemes for the structures, measuring their color diameters, and comparing with the above lower bounds, we make use of existing results from a version of the gossiping problem which is equivalent to our termination detection problem to argue about optimality. This version of the gossiping problem, by Liestman and Richards, uses exactly

[1]Liestman and Richards refer to this as the "standard model" [122].

the same edge-coloring technique as we have used here for the chain, the ring, and the mesh [122]. It is easy to see that the two problems—to find a coloring that would yield the shortest color diameter and to find a coloring that would lead to the minimum gossiping time—are equivalent. Therefore, we can use the gossiping results for edge-colored graphs to compare with the above lower bounds. In the following, if the gossiping time in some colored graph is optimal with respect to the corresponding lower bound (Table 7.2), then the termination delay due to our algorithm using the same coloring scheme is optimal or near optimal. Precisely, if we let g to be the gossiping time, then the termination delay is less than $g + 2\kappa$ communication operations. The coloring scheme that is used to arrive at the optimal gossiping time is exactly the optimal coloring scheme we need for our termination detection. Note that "gossiping time" in the following refers to that from using edge-coloring.

Liestman and Richards derived, among their many results, the following minimum gossiping times which are of relevance here. We use $g(G)$ to denote the minimum gossiping time for the structure G, and $g(G^c)$ the gossiping time for G with coloring c.

Theorem 7.3.1 (Liestman and Richards [122])

1. *For a chain of k nodes,* C_k*,* $g(C_k) = 2\lfloor (k-1)/2 \rfloor + 1$.
2. *For a ring of k nodes (k even),* R_k*,* $g(R_k) = k/2$.
3. *For a two-dimensional* $2 \times k$ *mesh* $M_{2,k}$*,* $g(M_{2,k}) = 3\lfloor (k-1)/2 \rfloor + 1$.

Note that in proving the above, Liestman and Richards gave an actual coloring scheme by using 2 colors for the chain and the ring, and by using 3 colors for the mesh [122]. They also showed that the minimum gossiping time is no larger than $2 \times \max\{k_1, k_2\}$ for a two-dimensional $k_1 \times k_2$ mesh by using an "alternate" coloring scheme with 4 colors. In the following, we sharpen the bound and show its optimality for the even square mesh. We also present a tight bound of gossiping time for the square torus.

Theorem 7.3.2 *For a two-dimensional* $k_1 \times k_2$ *mesh* M_{k_1,k_2}*,* $k_1, k_2 \geq 3$*, the minimum gossiping time is bounded as* $g(M_{k_1,k_2}) \leq 4\lfloor (k-1)/2 \rfloor + 2$*, where* $k = \max\{k_1, k_2\}$.

Proof. Suppose in a 4-color situation we color a chain with the sequence $\cdots 1313 \cdots$; then it is easy to verify that the gossiping time of such a chain matches the result of Theorem 5 of [122]—*i.e.*, its gossiping time is equal to $4\lfloor (k-1)/2 \rfloor + 1$, where k is the number of nodes in the chain. If instead we color the chain by the sequence $\cdots 2424 \cdots$, then its gossiping time becomes one unit more than the above—*i.e.*, $4\lfloor (k-1)/2 \rfloor + 2$—since the two colors 2, 4 are exactly one time step behind the colors 1, 3. Now the two-dimensional mesh in question is basically an assembly of horizontal and vertical chains, and its gossiping time is equal to the maximum of the gossiping times of these chains. Therefore, if we always color the longer dimension with $\cdots 1313 \cdots$ and the shorter dimension by $\cdots 2424 \cdots$, then $g_4(M^c_{k_1,k_2}) \leq 4\lfloor (k-1)/2 \rfloor + 2$, where $k = \max\{k_1, k_2\}$ and c denotes the alternate coloring scheme. □

Figures 7.3(a) shows an example of information propagation in a 4-color meshes using alternate coloring. The corner node with double circles corresponds to the node whose information will take the longest time to propagate to all other nodes. Using dashed ovals, we trace the propagation of information from this node to other nodes against time step numbers in the figure.

Corollary 7.3.1 *The above gossiping time based on alternate coloring of 4 colors is optimal when the mesh is an even square mesh.*

Proof. From the 8×8 mesh in Figure 7.3(a), it is clear that $g(M^c_{k,k}) = 4\lfloor (k-1)/2 \rfloor + 2 = 2k - 2$ for an even square 4-color mesh $M_{k,k}$, which matches the corresponding lower bound in Table 7.2. □

The upper bound of gossiping time for a two-dimensional mesh can be generalized to an n-dimensional $k_1 \times k_2 \times \ldots \times k_n$ mesh, $M_{k_1,k_2,\ldots,k_n}$. We label the edges in the ith dimension of the mesh, $i = 1, 2, \ldots, n$, with alternating i's and $(n+i-1)$'s. Based on this kind of colored meshes, we obtain the following results.

Theorem 7.3.3 *For an n-dimensional $k_1 \times k_2, \cdots, k_n$ mesh $M_{k_1,k_2,\ldots,k_n}$, where $k_1, k_2, \ldots, k_n \geq 3$, the minimum gossiping time is bounded as follows.*

$$g(M_{k_1,k_2,\ldots,k_n}) \leq 2n\lfloor (k-1)/2 \rfloor + n,$$

where $k = \max\{k_1, k_2, \ldots, k_n\}$.

Corollary 7.3.2 *The gossiping time based on alternate coloring for n-dimensional meshes is optimal when all the k_i's are equal to the same even number.*

Next, the torus structure. We consider even tori of which the number of nodes in each dimension is even. Such a torus can be colored with $2n$ colors using the alternate coloring scheme as above, where n is the number of dimensions. Figure 7.3(b) shows a trace of information propagation against time step numbers in a 6×8 colored torus.

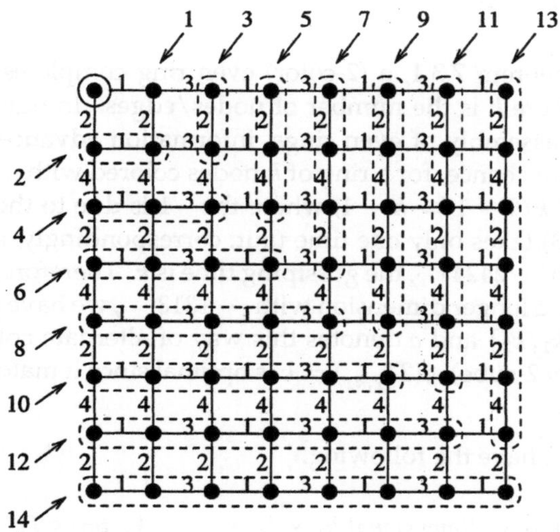

(a) Mesh 8 x 8

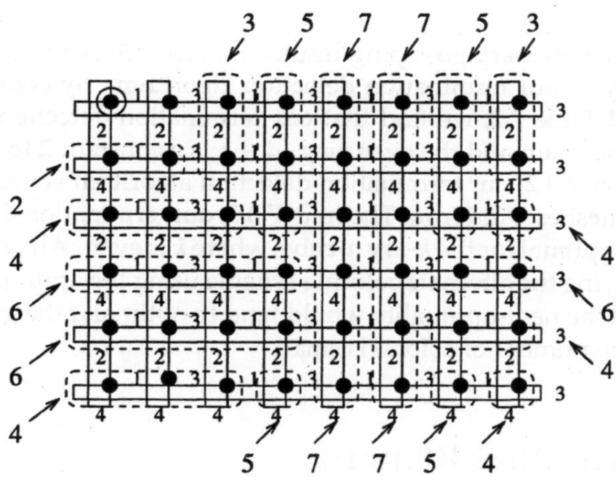

(b) Torus 6 x 8

Figure 7.3: Traces of information propagation across processors against time step numbers in different meshes

Theorem 7.3.4 *For a two-dimensional $k_1 \times k_2$ torus T_{k_1,k_2}, $k_1, k_2 > 2$ and are even, the minimum gossiping time is bounded as $g(T_{k_1,k_2}) \leq k$, where $k = \max\{k_1, k_2\}$. It is optimal when $k_1 = k_2$.*

Proof. From Theorem 7.3.1, a (2-color) even ring completes gossiping in $k/2$ time units, where k is the number of nodes/edges. In our 4-color torus here, which is an assembly of even rings, information advances one step in every two time units; hence, for a ring of k nodes colored with $\cdots 1313 \cdots$, the gossiping time is $2k/2 - 1 = k - 1$, where the -1 is due to the fact that the last step (a 1 or a 3) takes only one time unit; correspondingly, for a ring of k nodes colored with $\cdots 2424 \cdots$, the gossiping time is k. Therefore, if we always color the rings of the longer dimension with $\cdots 1313 \cdots$, we have $g(T^c_{k_1,k_2}) \leq k$, where $k = \max\{k_1, k_2\}$ and c denotes this way of alternate coloring. When $k_1 = k_2$ (*i.e.*, a k-ary 2-cube), $g(T^c_{k_1,k_2}) = k$ is optimal since it matches the lower bound in Table 7.2. □

Generalizing we have the following.

Theorem 7.3.5 *For an n-dimensional $k_1 \times k_2 \times \cdots \times k_n$ torus $T_{k_1,k_2,\ldots,k_n}$, where $k_1, k_2, \ldots, k_n$ are even, the minimum gossiping time is bounded as $g(T_{k_1,k_2,\ldots,k_n}) \leq nk/2$. It is optimal when $k_1 = k_2 = \cdots = k_n$ (i.e., a k-ary n-cube).*

With all the necessary gossiping results in place, we can now comment on the optimality of our termination detection algorithm. By comparing Theorem 7.3.1 and Table 7.2, we find that our termination detection algorithm is optimal for the chain and the even ring ($d - g$ is a constant 2 to 4 time steps). From Corollary 7.3.2, our termination detection algorithm is near-optimal for even square meshes. And from Theorem 7.3.5, our termination detection algorithm is near-optimal for the k-ary n-cube, where k is even. All of the above are valid by applying the alternate coloring scheme using the appropriate number of colors, and the near-optimality would tend to optimal if the graph's degree (and hence the number of colors) is small.

7.4 Concluding Remarks

We have shown that our simple termination detection algorithm based on edge-coloring is time-optimal for the chain, the even ring, the even square mesh of low degree, and the k-ary n-cube (k even) of low degree under the serial communication model (single exchange with a neighbor per node per time step). It is near-optimal for the other cases. From Table 7.2, we note that the numbers of time steps for the optimal cases under the serial model are actually equal to the respective absolute lower bounds for information dissemination in these structures regardless of the communication model (*e.g.*, a k-chain will need $k-1$ time steps to complete a gossip even under the most powerful communication model). Therefore, if we use the all-port communication model, our algorithm performs as well as the SSP algorithm or any other algorithm in these structures.

What is more, the proposed algorithm behaves consistently with the GDE load balancing procedure: during the communication step of an iteration phase, a processor updates its counter immediately after its every exchange with a neighboring process. Consequently, the control messages for termination detection can be piggybacked on the data messages of GDE load balancing. Hence, the communication overhead for termination detection is almost negligible in the implementation of the GDE method.

8

REMAPPING WITH THE GDE METHOD

A party of order or stability, and a party of progress or reform, are both necessary elements of a healthy state . . .

—JOHN STUART MILL

This chapter is devoted to the application of the GDE algorithm in the remapping of data parallel computations. As we have shown in Chapter 6 the inferiority of the diffusion method in static workload model, we will not discuss practical implementations of the diffusion method in this chapter.

8.1 Remapping of Data Parallel Computations

The mapping problem in parallel computations is concerned with how to distribute the workload or processes of a computation among the available processors so that each processor would have the same or nearly the same amount of work to do. In most cases, mapping is done prior to execution and is done only once—called *static* mapping. Static mapping can be quite effective for computations that have predictable run-time behaviors [68]. For computations whose run-time behavior is non-deterministic or not so predictable, however, performing mapping only once in the beginning is insufficient. For these cases, it might be better to perform the mapping more than once or periodically during run-time—this is called *dynamic remapping*. Dynamic remapping produces ideal load-balances at the cost of additional run-time overheads. A successful remapping mechanism must therefore try to produce enough benefits that would outweigh the overheads incurred. In this chapter, we present such a remapping mechanism [212] which is based on the GDE method. We demonstrate the effectiveness of this mechanism through incorporating it into the implementation of three major applications.

8.1.1 The Remapping Problem

A data parallel computation decomposes its problem domain into a number of sub-domains (data sets), and designates them to processes [68]. These processes simultaneously perform the same functions across different data sets. Because the sub-domains are connected at their boundaries, processes in neighboring sub-domains have to synchronize and exchange boundary information with each other every now and then. These synchronization points divide the computation into phases. During each phase, every process executes some operations that might depend on the results from previous phases. This kind of computations arises in a large variety of real applications. In a study of 84 successful parallel applications in various areas, it was found that nearly 83% used this form of data parallelism [66].

In data parallel applications, the computational requirements associated with different parts of a problem domain may change as the computation proceeds. This occurs when the behavior of the physical system being modeled changes with time. Such adaptive data parallel computations appear frequently in scientific and engineering applications such as those in molecular dynamics (MD) and computational fluid dynamics (CFD). A molecular dynamics program simulates the dynamic interactions among all atoms in a system of interest for a period of time. For each time step, the simulation calculates the forces between atoms, the energy of the whole structure, and the movements of atoms. Since atoms tend to move around in the system, simulation loads associated with different parts of the system change from one step to another with the change of the atom spatial positions. A computational fluid dynamics program calculates the velocity and the pressure of vertices in a moving object for the purpose of deriving its structural and dynamic properties. The object can be either a car, an airplane, a space-shuttle or an any other high-speed vehicle. It is first tessellated using a grid. Numerical calculations are carried out at grid points. In simulations that use adaptive griding to adjust the scale of resolution as the simulation progresses, computational workloads associated with different parts of a grid may change from phase to phase. To implement this kind of computations on a distributed memory multiprocessor, *static* domain decomposition techniques, such as strip-wise, box-wise, and binary decompositions [13], are often not satisfactory; they fail to maintain an even distribution of computational workloads across the processors during execution. Because of the need of synchronization between phases, a processor that has finished its work in the current phase has to wait for the more heavily loaded processors to finish their work before proceeding to the next phase (see Figure 8.1). Consequently, the duration of a phase is determined by the heavily loaded processors, and system performance may deteriorate in time. Figure 8.1 shows a typical scenario of the paradigm in a system of four processors. The horizontal scale corresponds to elapsed time (or computation time) of the processors; the vertical lines represent synchronization points at which a round of communications among the processors is due to begin. The shaded and the dark horizontal bars represent the communication time and the calculation time respectively. The dotted empty bars correspond to the idle times of the processors, which are the times spent in waiting for the next phase to come.

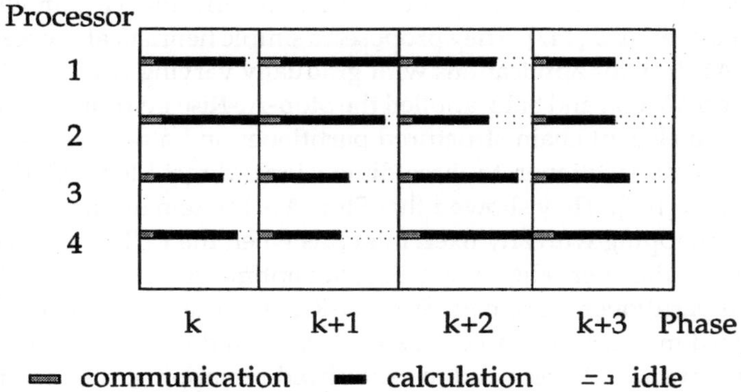

Figure 8.1: An illustration of time-dependent multiphase data parallel computations

To lessen the penalty due to synchronization and load imbalances, one must dynamically remap (re-decompose) the problem domain onto the processors as the computation proceeds. Remapping can be performed either afresh—*i.e.*, treating the current overall workload as if it is a new workload to be decomposed—or through adjusting boundaries created in the previous decomposition. The former approach can be viewed as dynamic invocation of a static decomposition. Since the global workload is to be taken as a whole for re-decomposition, the work is most conveniently performed by a designated processor which has a global view of the current state of affair. Such a centralized remapping can no doubt yield a good workload distribution because of the existence of global knowledge. However, the price to pay is the high cost of collecting the data sets from and communicating the re-decomposed data sets to the processors, which could be prohibitive, especially in large systems. Therefore, the second approach of adjusting boundaries from the previous phase, which can be easily performed in a decentralized, parallel fashion, is preferred. As each processor has to deal only with its nearest neighbors, much fewer data transfers would take place in the network as compared to the centralized approach. The difficulty lies in how to decide in a distributed way when a remapping should be invoked and how to adjust the sub-domain boundaries among processors (also in a distributed way) so that the result is a reasonably balanced workload.

8.1.2 Related Work

In the literature, much attention has been given to dynamic remapping of data parallel computations over past several years. Nicol and Saltz addressed the issue of when to invoke a remapping so that its performance gain will not be offset by its overhead [147]. They proposed a simple heuristical invocation policy, Stop-At-Rise, for applications with gradually varying resource demands. Most recently, Moon and Saltz applied the Stop-At-Rise invocation policy, coupled with an elegant chain-structured partitioner and a recursive coordinate bisection (RCB) partitioner, to three-dimensional direct Monte Carlo simulation methods [142]. They showed that Stop-At-Rise remapping is superior to periodic remapping with any fixed intervals when the RCB is applied, and is slightly worse than periodic remapping with optimal intervals when the chain-structured partitioner is applied. Stop-At-Rise invocation decision is made in a centralized manner and based on an assumption that the remapping cost is known in advance. Albeit valid in centralized remapping, the assumption is obviously not applicable to decentralized remapping.

De Keyser and Roose experimented with centralized re-partitioning in the calculation of dynamic unstructured finite element grids [108, 109]. The computation here is solution-adaptive in that the grids are refined according to the solution obtained so far. After the refinement of the grids, a global remapping is imposed. Dynamic remapping for solution-adaptive grid refinements was also considered by Williams [204]. He compared three complex parallel algorithms for carrying out the remapping, the ROB, the simulated annealing, and the eigenvalue recursive bisection, and concluded that the last one should be preferred.

More parallel grid partitioning algorithms based on existing sequential algorithms were developed in recent years. They include a parallel index-based algorithm [153], a parallel inertial algorithm [55], a parallel multilevel spectral algorithm [104], a parallel recursive bisection algorithm [198] and the unbalanced recursive bisection (a parallel variant of ROB) [100]. Most of these parallel algorithms take advantage of the recursive nature of their sequential versions, and exploit parallelism associated with the recursive step. They are efficient for initial grid partitioning. Since they are based on global knowledge of the entire grid, they might not be applicable to grid re-partitioning at runtime. Our GDE-based distributed refinement can complement these parallel partitioning algorithms. In [55], the authors proposed a distributed greedy refinement strategy, based on ideas described by Hammond [75], to complement their parallel inertial algorithm. The refinement strategy greedily improves the bisection resulted from the inertial partitions in a pairwise fashion. That is, all pairs of processors whose partitions share common edges exchange vertices so as to minimize cut sizes. Their parallel refinement strategy is essentially a dimension exchange algorithm applied to computational graphs.

In the context of image understanding, Choudhary *et al.* incorporated a remapping mechanism into a parallel motion estimation system [41, 40]. The system consists of several stages: convolution, thresholding and template matching. Remapping is invoked at the beginning of each stage, in which every processor would broadcast information about the subdomain it is working on to all others, and then do border adjustment based on the collected information. A similar idea based on global knowledge was implemented by Hanxleden and Scott [76]. They invoked remapping periodically in the course of a Monte Carlo dynamical simulation, and gained 10-15% performance improvement using the optimal remapping interval.

8.2 Distributed Remapping

Distributed remapping is the task to re-decompose the physical domain, which is spread over all the processors, to produce a better balance among computational workloads in the nodes while keeping the communication structure among these subdomains stable. Notice that the original communication structure, induced by the initial domain decomposition, is assumed to be optimal or near-optimal in the sense that the communications across subdomains are minimized, which therefore needs to be preserved in subsequent re-decompositions. Even though the analysis of the GDE method ignores the inter-processor communication overhead, the method is applicable to the computations where inter-processor communication costs are non-negligible. Basically, what the GDE load balancing ends up with are nearest neighbor communications that shift the loads across short distances. By adopting the approach of adjusting boundaries of the problem domain, the GDE balancing procedure preserves the communication locality and hence the stability of the original communication structure through the series of re-decompositions.

The problem domain can be treated as a group of *internal load distributions* together with a corresponding *external load distribution*. Every sub-domain in a node is represented by an internal load distribution for the computational requirements of its internal finer portions, and by an external integer value for its total workload. The remapping mechanism has two components: the *decision maker* and the *workload adjuster*. The decision maker is concerned only with the external load distribution, and is responsible for calculating the amount of workload inflow or outflow along each link of a node necessary for workload balancing. The workload adjuster is responsible for actually adjusting the borders of the problem domain according to the results of the decision maker.

The decision maker uses the GDE method with which a node iteratively balances its workload with its nearest neighbors until a uniform workload distribution is reached and detected. Note that the balance operator does not involve real workload. The workload is represented abstractly in this decision making process by simple integer variables: $WorkLoad$ for the node's workload before the decision making and $Load$ a temporary variable for workload during the process. We also introduce a vector $FlowTrace$ to keep track of the workload flows along each link of a node. Initially, each element $FlowTrace[i]$ is set to zero. For each sweep of the iterative decision making procedure, the amount of workload which is to be sent away or absorbed along a link i is added to $FlowTrace[i]$ as a positive or negative value respectively. Thus, at the end of the decision making, $FlowTrace$ records the inflow or outflow amount along each link.

Below, we outline the algorithm executed by the decision maker, which combines the GDE algorithm and the termination detection algorithm. Note that $LocalTerminated$ would become true in processor i when no change occurs in $FlowTrace[i]$ after a sweep of exchanges with the processor's neighbors.

Algorithm: *DecisionMaker*
  $State = 0;$
  $Load = WorkLoad;$

```
while (State ≤ Δ) {
    for (c = 1; c ≤ κ; c++) {
        if there exists an edge of color c {
            (InputState, InputLoad) = Exchange(c, State, Load);
            if (InputLoad > Load)
                temp = ⌊(InputLoad − Load) × λ⌋;
            else
                Flow[c] = ⌈(InputLoad − Load) × λ⌉;
            FlowTrace[c] = FlowTrace[c] + temp;
            Load = Load + temp;
            State = min{State, InputState};
        }
    }
    if (LocalTerminated)
        State = State + 1;
    else
        State = 0;
}
```

Applying the algorithm to the external load distribution in Figure 2.2, we obtain the inflow or outflow value for each link, as illustrated in Figure 8.2.

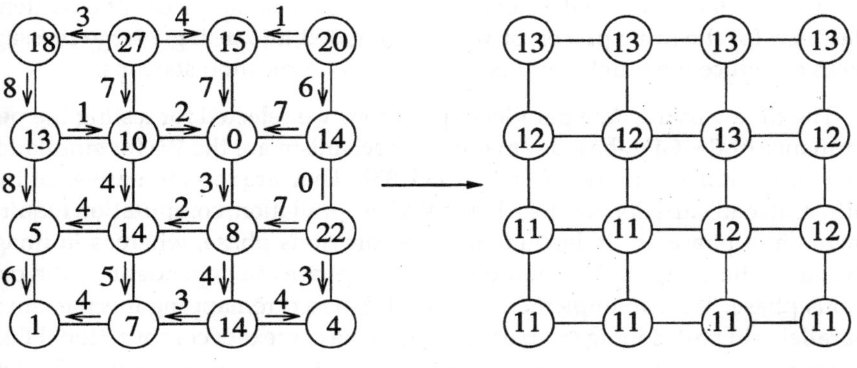

Figure 8.2: In/out-flow along each channel of a processor necessary for arriving at a global balanced state

Following the decision making, the workload adjuster of every node would start to work on its internal load distribution according to the *FlowTrace* vector generated by the decision maker. It involves selecting data set(s) to be split, transferring the split data sets between nodes, and merging of received data set(s) with the original sub-domain. In principle, the splitting and merging of data sets are such that the geometric adjacency of data points in the problem domain are kept intact—basically adjusting of borders. For strip-wise-partitioned sub-domains, this can be done rather conveniently through shifting rows (or columns) between neighboring sub-domains. Details of how this is done will be presented in Section 8.3 and Section 8.4 when the implementations of two real applications are discussed. In Section 8.5, we discuss a policy for splitting data items in grid partitioning and re-partitioning in computational fluid dynamics.

The data transfer module dominates the cost of remapping when the original distribution is severely imbalanced. Nearest-neighbor algorithms reduce the domain remapping operation to adjustment of sub-domain borders. Correspondingly, a processor may need to send and/or receive data along its communication channels at the same time. To exploit the parallelism in multi-port communications, we experimented with a multithreaded model for multi-port concurrent communications. We created a sender thread or receiver thread for each communication port. The local sub-domain is treated as a public data pool for all threads. Sender threads continually fetch data from the pool and receiver threads store data in the pool. One more thread was used for the pool management including the selection of data for sender threads and the combination of data from receiver threads with the original sub-domain.

The flow calculation module determines the communication pattern and communication volume along each channel. A processor usually needs to send many data items to the same neighbor. These small pieces of data items destined for the same processor were aggregated into a single large message so as to reduce the number of instances of communication startups.

The time-varying data parallel applications we selected for testing the performance of the GDE-based remapping mechanism are the WaTor simulation [51] and parallel thinning of images [85, 83]. They are representatives of two different load variation models: in the WaTor simulation, computation requirements in a phase are independent of the previous phase, whereas in image thinning, the computation requirements of a phase are dependent on the previous phase. We also implemented the GDE-based remapping mechanism in parallel grid partitioning/re-partitioning in the context of computational fluid dynamics. All experiments run on a group of T805-30 transputers. The first two were coded in INMOS Parallel C [124], and the third was in C under the Parix parallel operating system. The main metric in the first two experiments is the *improvement* in execution time due to remapping, denoted by η_{remap}, which is defined as

$$\eta_{remap} = \frac{t_{WithoutRemap} - t_{WithRemap}}{t_{WithoutRemap}} \times 100\%$$

where $t_{WithoutRemap}$ and $t_{WithRemap}$ are the execution times without and with remapping respectively. The metric in the application of grid partitioning/re-partitioning is the *improvement* in the quality of partitions due to refinement. Another metric of all experiments is the overhead of the remapping (repartitioning) mechanism.

8.3 Application 1: WaTor—A Monte Carlo Dynamic Simulation

WaTor is an experiment that simulates the activities of fishes in a two-dimensional periodic ocean. The name WaTor comes from the toroidal topology of the imaginary watery planet. Fishes in the ocean breed, move, eat and die according to certain non-deterministic rules. The simulation is Monte Carlo in nature, and can be used to illustrate many of the crucial ideas in dynamic time- and event-driven simulations.

In the simulation, the ocean space was divided into a fine grid which was structured as a torus. Fishes are allowed to live only on grid points, and move around within neighboring points in a simulation step. There are two kinds of fishes in the ocean: the *minnows* and the *sharks*. They adhere to the following rules as they strive to live.

1. Each fish is updated as the simulation progresses in a series of discrete time steps.
2. A minnow locates a vacant position randomly in up, down, left or right direction. If the vacant position is found, the minnow moves there. If it is mature with respect to the *minnow breeding age*, the minnow leaves a new minnow of age 0 in the original location.
3. A shark locates a minnow within its neighboring positions at first. If found, it eats the minnow and moves to that location. Otherwise, the shark locates a vacant position like what the minnow does. If the shark moves to a new location and it is mature with respect to the *shark breeding age*, a new shark of age 0 is left in its original location. If a shark has not eaten any minnows within a *starvation* period, it dies.

Since the ocean structure is toroidal, we implemented the WaTor algorithm on a ring-structured system (a ring is a special case of a torus). The parallel implementation decomposed the ocean grid into strips, and assigned each of them to a processing node. Each simulation step consists of three sub-steps:

1. *ExBound*: exchange of contents of grid points along a strip's boundaries;
2. *Update*: update of fishes in the strip;
3. *ExFish*: boundary-crossing of fishes that have to leave the strip.

The routine *Update* follows the above live-and-die rules for fishes. Fishes bound for neighboring strips are not transferred individually. Instead, they are held until the end of the *Update* procedure, and then bundled up to cross the boundaries in the routine *ExFish*. Thus, the duration of a simulation step T in a processor is the sum of the time spent in above three procedures. Since the boundary-crossing fishes are bundled and transferred in one message, every processor transmits the same number of messages to its neighbors and hence incurs approximately the same communication cost.

The simulation was done for a 256×256 ocean grid which was mapped onto 16 T805 transputers. And it was run for as many as 100 simulation steps. The *minnow breeding*, the *shark breeding* and the *shark starvation* parameters were set to be 7, 12, and 5 steps respectively. Initially, the ocean was populated by minnows and sharks generated from a random uniform distribution, which were distributed by rows among the 16 transputers. The total simulation time for 100 steps was 17.58 seconds.

The computational requirement of a processor is proportional to the density of fishes in the strip that it is simulating. The more fishes there are, the more computation time is needed for the update. Owing to the tendency of the fishes to form schools dynamically and owing to their unpredictable behaviors, the processor utilization of the processors, varies not so smoothly over time, as shown in the TIME curve of Figure 8.3. We applied remapping based on the GDE method periodically on the parallel simulation. Since the computational workload of a processor is proportional to the number of fishes in the strip, we used the latter as the measure of workload. The remapping procedure then tries to split the number of fishes between nodes as evenly as possible. Figure 8.3 (the FISH curve) also plots the processor utilization in terms of the number of fishes of each processor at various simulation steps. From the simulation data, it is observed that the variance of the computation time distribution changes with time and the change tendency is unpredictable. The close agreement in shape of the two curves confirms the reasonableness of measuring the computational load in terms of the number of fishes.

We examined the benefits of GDE-based remapping for various sizes of the remapping interval. Other than the remapping interval, the remapping cost relative to the computation time per simulation step is also an important parameter for determining the improvement due to remapping. The remapping cost at a processor i is the time $t_i^{decision}$ required for decision-making plus the time t_i^{adjust} spent in the workload adjustment. The latter is dependent on the internal fish distribution at the time the remapping is invoked and on the results of the decision making. Table 8.1 presents the scenario of a remapping instance which is invoked after the simulation has passed 30 steps. The distribution of number of fishes f_i^{pre} prior to the remapping is given in the second column. The third column presents the time $t_i^{decision}$, which is the prod-

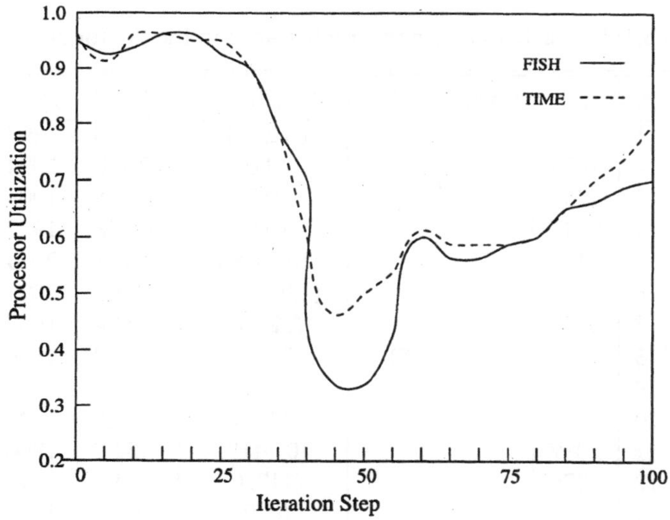

Figure 8.3: Processor utilization in the WaTor simulation at various simulation steps

uct of the number of iteration sweeps spent in decision making using the GDE method and a constant representing the time complexity of a sweep. The forth column gives the number of fishes that are migrated upwards (f_i^{up}) and downwards (f_i^{down}) due to the remapping. A positive number means "take" and a negative number means "give away". Correspondingly, the time spent in load adjustment t_i^{adjust} is presented in the sixth column. The last column is the distribution of fishes after remapping, f_i^{post}. All time items t_i in the table are in the unit of millisecond.

It can be seen from the table that the time for decision making $t_i^{decision}$ (= 2.75 milliseconds) is relatively insignificant when compared to the update time t_i^{update} (122 milliseconds on average) and that the cost of remapping is dominated by the time for load adjustment t_i^{adjust}. It is because the load adjustment procedure involves a number of time-consuming steps including memory allocation/deallocation and transmission of the fishes concerned.

The improvements due to remapping for different sizes of the remapping interval are plotted in Figure 8.4 (the curve of DR,EL=0; where DR stands for distributed remapping, and EL stands for extra workload). The horizontal scale is the number of simulation steps between two successive remapping instances; for example, a 20 means remapping is invoked once every 20 simulation steps. The curve shows that relatively frequent remapping gives an improvement of 7 – 15% in the overall simulation time. Because of its rather low

Table 8.1: Scenario of a remapping instance in the WaTor simulation

p_i	f_i^{pre}	$(NS, t_i^{decision})$	(f_i^{up}, f_i^{down})	t_i^{adjust}	f_i^{post}
1	2014		(-121, 0)	37.3	1893
2	2094		(0,0)	0.128	2094
2	1909		(0,0)	0.128	1909
4	1927		(0,0)	0.128	1927
5	2160		(0, -126)	33.8	2034
6	2123		(126, -228)	71.7	2021
7	1737		(228, 0)	71.4	1965
8	1727	(17, 2.75)	(0, 109)	25.2	1836
9	2042		(-109, 0)	25.2	1933
10	2132		(0, 0)	0.128	2132
11	2017		(0, -117)	34.9	1900
12	1876		(117, 0)	34.8	1993
13	1743		(0, 0)	0.128	1743
14	1848		(0, 122)	30.7	1970
15	1931		(-122, 139)	41.4	1948
16	2030		(-139, 121)	41.3	2012

cost, remapping is favorable even in the case that the simulation is interrupted by remapping once every simulation step. Conversely, less frequent remapping (*e.g.*, once every 30 to 50 steps) could end up with no improvement or even degradation of performance. It is because the load distribution across processors changes in a haphazard way over time. This is characteristic of WaTor simulations.

Since the decision making and the load adjustment are based on the number of fishes, the remapping cost does not change with the increase of the time a fish spends in a simulation step. Hence, remapping would be even more beneficial if a fish does some extra work in a simulation step. This "better" performance is shown in Figure 8.4: the cases of DR,EL=1 and DR,EL=2, in which the time for the update of a fish is increased by an extra load of 64 microseconds and 128 microseconds, respectively.

For comparison, we also gave improvements resulting from an efficient implementation of a centralized remapping method in the figure (the case of CR,EL=0; CR stands for centralized remapping). With the method, a designated processor takes the responsibility of making decisions according to the external load distribution [76]. This centralized version takes a much longer time (6.4 ms to 12.8 ms) to do decision making than the decentralized version based on GDE. From the figure, it can be measured that the GDE-based remap-

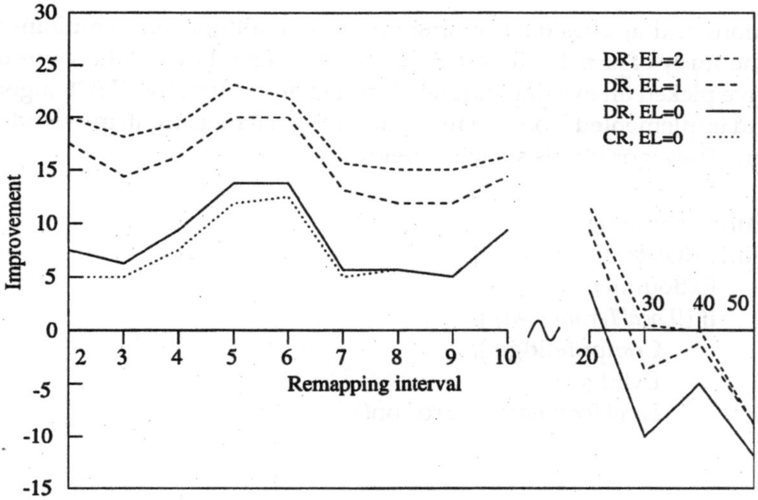

Figure 8.4: Improvement due to remapping for various interval sizes in the WaTor simulation

ping method, when frequently invoked, outperforms the centralized method by up to 40%.

8.4 Application 2: Parallel Thinning of Images

Thinning is a fundamental pre-processing operation to be applied over a binary image to produce a version that shows the significant features of the image (see Figure 8.5). In the process, redundant information is removed from the image. It takes as input a binary picture consisting of objects and a background which are represented by 1-valued pixels and 0-valued pixels respectively. It produces object skeletons that preserve the original shapes and connectivity. An iterative thinning algorithm performs successive iterations on the picture by converting those 1-valued pixels that are judged to be not belonging to the skeletons into 0-valued pixels until no more conversions are necessary. In general, the conversion (or survival) condition of a pixel, say P, is dependent upon the values of its eight neighboring pixels, as depicted below.

$$\begin{array}{ccc} NW & N & NE \\ W & P & E \\ SW & S & SE \end{array}$$

A parallel thinning algorithm decomposes the image domain into a number of portions and applies the thinning operator to all portions simultaneously. Since the study of parallel thinning algorithms itself is beyond the scope of this study, we picked an existing parallel thinning algorithm, the HSCP algorithm [85], and implemented it on a chain-structured system using strip-wise decomposition. The algorithm is sketched below.

```
Algorithm: Thinning
    while (!GlobalTerminated) {
        ExBound();
        if (!LocalTerminated) {
            ComputeEdge();
            ExEdge();
            LocalTerminated = Erosion();
        }
    }
```

At the beginning of each thinning iteration step, the boundary pixels of each strip are exchanged with those of the neighboring strips in the routine *ExBound*. The heart of the algorithm is the routine *Erosion* which applies the thinning operator to each pixel according to the following survival condition.

$$\begin{aligned} p \ \&\& \ & (!edge(P) \ || \\ & (edge(E) \ \&\& \ n \ \&\& \ s) \ || \\ & (edge(S) \ \&\& \ w \ \&\& \ e) \ || \\ & (edge(E) \ \&\& \ edge(SE) \ \&\& \ edge(S))) \end{aligned}$$

where a small letter denotes the pixel value at a location identified by the corresponding capital letter; the function *edge* tells whether a pixel is on the edge of an object skeleton. The *edge value* of a pixel is determined by the values of its surrounding pixels, and is computable in advance. The routine *ComputeEdge* is for computing the edge values of all pixels. The edge values of boundary pixels are exchanged in the routine *ExEdge*.

We used a typical image, that of a human body, as shown in Figure 8.5, to be the test pattern. The dots are 1-pixels, the white space is the 0-pixels, and the asterisks are the result of the thinning process. For the image of size 128 × 128, the number of iterations required by the thinning algorithm is 15. The thinning time (T) and other performance data of the algorithm (**Sp**: speedup, **E**: efficiency, **C**: communication cost) for various numbers of the processors (**N**) are tabulated in Table 8.2. The "efficiency" measures the effectiveness of using more processors to solve the same problem. The loss of the efficiency as the number of processors increases is due to inter-processor communication costs and load imbalances. From the thinning algorithm, we see that each thinning iteration step involves two communication operations

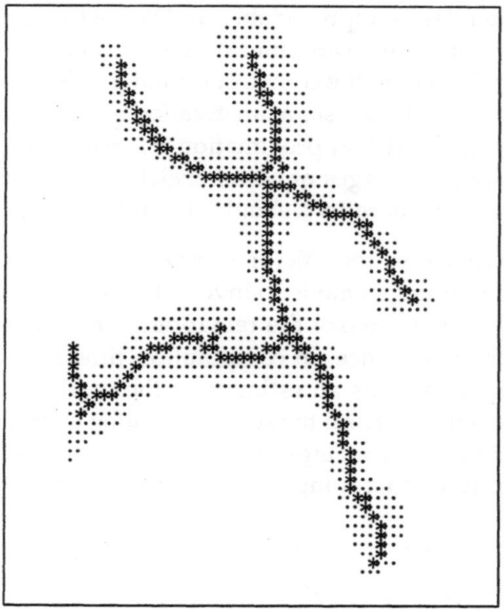

Figure 8.5: The image pattern and the thinning result

with neighboring nodes (in a chain, each node has one or two neighbors): the exchange of boundary rows and the exchange of edge values of boundary pixels. An exchange operator is made up of sending and receiving a fixed size message in parallel. It is measured that the operator uses about 0.64 milliseconds. The total communication time is thus about 19.2 milliseconds, which is the same for any number of processors. Its contribution in percentage to the overall thinning time is shown in the last row of Table 8.2.

Table 8.2: Performance of parallel thinning

N	1	2	3	4	5	6	7	8
T(sec.)	3.414	1.727	1.27	0.974	0.793	0.713	0.579	0.555
Sp	1	1.977	2.685	3.503	4.304	4.785	5.892	6.146
E	1	0.988	0.893	0.875	0.861	0.798	0.842	0.768
C(%)	—	1.112	1.510	1.970	2.318	2.691	3.313	3.457

We see that in parallel thinning, the computational requirement of a node is mainly dependent on the 1-pixels. The amount of conversions of 1-pixels to 0-

pixels in an iteration step is unpredictable, and hence the computational workload can be somewhat varied over time. We thus resort to dynamic remapping to balance the workload over the course of thinning. We approximate the computational workload of a processor at an iteration by the processing time spent in the previous iteration. This approximation is reasonable since erosion takes place gradually along the edges of object skeletons, and thus the processing times of two consecutive iterations should not differ by a great deal.

From the experience in the WaTor simulation, we tried two invocation policies for the remapping. One is to invoke the remapping once every two steps, and the other is to invoke the remapping only once at the beginning of the thinning process. Since no computation time is available before the first iteration step to serve as an estimate of the workload, we perform the remapping between the first and the second iteration step. Figure 8.6 plots the processor utilization U_k across eight processors at various iteration steps for cases with and without remapping.

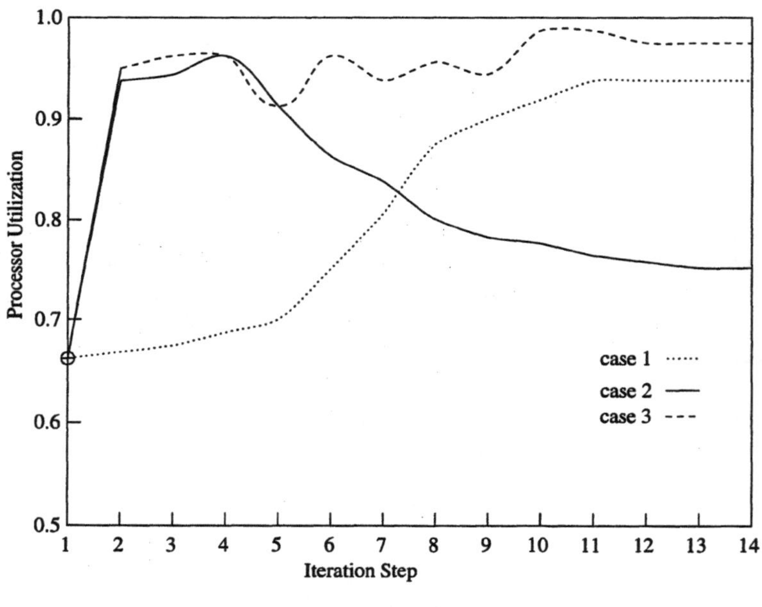

Figure 8.6: Processor utilizations at various iteration steps in the parallel thinning experiment

The curve for case 1 (without remapping) shows that the initial unbalanced workload distribution tends to uniform as the thinning algorithm proceeds. This points to the fact that the problem in question does not favor remapping. In fact, applying the once-at-the-beginning remapping to the problem (case 2) seems to degrade the overall performance: the initial balanced load distribution which is the result of the remapping tends to non-uniform afterwards. To preserve the uniform distribution, it seems necessary to invoke the remapping periodically (case 3). This time improvement is evident, as can be seen in the figure. Then in Figure 8.7, we show the improvement due to remapping (cases 2 and 3) in overall thinning time for different numbers of processors. Note that even though case 2 has seemed to be not so satisfactory in terms of processor utilization as shown in Figure 8.6, it does however reap performance gain in terms of thinning time most of the time, even outperforming case 3 in some instances.

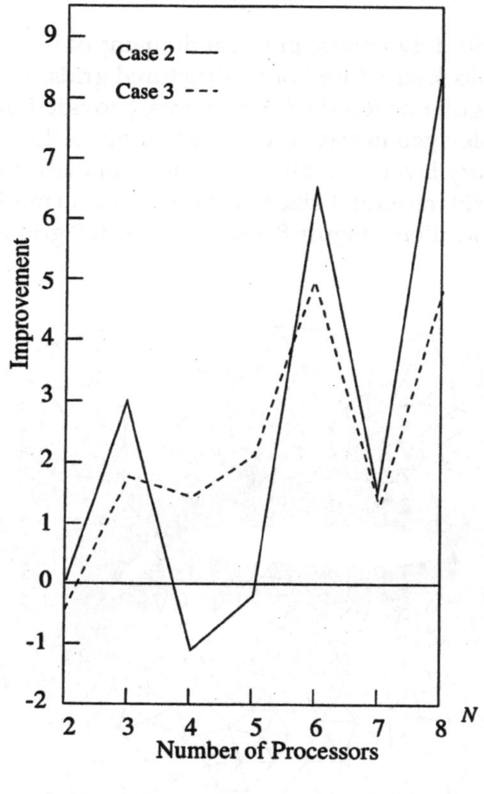

Figure 8.7: Improvement due to remapping for various numbers of processors in the parallel thinning experiment

From Figure 8.7, it is clear that the parallel thinning algorithm does benefit from remapping. Although the once-at-the-beginning remapping could sometimes outperform frequent remapping, the latter tends to give smoother performance throughout. As we have already pointed out, this particular test image is unfavorable so far as remapping is concerned because its workload distribution would tend to a uniform distribution as thinning progresses. Therefore, we consider the saving due to remapping of only a few percents in the overall thinning time in both cases satisfactory. In comparison with the interprocessor communication cost which accounts also for a few percents (see Table 8.2), this saving is significant.

8.5 Application 3: Parallel Unstructured Grid Partitioning

In computational fluid dynamics, physical domains of interest are tessellated using structured, block structured or unstructured grids. Unstructured grids, composed of triangular or tetrahedra elements, provide flexibility for tesselating about complex geometries and for adapting to flow features, such as shocks and boundary layers. Parallel numerical simulations require splitting the unstructured grid into equal-sized partitions so as to minimize the number of edges crossing partitions. Figure 8.8 shows an airfoil grid with 64 partitions.

Figure 8.8: A distribution of an unstructured mesh around an air-foil

Traditionally, grid partitioning is performed as a serial pre-processing step. For large unstructured grids, serial partitioning on a single processor may not be feasible due to memory or time constraints. Parallel partitioning is essential for reducing the pre-processing time. It is also desirable for handling load imbalance at run-time in simulations based on solution-adaptive griding.

We applied the GDE method to both grid partitioning and re-partitioning. The grid in consideration was first partitioned using a simple strategy, and then assigned to processors using Bokhari's simple mapping algorithm [21]. We experimented with two initial partitioning strategies: the recursive orthogonal bisection (ROB) and Farhat's algorithm [59]. The ROB algorithm recursively cuts the grid or sub-grids into two halves. It tends to generate balanced and well-shaped partitions but with a large cut size. Farhart's algorithm uses a breadth-first-search-based front technique to determine partitions one by one [60]. Starting from non-partitioned vertices which are connected to the boundary of partition $i-1$, it forms partition i according to the number of edges external to partition $i-1$. The algorithm produces compact and balanced partitions with a small cut size. Partitions generated by both strategies are not necessarily connected. We refined the distribution using the GDE method according to the geometric information of vertices with respect to the *cut size* (the number of cut edges).

8.5.1 Flow Calculation

Initial partitioning of a physical domain results in a computational graph, where vertices represent partitions and edges reflect neighboring relationships between partitions. The workload of a partition is defined as the total number of grid points inside the partition. The GDE method is readily applicable to the flow calculation in the case that the network graph matches well with the computation graph. In the case that the computational graph is different from the network graph, however, the GDE method on the network graph may generate a load flow along an edge between a pair of directly connected processors whose sub-domains are geometrically disconnected. Figure 8.9(a) shows such a computational graph mapped onto a 2×4 mesh. Network links $(2,7)$ and $(3,6)$ do not match with any edges of the computational graph. Load migration along such mis-matched links would lead to bad partition shapes and to non-connected partitions.

We handled this problem by de-routing flows on mis-matched links to a sequence of edges that are on the shortest path to the destination of flows. In Figure 8.9(b), for example, the flow on link $(7,2)$ is de-routed to the path $(7,3,1)$ in the computational graph. The flow on link $(3,6)$ is de-routed to the path $(3,5,6)$. Notice that flow de-routing may result in undesirable cyclic traffic such as those along the path $(7,3,5,6,7)$ in Figure 8.9(b). This cyclic path can be easily eliminated, as shown in Figure 8.9(c), by subtracting certain flows from all links in the path.

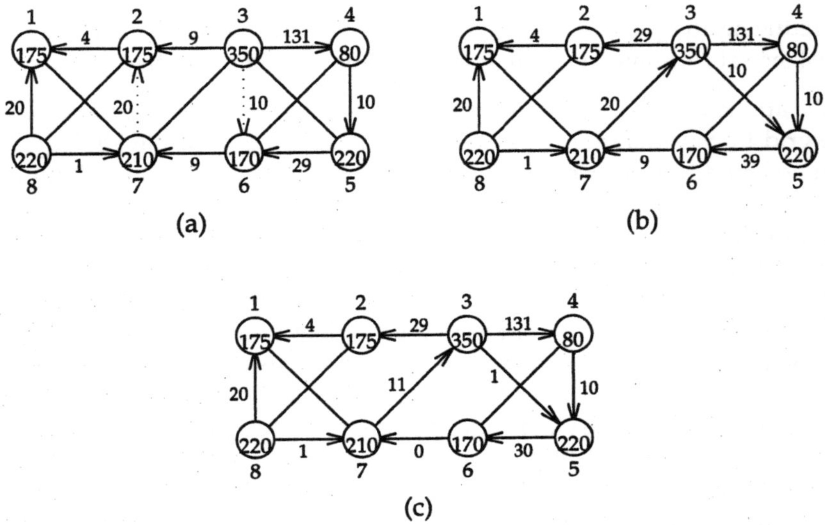

Figure 8.9: Workload de-routing for the GDE method applied to arbitrary networks—(a) mesh with mis-matched links; (b) flows along the mis-matched links de-routed; (c) after elimination of cyclic traffic

8.5.2 Selection of Vertices for Load Migration

Selection of data sets to be split should be such that the geometric adjacency of data points in the problem domain is preserved. The fundamental idea behind the selection policy is the concept of gain associated with switching a grid point between different partitions. As in the Kernighan-Lin local refinement algorithm [54, 106], the gain for a point v was simply defined as the net reduction in the number of cut edges if the grid point were to switch sets. That is,

$$gain(v) = \sum_{(v,u) \text{ is an edge}} \begin{cases} 1 & \text{if P(u) = P(v)} \\ -1 & \text{otherwise} \end{cases}$$

where $P(u)$ and $P(v)$ are the current partitions in which vertices u and v, respectively, reside.

8.5.3 Experimental Results

We experimented with the GDE-based refinement for grid partitioning [53]. Table 8.3 summarizes the improvement in cut size due to GDE-based refinement for partitioning of three 2-D finite element unstructured grids onto 8 or 32 processors. The AIRFOIL grid has 4253 vertices and 12289 edges, the CRACK grid has 10240 vertices and 30380 edges, and the BIG grid has 15606 vertices and 45878 edges [75]. From this table, it can be seen that the GDE-based refinement strategy improves the quality of initial partitions by a factor of 15% to 25% in most cases.

Table 8.3: Improvements in cut size due to GDE-based refinement in the partitioning of unstructured graphs

	AIRFOIL		CRACK		BIG	
	8	32	8	32	8	32
ROB	272	870	556	1405	709	1950
ROB+GDE	207	666	463	1154	535	1478
Improvement (%)	23.9	23.3	16.7	17.9	24.5	24.2
Farhat	423	684	611	1483	848	1454
Farhat+GDE	329	639	437	1146	719	1384
Improvement (%)	22.2	6.6	28.0	22.7	15.2	4.8

Table 8.4 presents the quality and efficiency of our parallel partitioning mechanism, together with those from other well-known sequential algorithms. In the table, KL is the Kernighan-Lin algorithm, IN the inertial algorithm, SB the spectral bisection algorithm, ML the multilevel algorith, and GDE the GDE-based refinement algorithm. The inertial method (IN) employs a

Table 8.4: Comparison of various algorithms in terms of cut size and running time in seconds for mapping various unstructured grids onto 16 processors

	AIRFOIL		CRACK		BIG	
	CutSize	Time	CutSize	Time	CutSize	Time
IN	503	0.20	797	0.45	1219	1.05
IN+KL	400	0.86	639	2.03	995	3.31
SB	372	21.29	671	74.14	863	124.8
SB+KL	309	24.20	577	82.60	675	131.3
ML+KL	325	2.98	615	6.47	605	8.05
Farhat+GDE	382	1.96	660	4.30	913	3.55

physical analogy in which the grid points are treated as point masses and the grid is cut with a plane orthogonal to the principal inertial axis of the mass distribution. The spectral bisection method (SB) partitions a grid by considering an eigenvector of an associated matrix to gain an understanding of global properties of the grid. Both methods are complemented by a Kernighan-Lin (KL) local refinement algorithm. The multilevel method accelerates the spectral method by coarsening the grid down to a smaller graph. Partitions of the small graph resulted from the spectral method are projected back towards the original grid. All these sequential methods are available in the Chaco library [82], and the evaluation was done on a Sun Sparc 10/50 with 96 MB memory. The parallel algorithm ran on a Parsytec T805 transputer-based GCel system. The T805 transputer is about 17 times slower than the Sparc machine; the timing performance in the table has been scaled to take this into account. From this table, it can be seen that the inertial method is fast, but produces partitions of relatively low quality. The spectral method produces excellent partitions at a very slow speed. The GDE-based refinement strategy, coupled with a simple Farhat partitioner, outperforms the inertial method in quality. It produces partitions comparable to the spectral method, and runs an order of magnitude faster.

8.6 Concluding Remarks

In this chapter, we have reported on the implementation of the GDE method for periodic remapping in two data parallel applications. In the WaTor simulation of a 256 × 256 toroidal ocean running on 16 processors, it is found that frequent remapping leads to about 20% improvement in simulation time over static mapping, and it outperforms centralized remapping by a factor of 50%. In parallel thinning of a 128 × 128 image on 8 processors, the policy of frequent remapping still saves about 5% thinning time although the test image is unsuitable for remapping. We consider these gains in performance due to remapping satisfactory because our test problems are themselves balanced in statistical sense—*i.e.*, the mean and variance of the workload distribution are more or less homogeneous across the domain, and the imbalances are mainly due to statistical fluctuations. We believe this is typical of many real data parallel problems. For other problems that have substantial imbalances (simulation of timed Petri nets, for instance), improvements on the order of hundreds of percents could sometimes be observed.

We have also presented an implementation of the GDE method for grid partitioning/re-partitioning in the context of computational fluid dynamics. It is found that the GDE-based parallel refinement method, coupled with simple geometric approaches, produces partitions comparable in quality to results from the best serial algorithms.

The GDE method is readily applicable to flow calculation in the case that the underlying network graph matches well with the computational graph generated from applications, such as in the first two applications we experimented.

In the case that the computational graph is different from the network graph, as we have encountered in the third experiment, we employed a de-routing strategy to redirect traffic on mis-matched network links to a different path in the computational graph in order to preserve communication locality. An alternative approach is to apply the GDE method directly to the computational graph, as illustrated in Figure 8.10(a). Figure 8.10(b) is the result of eliminating the circular traffic flows in Figure 8.10(a). Flow calculation on the computational graph can also be performed serially.

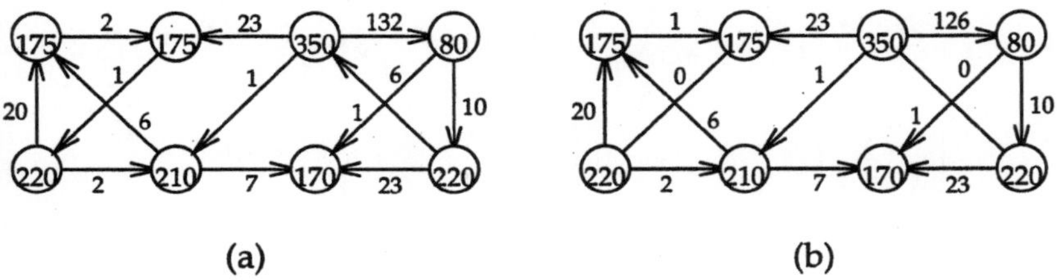

Figure 8.10: Flows along each edge of a computational graph for arriving at a global balanced state; (b) results from eliminating circular traffic paths in (a)

9

LOAD DISTRIBUTION IN COMBINATORIAL OPTIMIZATIONS

A state of balance is attractive only when one is on a tight rope; seated on the ground, there is nothing wonderful about it.

—ANDRÉ GIDE

This chapter reports the application of the GDE and the diffusion methods in combinatorial optimizations. A combinatorial optimization is the process of finding optimal or suboptimal solutions in a defined problem space. It arises from a large variety of applications in various areas in operational research and artificial intelligence. Examples are task planning and scheduling, capital investment, layout of VLSI chips, robot motion planning and game playing. Unlike the data parallel applications discussed in Chapter 8, the combinatorial optimization problem is characterized by an unpredictably varying unstructured search space. Its parallel execution relies on load balancing strategies to distribute the problem space recursively at run-time.

From the viewpoint of a load distribution strategy, parallel optimizations fall in the asynchronous category as shown in Figure 1.3 of Chapter 1. A processor initiates a balancing operation when it becomes lightly loaded or overloaded. Unlike remapping in time-varying multiphase data parallel computations, the objective of the data distribution strategies is to ensure that there exist no idle processors while others are heavily loaded, as opposed to keeping all processors to have more or less the same amount of load. We implement the algorithms and incorporate them into a portable branch-and-bound library (PPBB). The PPBB library, developed at University of Paderborn, Germany, subsumes the architecture-dependent features so as to relieve the programmer of architecture-dependent parallelization tasks and to ensure the efficiency of the parallel implementation automatically [190].

9.1 Combinatorial Optimizations

A combinatorial optimization problem is essentially the problem of finding a minimum-cost path from an initial node to a goal node in a state space graph. Each node of the graph represents an internal state of the object whose behavior is to be optimized. The initial and goal nodes correspond to the initial state and the final acceptable state of the object, respectively. Each edge represents a possible way of state change. A path from the initial node to a goal node is a feasible solution to the optimization problem. The cost of a path is defined in terms of the costs associated with the edges along the path.

For example, consider an 8-puzzle problem. There are eight tiles, numbered one through eight, on a 3×3 board having nine slots. Each tile occupies one slot. One of the slots is left empty. A tile adjacent to the empty slot in the horizontal or vertical direction can be moved into the empty slot, leaving its original slot empty. Given an initial tile configuration, the puzzle problem is to determine a shortest sequence of moves that would change the initial configuration to the configuration where the tiles are in row-major order. Following is a tile configuration and the goal in the 8-puzzle problem.

2	3	5
4	1	6
7	8	

$\longrightarrow$

1	2	3
4	5	6
7	8	

Treating a tile configuration as an internal state and defining the cost of a path as the length of the path, the puzzle problem is to find a shortest path from an initial state to the goal state in a state space graph.

9.1.1 Branch-and-Bound Methods

Given an initial condition and some objective function for minimization, there may exist a large number of feasible solutions. Branch-and-bound is an efficient search technique that avoids exhaustive search of all feasible solutions [121]. Its basic scheme is to reduce the search space by dynamically pruning unsearched state space areas which cannot yield better results than solutions already found according to information about the optimality of partial solutions.

In the 8-puzzle problem, for example, the goal configuration can be reached from an initial configuration through various sequences of tail moves. A branch-and-bound algorithm in the 8-puzzle problem searches the state space and maintains a data structure recording the shortest path found so far in the search process. It prunes an unsearched space portion rooted at a node x if it finds that the segment of edges from the initial node to the node x is not shorter than the current shortest path. It is because any extension of the segment stemming from the node x will not generate better solutions. Upon termination, the current shortest path is a globally optimal solution.

A branch-and-bound algorithm consists of three fundamental components: a branching procedure, a bounding procedure and a selection rule. Regard the search process associated with an internal node in the state space graph as a subproblem. The branching procedure recursively expands a (sub)problem into subproblems such that an optimal solution to the problem can be found by solving each of its subproblems. The bounding procedure computes a lower bound on the cost of an optimal solution for each subproblem to be expanded and uses it to determine whether or not further exploration of the subproblem is necessary. The branching and bounding procedures are problem-dependent. In the 8-puzzle problem, for example, the branching procedure expands a configuration in the state space graph into a set of subsequent configurations. Each subsequent configuration is generated by a move of a tile adjacent to the empty slot. The lower bound of a subproblem is the length of the segment from the initial configuration to the configuration the subproblem is associated with.

The selection rule is used to decide the order by which subproblems are branched on. It is problem-independent and exhibits greater flexibility in the design of branch-and-bound algorithms. It can be either a depth-first, best-first or a randomized rule. The randomized rule randomly selects a subproblem to expand. If this subproblem is unable to be expanded further, the algorithm backtracks and randomly selects a subproblem from the rest. The advantage of this rule is that it expands the minimum number of subproblems that are branched on [97]. The depth-first rule branches first on the most recently generated subproblems. Its major advantage is that its storage requirement is linear only in the depth of the state space being searched [121]. In a best-first search algorithm, the subproblems to be expanded are sorted according to certain heuristic evaluation function that measures how likely each subproblem will yield a solution [196]. The most promising subproblem is branched on first.

In the 8-puzzle problem, for example, a common heuristic evaluation function $l(x)$ on a configuration x is $g(x) + h(x)$, where $g(x)$ is the number of tile moves made so far and $h(x)$ is the sum of Manhattan distances between the current configuration and the goal configuration of all tiles. The Manhattan distance between two tiles at locations (x_1, y_1) and (x_2, y_2) is defined as $|x_1 - x_2| + |y_1 - y_2|$. The best-first branch-and-bound algorithm using the heuristic function $l(x)$ is also called an A^* algorithm. Figure 9.1 presents a portion of the search space graph of the 8-puzzle problem using the A^* algorithm. Previous studies showed that the best-first branch-and-bound algorithm is most attractive in terms of time complexity.

A branch-and-bound algorithm generates and prunes state nodes dynamically. The state space graph is highly unstructured. Its structure also changes unpredictably. A parallel branch-and-bound algorithm thus requires an extra load distribution rule to distribute the subproblems among processors at runtime. The simplest strategy is to maintain a heap to keep all the subproblems that need to be considered. Subproblems generated by all the processors are stored in this heap. When a processor runs out of work, it gets its next piece of work from the heap. Such a strategy based on a centralized heap works efficiently in small-scale shared-memory systems [141]. In distributed memory multiprocessors, however, maintaining a centralized heap incurs not only a severe accessing bottleneck but also heavy communication costs in transferring subproblems across the network. To alleviate the bottleneck problem and to minimize the communication cost, a decomposite approach is commonly favored. In this approach, each processor maintains a local heap to keep the assigned subproblems, and executes a serial branch-and-bound algorithm for evaluating the subproblem locally. When a processor is overloaded or lightly loaded, it initiates a load balancing operation in an attempt to balance its workload with others. The load distribution rule plays a crucial role in decomposite branch-and-bound algorithms.

The distribution rule is orthogonal to the selection rule. A load distribution algorithm can be used together with any selection rule. This chapter focuses on decomposite best-first branch-and-bound computations. We apply the Averaging Dimension Exchange (ADE) and the Averaging Diffusion (ADF) al-

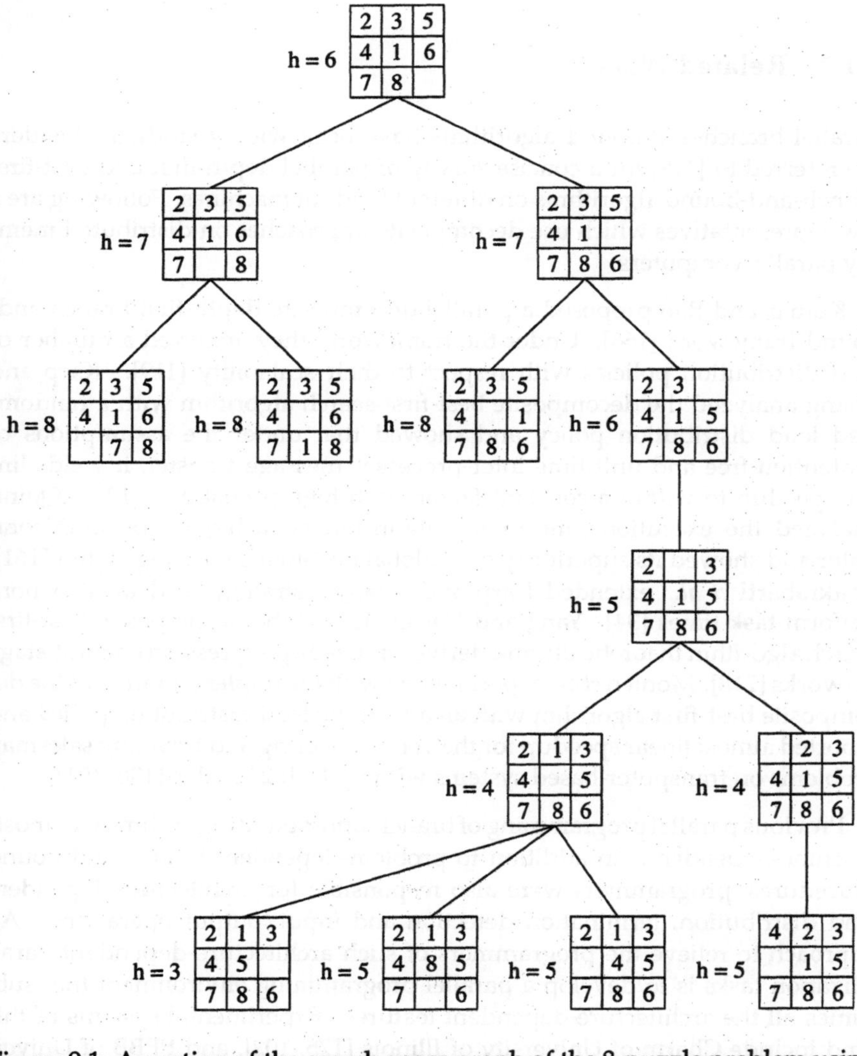

Figure 9.1: A portion of the search space graph of the 8-puzzle problem using a best-first branch-and-bound method

gorithms, together with two other popular nearest-neighbor algorithms: randomized allocation (RAND) and adaptive contracting withing neighborhood (ACWN), for the distribution of subproblems.

9.1.2 Related Work

Parallel branch-and-bound algorithms have been widely studied. Readers are referred to [118] for a concise survey of parallel depth-first and best-first branch-and-bound algorithms on different kinds of machines. Following are a few representatives which use decomposite approaches on distributed memory parallel computers.

Kumar and Rao proposed a parallel decomposite depth-first branch-and-bound framework [166]. Under the framework, they analyzed a number of load distribution policies with respect to their scalability [119]. Karp and Zhang analyzed the decomposite best-first search algorithm with a randomized load distribution policy and showed that under the assumptions of contention-free and unit time inter-processor message transfer, it yields linear speedup to within a constant factor, with high probability [103]. Quinn analyzed the execution time of the algorithm on a hypercube multicomputer and showed its superiority over global best-first search algorithm [161]. Chakrabarti *et al.* extended Karp and Zhang's strategy to deal with non-uniform task times [34]. Yang and Das evaluated the decomposite best-first search algorithm theoretically and derived a speedup expression on multistage networks [218]. Monien *et al.* experimented with the implementation of the decomposite best-first algorithm with an averaging load distribution policy and reported almost linear speedup for the vertex covering and traveling salesman problems on transputer-based systems with up to 1024 nodes [130, 191].

Previous parallel programming of branch-and-bound algorithms was mostly machine-dependent. In addition to problem-dependent branch and bound procedures, programmers were also responsible for architecture-dependent load distribution, termination detection and input/output operations. An approach to relieve the programmers of such architecture-dependent parallelization tasks is to develop a parallel programming environment that subsumes all the architecture-dependent features. Experimental systems of this kind include Charm of University of Illinois [175, 102], and PPBB of University of Paderborn [190]. In [177], Sinha and Kale tested the performance of two nearest-neighbor load balancing algorithms: the randomized allocation (RAND, for short) [103, 34] and and adaptive contracting within neighborhood (ACWN, for short) [101] in the Charm environment. They showed that the ACWN outperformed the RAND in general tree-structured computations. In [217], Xu *et al.* considered the averaging dimension exchange (ADE) and the averaging diffusion (ADF) methods, in addition to the RAND and ACWN algorithms, in the PPBB environment. PPBB is a parallel programming library for decomposite best-first branch-and-bound computations. With the support of the PPBB library, programmers only need to implement the branching and the bounding procedures. We tested the performance of the above algorithms when applied to set partitioning problems and found that both the ADE and ADF methods have better performance than the RAND and ACWN algorithms.

9.2 A Parallel Branch-and-Bound Library

PPBB is a portable parallel branch-and-bound library, developed to relieve the programmers of architecture-dependent parallelization tasks and ensure the efficiency of parallel implementation automatically. It comprises a heap management and a termination detection module and a decentralized mechanism for load distribution.

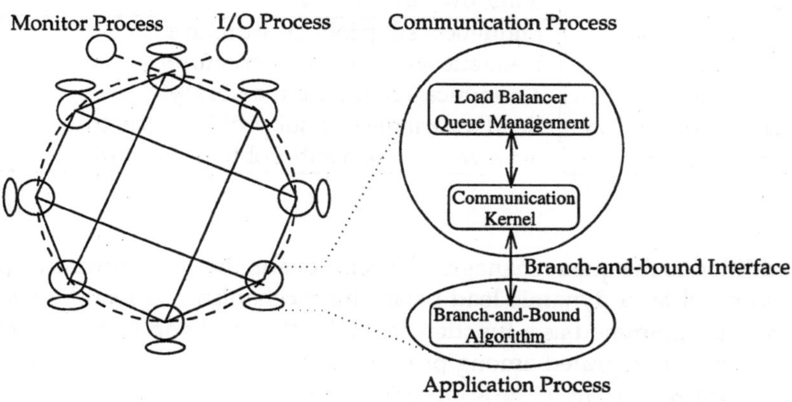

Figure 9.2: Architecture of the PPBB library

Figure 9.2 presents the architecture of the PPBB library. It encapsulates the architecture-dependent components by a *communication process*. The branch-and-bound algorithm is programmed as an *application process*. Each processor executes concurrently a pair of communication and application processes. The communication process provides run-time support for the application process. There is one processor serving as the supervisor of the computation. Its communication process is connected to an extra I/O process and an extra monitor process. The I/O process, serving as an interface to the outside, performs the input/output functions of the branch-and-bound algorithm and serves as a bypass for data for all other processes. The solid lines represent physical communication channels between processors, through which communication processes exchange load information, and transfer subproblems for load balancing. The dashed lines represent a virtual ring used in distributed termination detection and input/output data transmission.

The application and communication processes in a processor are coupled through a branch-and-bound interface. Table 9.1 lists a number of primitive functions provided in the interface. The application process repeatedly fetches subproblems for expansion from the queue managed by the local communication process, and inserts newly generated subproblems into the queue.

Table 9.1: Branch-and-bound interface between the application process and the communication process in the PPBB library

ppbb_Init	Initialize and start the library
ppbb_NProcs	Determine the number of application processes
ppbb_MyId	Determine process identification number
ppbb_End	Shutdown the library
ppbb_Enq	Enqueue a subproblem structure
ppbb_Deq	Dequeue a subproblem structure
ppbb_Bound	Announce a bound to the library
ppbb_spGet_<...>	Read a variable of a subproblem structure
ppbb_spSet_<...>	Set a variable of a subproblem structure

In addition to the queue management component, the communication process also provides a dynamic load balancing mechanism. A load balancing strategy is programmed as a function called by the local application process. Subproblems are migrated among processors through a communication kernel, which is transparent to the application process.

9.3 Load Distribution Strategies

9.3.1 Workload Evaluation and Workload Split

Recall from Chapter 1 that every load balancing algorithm has to resolve the issues of workload evaluation, workload information exchange, initiation of a balancing operation, location of balancing partners, and selection of processes for migration. The first and last issues are problem-dependent, and need to be resolved using problem-specific knowledge.

In parallel decomposite branch-and-bound computations, each processor maintains a local heap to keep the subproblems to be expanded. Obviously, the heap size—the number of subproblems in a processor—could be a workload index.

Since subproblems in a branch-and-boundcomputation have different computational requirements, the heap size as a workload index may not be accurate. It is known that the bounding procedure computes a lower bound on the cost of an optimal solution for each subproblem to be expanded. The lower bound of a subproblem partly reflects its grain size. The smaller the lower bound, the larger grain size the subproblem may have. Let $g(x)$ be the lower bound of a subproblem x. Define *weight* of the subproblem x as $-g(x)$ and *heap weight* as the largest weight of subproblems in a heap. Heap weight could be another workload index. We have therefore the following three possible workload indices in parallel branch-and-bound computations.

- Load measurement in terms of heap size;
- load measurement in terms of heap weight;
- load measurement in terms of both heap size and weight.

In parallel branch-and-bound computations, each process solves a subproblem. The subproblem is a basic unit of migration. Subproblems are independent of each other. They may be executed on any processor in any order. Thus, any subproblems in a heap and newly generated subproblems can be candidates for migration. The only factor we should consider is the subproblem weight. There are four possible selection policies:

- newly generated subproblem;
- the subproblem with the largest weight in the local heap;
- the subproblem with the smallest weight in the local heap;
- randomly selected subproblem.

9.3.2 Nearest-Neighbor Algorithms

Following are a number of nearest-neighbor load balancing algorithms using different load indices and selection rules: the RAND, the ACWN, the prioritized RAND (PRAND), the prioritized ACWN (PACWN), the ADE, and the ADF algorithms. If needed, they use on-state-change policy for exchanging workload information between processors.

With the RAND policy, a load distribution operation is performed once a subproblem is generated, and the newly generated subproblem is then sent out to a randomly selected neighbor. An advantage of this policy is simplicity of implementation. No local load information needs to be maintained, nor any load information to be sent to other processors. Theoretical analyses have shown that the randomized allocation gives respectable performance under the assumption of unit time inter-processor transfer [34, 103]. In practice, however, its performance will be greatly degraded by the communication costs incurred in subproblem migrations.

The ACWN policy differs from the RAND in the choice of the destination when a newly generated subproblem is required to be migrated out. It always selects the least loaded nearest neighbor as the recipient of the subproblem. A processor that receives a subproblem keeps it in its local heap if it finds its own load to be less than that of its least loaded neighbor. Otherwise, it forwards the subproblem to its least loaded neighbor. Thus, a newly generated subproblem travels along the steepest load gradient to a local minimum. With the ACWN policy, each processor is required to maintain its local load information, and adjacent processors need to exchange their load information periodically.

In both the RAND and ACWN strategies, only those newly generated subproblems are allowed for migration. The rationale behind these two strategies is that of an implicit assumption that all subproblems are uniform in terms of their computational requirements. In view of the non-uniformity of subproblems in branch-and-bound computations, the PRAND and PACWN algorithms take into account the lower bound information in load evaluation and index the workload of a processor by the weight of its heap.

Like the RAND and ACWN, both prioritized algorithms are initiated on the generation of a new subproblem. The subproblem is first inserted in the local heap. Then, the PRAND selects the second largest weighted subproblem in the heap and transfers it to a randomly selected neighbor, while the PACWN transfers the second largest weighted subproblem to its least loaded neighbor.

Both the ADE and the ADF strategies follow the same idea of local averaging in every load distribution operation. They differ in their way of averaging. In the ADE policy, a processor in need of load distribution "balances" its workload with one of its neighbors. In the ADF policy, the processor balances its workload with all its neighbors. Since the computational load of a processor is mainly determined by the weight and the size of its local heap, a balancing operation of both strategies comprises two steps: (1) to balance the heap weights of processors through migrating the second largest weighted subproblem; (2) to balance the heap sizes through migrating the smallest weighted subproblem.

9.4 Performance Evaluation

We evaluated the efficiency and scalability of load distribution strategies in different machines. We used the set partition problem (SPP for short) as the test problem. It is a well-known combinatorial optimization problem arising in a broad range of applications. Examples includes crew scheduling, truck scheduling, information retrieval, circuit, capacity balancing, capital investment, facility location, political districting, and radio communication planning. We implemented the branch-and-bound algorithm suggested by Chan and Yano [36]. The test instances were provided by the OR-Lib at Imperial College of Science, Technology and Medicine. Each data point obtained is the average of 10 runs.

SPP is a zero-one integer program formulated as follows:

$$\begin{array}{ll} \text{minimize} & \sum_{j=1}^{n} C_j x_j \\ \text{subject to} & \sum_{j=1}^{n} a_{ij} x_j = 1, i \in I \\ & x_j = \{0,1\}, j \in J \\ \text{where} & a_{ij} \in \{0,1\} \\ & I = \{1,\ldots,m\}, J = \{1,\ldots,n\} \end{array}$$

Our experiments were conducted on a PowerPC 601-based parallel computer Parsytec GC/PowerPlus and on a transputer T805-based parallel system Parsytec GCel, both installed in the Paderborn Center for Parallel Computing (PC^2). Both of them belong to the class of distributed memory two-dimensional mesh structured multiprocessors. They differ in their processing node performance.

9.4.1 Implementation on a GC/PowerPlus System

In the GC/PowerPlus system, each processing node consists of two 80MHz PowerPC 601s and four communication engines based on transputer T805, as illustrated in Figure 9.3. Each processing node has 80MB memory.

In the GC/PowerPlus system, we implemented the PPBB in two different models: *multi-threaded model* and *single-threaded model*. Recall that a parallel branch-and-bound computation under the support of PPBB comprises an application process and a communication process at each processing node. In the multi-threaded model, each PowerPC processor executes these two processes concurrently. Each process is implemented as a thread. In contrast, in

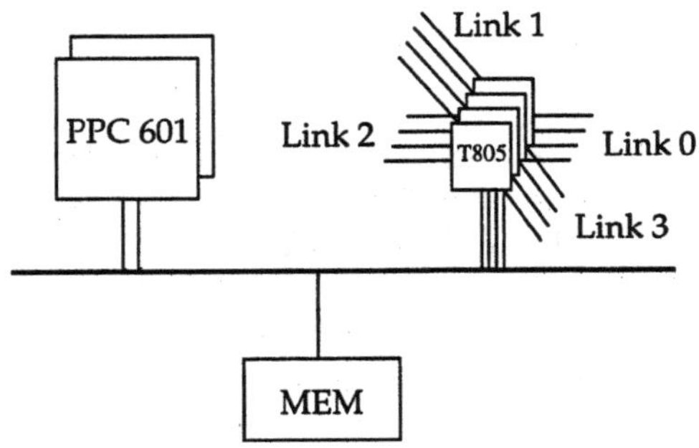

Figure 9.3: The structure of a processoring element of the GC/PowerPlus

the single-threaded model, the dual processors of a processing node execute these two processes separately. The processor executing the communication process takes the responsibility of local heap management, load distribution and message passing between processors. Another processor is fully dedicated to branch-and-bound algorithms. Evidently, the single-threaded implementation model should be more efficient than the multi-threaded model if the communication processor is counted only as a co-processor. The difference between their efficiencies reflects the overhead of the PPBB run-time support including the overhead in load distribution.

We used a large problem instance, *scpa1*, with 3000 columns and 120 rows in this experiment. Its sequential run in a single processor takes 1155 seconds. In the multi-threaded implementation model, its parallel execution times with different load distribution strategies are tabulated in Table 9.2. Figure 9.4 plots the speedup of the corresponding parallel implementation.

Table 9.2: Execution time in the multi-threaded implementation model on the GC/PowerPlus system

Processors	4	8	16	32
ADF	310.6	158.3	76.3	38.1
ADE	305.5	165.7	77.0	36.7
PACWN	324.4	164.1	82.4	42.8
ACWN	345.1	200.4	97.5	58.6
PRAND	361.9	185.9	100.1	65.0
RAND	348.5	201.5	111.3	85.2

From Figure 9.4, it can be seen that both the LADE and LADF algorithms lead to almost full parallel efficiency in a parallel computer with up to 32

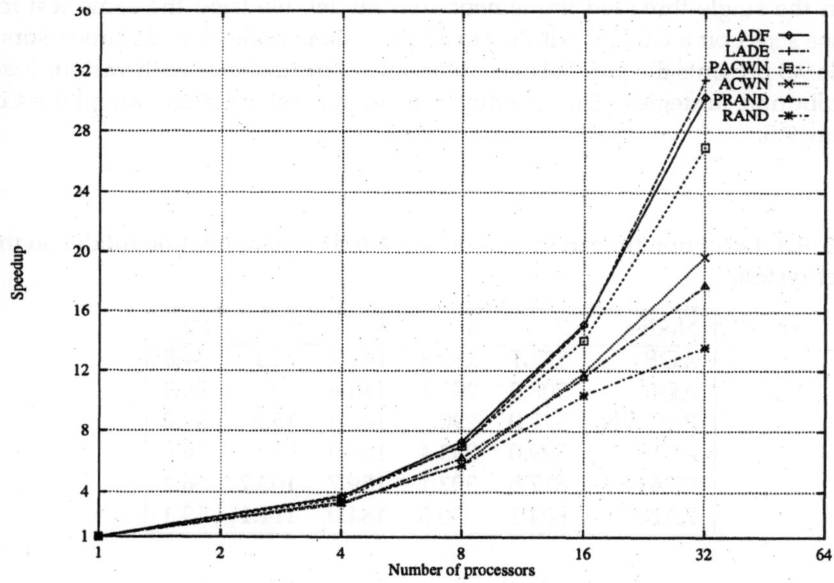

Figure 9.4: Speedups of parallel branch-and-bound algorithms with various distribution strategies in the multiple-threaded implementation model on a GC/PowerPlus system

processors. They outperform the other two classes of iterative load balancing algorithms. Their superiority is significant in large-scale systems.

Both the RAND and ACWN algorithms perform well when a system is saturated, but their performance degrades when the system size increases. The superiority of the ACWN algorithm to the RAND algorithm is consistent with the findings by other researchers [177]. It can also be seen that the prioritized variants of the RAND and ACWN algorithm are much better. Using the weight information in decision-making, the PRAND and the PACWN strategies gain 10% to 15% improvements over the RAND and the ACWN, respectively.

In the single-threaded implementation model, we tried the same test instance *scpa*1 on a GC/PP with up to 32 processing nodes (*i.e.*, 64 processors). Table 9.3 presents the parallel execution time of the instance with various load distribution strategies. The speedups due to parallel execution are plotted in Figure 9.5.

Table 9.3: Execution time in the single-threaded implementation model on the GCel system

Nodes	2	4	8	16	32
ADF	572.7	286.2	142.7	72.1	34.8
ADE	508.3	293.1	146.6	69.5	36.3
PACWN	577.0	290.7	146.0	75.3	39.0
ACWN	599.0	293.4	160.9	77.2	46.4
PRAND	617.5	302.1	159.7	103.2	56.4
RAND	604.2	300.3	184.0	114.1	69.1

From Tables 9.2 and 9.3, it can be seen that the PPBB run-time support with the ADE, the ADF and the PACWN strategies incurs as little as 10% of the execution time in systems with 16 or 32 processors. Moreover, the overhead percentage decreases with the increase of the system-scale. The ACWN, the RAND and the PRAND strategies, however, incur an overhead of as much as 15% to 20%.

Finally, we should note that the anomaly that the parallel efficiency of the ADE and the ADF in Figure 9.5 exceeds one in certain situations is due to the fact that the test instance has more than one optimal solution. A sequential algorithm solves subproblems in a fixed execution order, and always obtains a certain optimal solution first. In parallel implementation of a branch-and-bound algorithm, however, the execution order of subproblems is different from run to run. An earlier discovery of an optimal solution results in higher efficiency because the newly obtained optimal bound will cut off the remaining subproblems more swiftly.

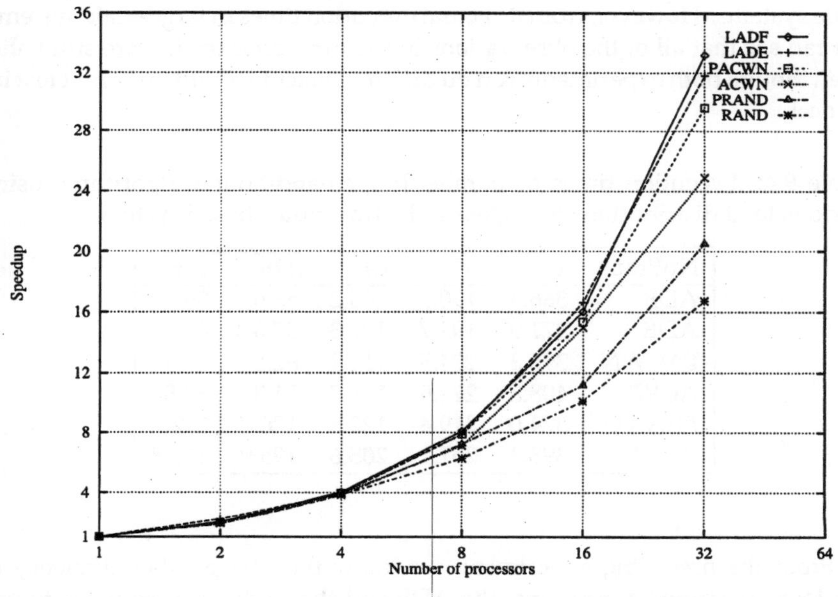

Figure 9.5: Speedups of parallel branch-and-bound algorithms with various distribution strategies in the single-threaded implementation model on a GC/PowerPlus system

9.4.2 Implementation on a Transputer-based GCel System

In the Parsytec GCel system, each processing node is a 30MHz T805 with 4MB local memory. In this experiment, we evaluated load distribution strategies on the Parsytec GCel with up to 256 processors. Because of the limitation of transputers in computational power and memory size, we choose a small test instance from the OR-Lib, *scp41*, with 1000 columns and 120 rows.

Table 9.4 presents the execution time of parallel branch-and-bound algorithms with various load distribution strategies. Since each transputer has only 4MB local memory, we are unable to run the test instance in very small-scale systems. However, from its actual execution times in large-scale systems, we can see that all of the observations in the preceding section are still valid, even though both experiments run on different machines with different test instances.

Table 9.4: Execution times of parallel branch-and-bound algorithms using various load distribution strategies on the transputer-based system

NoProc	16	32	64	128	256
ADF	366.4	190.7	105.2	58.6	39.1
ADE	371.9	192.7	102.3	57.6	41.3
PACWN	396.3	204.5	112.8	62.8	44.9
ACWN	408.8	222.9	148.7	71.3	57.5
PRAND	374.0	219.4	122.8	126.7	112.7
RAND	393.3	257.1	205.6	195.9	179.8

From the preceding experiment, we know that the parallel efficiency of the local averaging algorithms, the ADF and the ADE, approximates to one in systems with up to 32 processors. From Table 9.4, we find their parallel efficiency in a system with 256 nodes relative to the efficiency in a system with 16 nodes to be about 0.58. It follows that parallel implementation with the local averaging algorithms obtains a speedup of 148.5. Similarly, according to the efficiencies of different load distribution strategies on the GC/PP with 16 processors, we plot the speedups of different strategies in Figure 9.6.

9.5 Concluding Remarks

In this chapter, we have reported the implementation of the average dimension exchange (ADE) and the average diffusion (ADF) algorithms, together with a randomized algorithm (RAND) and an adaptive contracting within

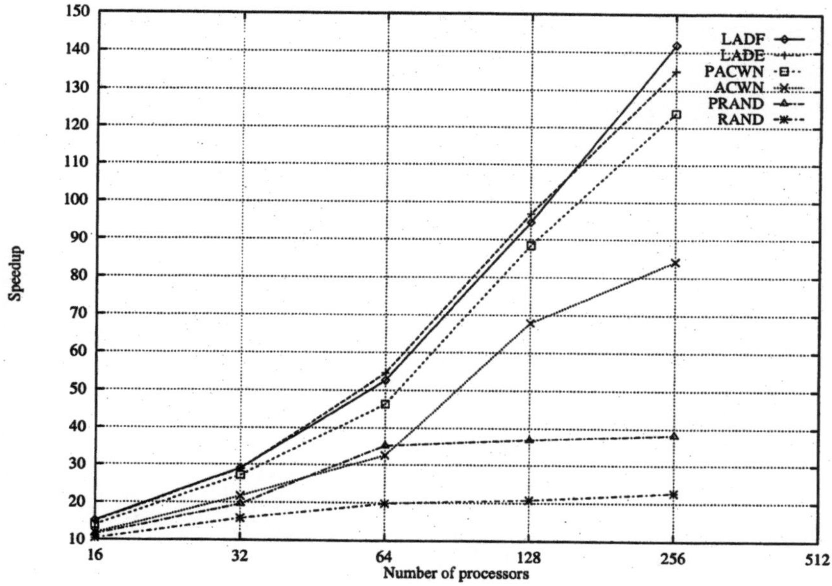

Figure 9.6: Speedups of parallel branch-and-bound algorithms with various distribution strategies on a GCel system

neighborhood (ACWN) algorithm and their respective prioritized versions, PRAND and PACWN, for load distribution in parallel branch-and-bound computations. These strategies were incorporated in the framework of a portable branch-and-bound library. Their performance was tested in the solution of set partitioning problems on a PowerPC-based GC/PowerPlus parallel computer and a transputer-based GCel system. It has been found that both the ADF and the ADE strategies outperform others significantly in large-scale systems and that they lead to an almost linear speedup on the GC/PowerPlus with up to 32 nodes and a speedup of 146.8 on the GCel with up to 256 nodes. It has also been found that the RAND and the ACWN strategies improve greatly when the bound of subproblems is considered in load distribution. Using this bound information in estimating processors' workloads, the PRAND and the PACWN strategies gained 10 to 15% improvements over the RAND and the ACWN strategy, respectively.

10

CONCLUSIONS

As peace is the end of war, so to be idle
is the ultimate purpose of the busy.
—SAMUEL JOHNSON

10.1 Summary of Results

We have examined a class of nearest-neighbor algorithms for load balancing in distributed memory parallel computers. The focus has been on two closely related methods: the dimension exchange method and the diffusion method. They are very simple algorithmically but turn out to be quite effective when applied to parallel computers.

10.1.1 Theoretical Optimizations

With the dimension exchange method, a processor equalizes its workload (a balance operation) with those of its nearest neighbors one by one, and the most recently computed value is always used in the next balance operation. Based on an observation that "equal splitting" of workload between a pair of processors in each balance operation does not necessarily lead to the fastest convergence rate in arriving at a global balanced state, we have presented the generalized dimension exchange (GDE) method. It is a refinement of the dimension exchange method with the addition of an exchange parameter λ to control the workload splitting. It was expected that through adjusting this parameter, the load balancing efficiency may be improved. We have carried out an analysis of the GDE method using linear system theory, and derived a necessary and sufficient condition for its convergence. We have also presented a sufficient condition *w.r.t.* the structure of the system network for the optimality of the original dimension exchange method. Among networks that have this property are the hypercube and the product of any two networks having the property.

For the other popular structures, the mesh and the torus, the optimal exchange parameter is critically dependent on their scales. We have derived their optimal exchange parameters for even-order cases, and uncovered the relationships between their convergence rates:

- For an n-D $k_1 \times k_2 \times \ldots \times k_n$ mesh and an n-D $2k_1 \times 2k_2 \times \ldots \times 2k_n$ torus. their optimal exchange parameters are equivalent to to $1/(1+\sin(\pi/k))$, where $k = \max\{k_i, 1 \leq i \leq n\}$.
- For tori and meshes of even order (even in each dimension), the convergence rate depends only on the largest dimension. the more vertices the largest dimension has, the slower the convergence rate.
- The convergence rate of a mesh whose largest dimension has k vertices is the same as a torus whose largest dimension has $2k$ vertices.

With the diffusion method, a processor balances its workload with those of its nearest neighbors all at the same time rather than one by one as in the dimension exchange method. Its efficiency depends on the diffusion parameter. Similarly, we have derived the optimal diffusion parameters for the structures of ring, torus, chain and mesh using circulant matrix theory.

We have validated the results through statistical simulation experiments. The simulation experiments show a significant performance improvement due to the optimal exchange and diffusion parameters.

Furthermore, we have made a comparison between the dimension exchange method and the diffusion method in different situations: global load balancing versus load sharing objectives; one-port versus all-port communication models; static versus dynamic workload models; synchronous versus asynchronous implementations. It turns out that the dimension exchange method outperforms the diffusion method in the one-port communication models. In particular, the optimally-tuned dimension exchange method is best suited for synchronous global load balancing regardless of its underlying communication models. The strength of the diffusion method is in asynchronous load balancing in the all-port communication model.

10.1.2 Practical Implementations

On the practical side, we have experimented with the dimension exchange and the diffusion methods in various applications for the purposes of global load balancing and load sharing. We have implemented the GDE method for periodic remapping in two time-dependent multiphase data parallel computations: a parallel Monte Carlo simulation and a parallel image thinning algorithm. The experimental results show that GDE-based remapping leads to substantial improvements in execution time in both cases. The GDE method has also been used for parallel partitioning of unstructured finite-element graphs. We have devised a de-routing technique to deal with mis-matched communication channels between the data dependency graph and the system graph. Experimental results show that the GDE-based parallel refinement, coupled with simple geometric partitioning approaches, produces partitions comparable in quality to those from the best serial algorithms.

The last application is parallel combinatorial optimizations. We have experimented with the dimension exchange and the diffusion methods for distributing dynamically generated workloads in the search process. We have tested their performance in the solution of set partitioning problems on two distributed memory parallel computers and found that both methods lead to an almost linear speedup in a system with 32 processors and a speedup of 146.8 in a system with 256 processors. These two methods give the best results among all the methods we tried.

10.2 Discussions and Future Research

The study we have reported here opens up a lot of interesting and challenging research opportunities.

The GDE and the diffusion methods. In the analysis of the GDE method, we limited our scope to the higher-dimensional torus and mesh which are of even order in every dimension. Through simulation, we showed that results for the even cases are applicable approximately to the non-even cases. From the viewpoint of theory and for completeness, however, it is worthwhile to continue on with the analysis of the GDE method for the non-even cases.

In the last section of Chapter 3, we extended the GDE method by employing different exchange parameters for different edges, and showed that there exist a set of parameters which maximize the convergence rate of the load balancing. The diffusion method should also have the potential of better performance by using different diffusion parameters for different edges. The derivation of such optimal sets in arbitrary structures is hard. For some specific structures (product of graphs, for instance), however, it might be possible to work out a set of near-optimal parameters, each of which is for a subset of the edges. Some sort of block iteration methods [195] could be used in the analysis.

The results we obtained in this study are for a number of popular structures which are but a small subset of all possible interconnection structures. It will be useful to create and maintain a catalog of structures versus their optimal parameters. Given a new structure, however, it might not be an easy task to try to derive its optimal parameter, as we have demonstrated in this work. An alternative would be to develop some general method so that the parameter for the structure in question can be estimated if not derived exactly based on similar structures that are in the catalog. A more ambitious project would be to identify the most basic graph components, parameterized perhaps by size, degree, *etc.*, and their optimal load balancing parameters, and use them as generators for practical interconnection structures.

Related to the above is load balancing in a subgraph. It is now a common practice to partition a multicomputer into sections, each of which to be assigned on demand to a different application. The partitioning can be such that the resulting pieces are neatly tiled and have one of those regular shapes, or it is done in a haphazard way. In either case, it is unlikely that the original parameter for the parent graph would still be optimal for these subgraphs. The question is: Would the original parameter still be acceptable? If not, what parameter value should be used for such a subgraph?

Run-time complexity. The main thrust of this study has been on analyzing the asymptotic convergence rates of the methods in the mesh and torus structures. Their convergence rates determine the upper bound of their run-time complexities. In [184], the authors present both lower and upper bounds of the run-time complexity of the diffusion method in arbitrary structures. These bounds however are too rough for system designers to estimate the cost of load balancing. For practical reasons, it is essential that the actual number of communication steps required to reduce the load imbalance by a certain factor is known in advance. This number can be determined based on the full eigenvalue spectrum of the characteristic matrix (the GDE matrix, for instance) of a load balancing algorithm. In [81], the authors derive such a number for a special form of the diffusion method in 3-D meshes. Further work can be performed along this line so that practical questions such as the following may be answered for optimally-tuned GDE and diffusion methods:

- If the variance (and perhaps other characteristics) of the initial workload distribution is known, what will be the number of sweeps required by the methods to arrive at the balanced state?
- If the number of sweeps is restricted to be within a certain limit, what degree of balancing can the methods achieve?

In fact, one practical advantage of iterative nearest-neighbor algorithms is that by varying the number of iterative steps, one can get different qualities of balancing result, provided that the algorithms are convergent. Although through simulation, one can easily obtain the answer, it would be even better if this information can be captured by compact equations derived through theoretical analysis. Given such information, programmers can then decide on the threshold (*i.e.*, degree of balancing) required for their applications in light of the cost, the number of iterative steps, that would be incurred.

Using fewer steps, our algorithms achieve the effect of local balancing in which a processor's load is balanced within its vicinity but not the entire network. This could well be the intention of the application programmer as for some applications, a balance over the entire network is really not that necessary; also, too much load migration across long distances might be too costly. A localized balancing result implies that the processors' workloads are mostly migrated to within their vicinity. With the programmer prescribing the number of steps to iterate, the termination detection component becomes unnecessary, and the programmer can enjoy using the simplest form of the GDE or diffusion algorithm.

Local and hierarchical balancing. It is evident from the theoretical as well as simulation results in previous chapters that the GDE and the diffusion methods would deteriorate in performance as the size of the network increases. This is not unexpected as what these methods are trying to do is to achieve a global balance. In practice, whether it is always necessary to produce a global balance at every remapping instance is questionable, as has been discussed above. In addition to local balancing which tries to balance loads that are within a processor's vicinity, another possible direction when dealing with massively parallel systems is to consider hierarchical schemes which produce local balances in various subsections of the system, and then depending on the needs, perform further balancing among subsections, and so on—basically a divide-and-conquer kind of strategy. Horton has made an attempt along this line by proposing a multi-level diffusion method [90]. Willibeek-LeMair and Reeves have also included a hierarchical scheme in their comparative study [203].

Decentralized vs. centralized methods. Distributed methods are generally preferred over centralized methods. Wu and Shu, however, proposed a modification of the dimension exchange method which requires some form of centralization [207]. They called the method direct dimension exchange (DDE). The "directness" of this method lies in its calculation of the load average (along every dimension) explicitly and directly instead of iteratively as in our methods. Note that our methods do not set out to calculate the load average as one of their tasks; the load average is implicitly calculated along with the recording of the give/take information during the execution of the GDE or diffusion method. In fact, as discussed before, the application in question might not even require a perfect average to be computed; the DDE method would lack this flexibility.

For a k-ary n-cube, the DDE method considers the dimensions in turn. For the set of rings in each dimension, a centralized algorithm is applied to each ring, which computes and then broadcasts the load average; each node of the ring then gives away or takes in the necessary amount of load according to the average. This transferring of tasks can in fact be delayed till the end by recording the give/take information at every node, like what is done in the GDE or diffusion method. One drawback of the centralized method is that one of the nodes in a ring would need to serve as the leader and execute a different algorithm than the other nodes; a large cube has many such rings. Should any one of the leaders go wrong, the entire load balancing operation would be affected; whereas in the GDE case, every node executes the same simple algorithm independently, and malfunctioning of a node would not have impact on the other nodes.

In terms of performance, it is not entirely clear that one is better than the other. Wu and Shu claimed that DDE is superior in terms of a number of measures, which however is not adequately supported. First of all, regarding load difference, the DDE method does not necessarily have the advantage, as the load difference is relative to the magnitude of the load indices; to achieve a smaller load difference (if at all necessary), one can always choose larger load indices in the GDE method. Then, regarding the message and time complexities, for every step within a sweep, a node in the GDE method would send and receive one message; based on the load index received, it computes the new load index and records, if applicable, the amount of load it should thus give away. In the full-duplex, one-port model, such a step would take one time step; and two time steps in the weak hypercube model [158]. In the DDE case, to compute and broadcast the load average for a ring, one of the messages has to go through at least half of the ring, and back. The time complexity of this phase (flow calculation) of the DDE algorithm is $O(kn)$ for the k-ary n-cube, against $O(sn)$ of the GDE method, where s is the number of sweeps needed for arriving at the balanced state. Which is better (and in what situations) has yet to be determined through a more comprehensive and detailed study.

In fact, the flow calculation phase might not be that crucial as the actual migration of tasks which follows could take up the largest share of the overall time. Some meaningful future work will be needed along this line to examine the characteristics of the per-node flow (give/take) information generated from the execution of the GDE method, and compare the GDE and the DDE method in this regard. The ultimate measure would be the number of tasks that need to be transferred. A good algorithm would not transfer tasks unnecessarily (*i.e.*, "task thrashing") and would try to transfer away as few tasks as possible. Clearly, the GDE method would not cause task thrashing, at least not between direct neighbors.

Asynchronous models. Other problems that deserve further studies are related to the assumptions we made in the analysis. The multicomputer we considered was assumed to be based on the synchronous communication model. On a different track altogether, there is this rather wide open area of studying nearest-neighbor load balancing methods in asynchronous communication systems. In an asynchronous system, each processor might maintain a set of outdated information about of its neighbors' workloads because of communication delays. Moreover, it is conceivable that some workloads might be in transit at certain times. All these result in certain difficulty in the convergence analysis of the asynchronous versions of the nearest-neighbor load balancing methods we presented here. Not too long ago, Bertsekas and Tsitsiklis studied the asynchronous version of the diffusion method, and presented the sufficient condition for its convergence [16]. However, the problem of determining the optimal convergence rate of the method remains unsolved. Major undertaking is necessary for analyzing the asynchronous version of the GDE method and for comparing the asynchronous methods their synchronous counterparts. In fact, the nearest-neighbor load balancing procedure resembles the fixed point problem in dynamic contexts [15, 134, 193]. It might be feasible to answer some of these questions concerning load balancing for asynchronous systems through using the techniques for distributed asynchronous computation of fixed points.

The parallel computation we assumed is made up of a large number of independent processes, and hence the communication cost between nodes was ignored in our analysis. Evidently, it is rather hard to thoroughly analyze the nearest-neighbor methods if the general computation model with arbitrary communication requirements between processes is considered. It is partly because the total workload in the system may vary greatly due to process migration if the communication cost is to be treated as some kind of workload or a parameter of the workload. For example, the workload of a node with two tightly coupled processes may increase when one of the processes is sent away according to the load balancing decision. However, for the simple model of chain structured parallel computations, as in [22, 38, 148], the nearest-neighbor load balancing procedure should be analyzable. It is worth making such an effort because the nearest-neighbor procedure is a promising solution for the mapping problem.

A run-time system. Finally, on the practical side, it would be rather interesting to try to implement a powerful run-time support that does automatic dynamic remapping using GDE for time-dependent data parallel applications. This support mechanism could either perform the remapping periodically or try to detect imbalances on the fly and perform a remapping only when the system workload exhibits a certain degree of imbalance. Unlike a user library such as the PPBB library described in Chapter 9 or the Concurrent Graph Library [188], the run-time support can be made a resident part of the system and as a privileged layer of the operating system. The advantage is that it can quickly access low-level information related to processes when making load balancing decisions. On the other hand, the programmer would be relieved of the burden to link extra library code (and relink when the library is upgraded).

References

[1] D. Abramson. A very high speed architecture for simulated annealing. *IEEE Computer*, 25(5):27–36, May 1992.

[2] T. Agerwala et al. SP2 system architecture. *IBM Systems Journal*, 34(2), 1995.

[3] I. Ahmad and A. Ghafoor. Semi-distributed load balancing for massively parallel multicomputer systems. *IEEE Transactions on Software Engineering*, 17(10):987–1004, October 1991.

[4] I. Ahmad, A. Ghafoor, and G. Fox. Hierarchical scheduling of dynamic parallel computations on hypercube multicomputers. *Journal of Parallel and Distributed Computing*, pages 317–329, March 1994.

[5] G. S. Almasi and A. Gottlieb. *Highly Parallel Computing*. The Benjamin/Cummings Pub. Co., second edition, 1994.

[6] T. E. Anderson, D. E. Culler, and D. A. Patterson. A case for NOW (Networks of Workstations). *IEEE Micro*, 15(1):54–64, February 1995.

[7] Kuck & Associates, Inc. *KAP/Concurrent User's Guide*, May 1990.

[8] W. C. Athas and C. L. Seitz. Multicomputers: Message–passing concurrent computers. *IEEE Computer*, 21(8):9–24, August 1988.

[9] F. Meyer auf der Heide, B. Oesterdiekhoff, and R. Wanka. Strongly adaptive token distribution. *Algorithmica*, 15:413–427, 1996.

[10] S. A. Baker and K. R. Milner. A process migration harness for dynamic load balancing. In *Proceedings of World Transputer User Group (WoTUG) Conference*, pages 52–61, 1991.

[11] K. M. Baumgartner and B. W. Wah. Computer scheduling algorithms: Past, present, and future. *Information Science*, 57–58:319–345, 1991.

[12] Y. Ben-Asher, A. Cohen, A. Schuster, and J. F. Sibeyn. The impact of task-length parameters on the performance of the random load-balancing algorithm. In *Proceedings of 6th International Parallel Processing Symposium*, pages 82–85, March 1992.

[13] M. J. Berger and S. H. Bokhari. A partitioning strategy for nonuniform problems on multiprocessors. *IEEE Transactions on Computers*, 36(5):570–580, May 1987.

[14] A. Berman and R. J. Plemmons. *Nonnegative matrices in the mathematical sciences*. Academic Press, 1979.

[15] D. P. Bertsekas and J. N. Tsitsiklis. Converence rate and termination of asynchronous iterative algorithms. In *Proceedings of 1989 International Conference on Supercomputing*, pages 461–470, 1989.

[16] D. P. Bertsekas and J. N. Tsitsiklis. *Parallel and distributed computation: Numerical methods*. Prentice-Hall, 1989.

[17] J. B. Boillat. Load balancing and poisson equation in a graph. *Concurrency: Practice and Experience*, 2(4):289–313, December 1990.

[18] J. B. Boillat and P. G. Kropf. A fast distributed mapping algorithm. In *Lecture Notes on Computer Science, 457*. Springer-Verlag, Berlin, 1990.

[19] J. E. Boillat. Fast load balancing in Cayley graphs and in circuits. In *Proceedings of Workshop on Graph-Theoretic Concepts in Computer Science*, pages 315–326, 1993.

[20] S. H. Bokhari. On the mapping problem. *IEEE Transactions on Computers*, 30(3):550–557, 1981.

[21] S. H. Bokhari. *Assignment Problems in Parallel and Distributed Computing*. Kluwer Academic Publishers, 1987.

[22] S. H. Bokhari. Partitioning problems in parallel, pipelined, and distributed computing. *IEEE Transactions on Computers*, 37:48–57, January 1988.

[23] S. H. Bokhari. A network flow model for load balancing in circuit-switched multicomputers. *IEEE Transactions on Parallel and Distributed Systems*, 4(6):649–657, June 1993.

[24] S. W. Bollinger and S. F. Midkiff. Heuristic techniques for processor and link assignment in multicomputers. *IEEE Transactions on Computers*, 40(3):325–333, March 1991.

[25] F. Bonomi and A. Kumar. Adaptive optimal load balancing in a heterogeneous multiserver system with a central job scheduler. *IEEE Transactions on Computers*, 39(10):1232–1250, October 1990.

[26] V. Borkar and P. Varaiya. Asymptotic agreement in distributed estimation. *IEEE Transactions on Automatic Control*, 27:650–655, 1982.

[27] N. S. Bowen, C. N. Nikolaou, and A. Ghafoor. On the assignment problem of arbitrary process systems to heterogeneous distributed computer systems. *IEEE Transactions on Computers*, 41(3):257–273, March 1992.

[28] A. Broder and E. Shamir. On the second eigenvalue of random regular graphs. In *Proceeings of 28th IEEE Foundations of Computer Science Conference*, pages 286–294, 1987.

[29] R. M. Bryant and R. A. Finkel. A stable distributed scheduling algorithm. In *Proceedings of International Conference on Distributed Computing Systems*, pages 314–323, 1981.

[30] T. L. Casavant and J. G. Kuhl. Analysis of three dynamic load-balancing strategies with varying global information requirements. In *Proceedings of 7th International Conference on Distributed Computing Systems*, pages 185–192, September 1987.

[31] T. L. Casavant and J. G. Kuhl. Effects of response and stability on scheduling in distributed computing systems. *IEEE Transactions on Software Engineering*, 14(11):1578–1587, November 1988.

[32] T. L. Casavant and J. G. Kuhl. A taxonomy of scheduling in general-purpose distributed computing systems. *IEEE Transactions on Software Engineering*, 14:141–154, May 1988.

[33] T. L. Casavant and J. G. Kuhl. A communicating finite automata approach to modeling distributed computation and its application to distributed decision-making. *IEEE Transactions on Computers*, 39(5):628–639, May 1990.

[34] S. Chakrabarti, A. Ranade, and K. Yelick. Randomized load balancing for tree-structured computation. In *Proceedings of Scalable High Performance Computing Conference*, pages 666–673, May 1994.

[35] T. F. Chan and R. S. Tuminaro. Design and implementation of parallel multigrid algorithms. In *Multigrid Methods: Theory, Applications, and Supercomputing*, pages 101–115. Marcel Dekker, 1988.

[36] T. J. Chan and C. A. Yano. A multiplier adjustment approach for the set partitioning problem. *Operations Research*, 40(1):40–47, January-February 1992.

[37] V. Chaudhary and J. K. Aggarwal. A generalized scheme for mapping parallel algorithms. *IEEE Transactions on Parallel and Distributed Systems*, pages 328–346, March 1993.

[38] H.-A. Choi and B. Narahari. Algorithms for mapping and partitioning chain structured parallel computations. In *Proceedings of International Conference on Parallel Processing*, volume 1, pages 625–628, 1991.

[39] T. C. K. Chou and J. A. Abraham. Load balancing in distributed systems. *IEEE Transactions on Software Engineering*, 8(4):401–412, July 1982.

[40] A. N. Choudhary, B. Narahari, and R. Krishnamurti. An efficient heuristic scheme for dynamic remapping of parallel computations. *Parallel Computing*, 19:621–632, 1993.

[41] A. N. Choudhary and R. Ponnusamy. Run-time data decomposition for parallel implementation of image processing and computer vision tasks. *Concurrency: Practice and Experience*, 4(4):313–334, June 1992.

[42] Y.-C. Chow and W. H. Kohler. Models for dynamic load balancing in homogeneous multiple processing systems. *IEEE Transactions on Computers*, 36, May 1982.

[43] R. Chowkwanyun and K. Hwang. Multicomputer load balancing for concurrent lisp execution. In K. Hwang and D. Degroot, editors, *Parallel Processing for Supercomputers and Artifical Intelligence*, pages 325–365. McGraw-Hill Publishing Co., 1989.

[44] Thinking Machines Co. *The Connection Machine CM-5 Technical Summary*, 1992.

[45] Intel Corporation. Intel Paragon supercomputer product brochure. `http://www.ssd.intel.com/paragon.html`.

[46] Intel Corporation. The Intel Pentium Pro processor. `http://www.intel.com/procs/ppro/`.

[47] G. Cybenko. Load balancing for distributed memory multiprocessors. *Journal of Parallel and Distributed Computing*, 7:279–301, 1989.

[48] R. Cypher and J. L. C. Sanz. *The SIMD Model of Parallel Computation*. Springer-Verlag, 1994.

[49] W. J. Dally. Performance analysis of k-ary n-cube interconnection networks. *IEEE Transactions on Computers*, 39(6):775–785, June 1990.

[50] P. J. Davis. *Circulant matrices*. John Wiley and Sons, 1979.

[51] A. K. Dewdney. Computer recreations. *Scientific American*, 251(6):14–22, December 1984.

[52] R. Diekmann, R. Lũling, and J. Simon. A general purpose distributed implementation of simulated annealing. In *Proceedings of 4th IEEE Symp. on Parallel and Distributed Processing*, pages 94–101, December 1992.

[53] R. Diekmann, D. Meyer, and B. Monien. Parallel decomposition of unstructured FEM-meshes. In *Proceedings of 2nd International Workshop on Parallel Algorithms for Irregularly Structured Problems*, pages 199–215. Springer LNCS 980, 1995.

[54] R. Diekmann, B. Monien, and R. Preis. Using helpful sets to improve graph bisecitons. In Sotteau Hsu, Rosenberg, editor, *Interconnection Networks and Mapping and Scheduling Parallel Computations*, pages 57–73. DIMACS, 1995.

[55] P. Diniz, S. Plimpton, B. Hendrickson, and R. Leland. Parallel algorithms for dynamically partitioning unstructured grids. In *Proc. of the 7th SIAM conf. on Parallel Processing for Scientific Computing*, pages 615–620, 1995.

[56] D. L. Eager, E. D. Lazowska, and J. Zahorjan. Adaptive load sharing in homogeneous distributed systems. *IEEE Transactions on Software Engineering*, 12(5):662–675, May 1986.

[57] D. L. Eager, E. D. Lazowska, and J. Zahorjan. A comparison of receiver-initiated and sender-initiated adaptive load sharing. *Performance Evaluation*, 6(1):53–68, March 1986.

[58] O. Eriksen. A termination detection protocol and its formal verification. *Journal of Parallel and Distributed Computing*, 5:82–91, 1988.

[59] C. Farhat. A simple and efficient automatic FEM domain decomposer. *Computers and Structures*, 28(5):579–602, 1988.

[60] C. Farhat and H. D. Simon. TOP/DoMDEC—A software tool for mesh partitioning and parallel processing. Technical Report Tech. Rep. RNR-93-011, NASA Ames, 1993.

[61] A.M. Farley and A. Proskurowski. Gossiping in grid graphs. *Journal of Combinatorics, Information and System Sciences*, 5(2):161–172, 1980.

[62] D. G. Feitelson and L. Rudolph. Distributed hierarchical control for parallel processing. *IEEE Computer*, 23(5):65–77, May 1990.

[63] D. Ferrari and S. Zhou. An empirical investigation of load indices for load balancing applications. In *Proceedings of Performance'87*, pages 515–528, 1987.

[64] D. Ferrari and S. Zhou. An empirical investigation of load indices for load balancing applications. In *Proceedings of 12th Annual International Symposium on Computer Performance Modeling, Measurement and Evaluation*, pages 515–528, 1987.

[65] S. Fiorini and R. J. Wilson. Edge-coloring of graphs. In L. W. Beineke and R. J. Wilson, editors, *Selected Topics in Graph Theory*, pages 103–125. Academic Press, 1978.

[66] G. C. Fox. Applications of parallel supercomputers: Scientific results and computer science lessons. In *Natural and Artifical Parallel Computation*. The MIT press, Cambridge, 1990.

[67] G. C. Fox, W. Furmanski, J. Koller, and P. Simic. Physical optimization and load balancing algorithms. In *Proceedings of Conference on Hypercube Concurrent Computers and Applications*, pages 591–594, 1989.

[68] G. C. Fox, M. A. Johnson, G. A. Lyzenga, S. W. Otto, J. K. Salmon, and D. W. Walker. *Solving problems on concurrent processors*, volume 1. Prentice-Hall, 1988.

[69] G. C. Fox, A. Kolawa, and R. Williams. The implementation of a dynamic load balancer. In *Proceedings of Hypercube Multiprocessors*, pages 114–121. SIAM, 1987.

[70] N. Francez. Distributed termination. *ACM Transactions on Programming Languages Systems*, 2:42–45, January 1980.

[71] M. Furuichi, K. Taki, and N. Ichiyoshi. A multi-level load balancing scheme for OR-parallel exhaustive search programs. *SIGPLAN Notices*, 25(3):50–59, March 1990.

[72] A. Geist et al. *PVM (Parallel Virtual Machine)—A User's Guide and Tutorial for Network Parallel Computing*. MIT Press, 1994.

[73] B. Ghosh and S. Muthukrishnan. Dynamic load balancing in distributed networks by random matchings. In *Proceedings of 6th ACM Symposium on Parallel Algorithms and Architectures*, 1994.

[74] R. H. Halstead and S. A. Ward. MuNet: A scalable decentralized architecture for parallel computation. In *Proceedings of IEEE 7th Annual Symposium on Computer Architecture*, 1980.

[75] H. W. Hammond. *Mapping unstructured grid computations to massively parallel computers*. PhD thesis, Rensselaer Polytechnic Institute, 1992.

[76] R. V. Hanxleden and L. R. Scott. Load balancing on message passing architectures. *Journal of Parallel and Distributed Computing*, 13(3):312–324, November 1991.

[77] M. Harchol-Balter and A.B. Downey. Exploiting process lifetime distributions for dynamic load balancing. In *Proceedings of ACM Conference on Measurement and Modeling of Computer Systems (SIGMETRICS '96)*, pages 13–24, May 1996.

[78] A. J. Harget and I. D. Johnson. Load balancing algorithms in loosely-coupled distributed systems: A survey. In H. S. M. Zedan, editor, *Distributed Computer Systems: Theory and Practice*, pages 85–108. Butterworths, 1990.

[79] C. Hazari and H. Zedan. A distributed algorithm for distributed termination. *Information Processing Letters*, 24:293–297, 1987.

[80] S.M. Hedetniemi, S.T. Hedetniemi, and A.L. Liestman. A survey of gossiping and broadcasting in communication networks. *Networks*, 18:319–349, 1988.

[81] A. Heirich and S. Taylor. A parabolic load balancing algorithm. In *Proceedings of International Conference on Parallel Processing (ICPP'95)*, volume 3, pages 192–202, 1995.

[82] B. Hendrickson and R. Leland. The Chaco user's guide. Technical Report SAND 93–2339, Sandia National Lab., USA, 1993.

[83] S. Heydorn and P. Weidner. Optimization and performance analysis of thinning algorithm on parallel computers. *Parallel Computing*, 17:17–27, 1991.

[84] High Performance Fortran Forum. *High Performance Fortran Language Specification*, November 1994.

[85] C. M. Holt, A. Stewart, M. Clint, and R. D. Perrott. An improved parallel thinning algorithm. *Communications of ACM*, 30(2):156–160, February 1987.

[86] J.-W. Hong, X.-N. Tan, and M. Chen. From local to global: An analysis of nearest neighbor balancing on hypercube. In *Proceedings of ACM–SIGMETRICS*, pages 73–82, May 1988.

[87] J.-W. Hong, X.-N. Tan, and M. Chen. Dynamic cyclic load balancing on hypercube. In *Proceedings of Conference on Hypercube Concurrent Computers and Applications*, pages 595–598, 1989.

[88] R. M. Hord. *Parallel Supercomputing in SIMD Architectures*. CRC Press, 1990.

[89] R. A. Horn and C. R. Johnson. *Matrix analysis*. Cambridge University Press, 1985.

[90] G. Horton. A multi-level diffusion method for dynamic load balancing. *Parallel Computing*, 19:209–218, 1993.

[91] S. H. Hosseini, B. Litow, M. Malkawi, J. McPherson, and K. Vairavan. Analysis of a graph coloring based distributed load balancing algorithm. *Journal of Parallel and Distributed Computing*, 10:160–166, 1990.

[92] K. Hwang. *Advanced Computer Architecture: Parallelism, Scalability, Programmability*. McGraw-Hill, Inc., 1994.

[93] K. Hwang et al. A Unix-based local computer network with load balancing. *Computer*, 5(4):55–65, April 1982.

[94] Cray Research, Inc. The CRAY T3E scalable parallel processing system. `http://www.cray.com/PUBLIC/product-info/T3E/`.

[95] Parsytec, Inc. Products information. `http://www.parsytec.de` or `http://www.parsytec.com`.

[96] M. A. Iqbal, J. H. Saltz, and S. H. Bokhari. A comparative analysis of static and dynamic load balancing strategies. In *Proceedings of International Conference on Parallel Processing*, pages 1040–1047, 1986.

[97] V. K. Janakiram, D. P. Agrawal, and R. Mehrotra. A randomized parallel branch-and-bound algorithm. In *Proceedings of International Conference on Parallel Processing*, pages 69–75, 1988.

[98] J. JáJá and K.-W. Ryu. Load balancing on the hypercube and related networks. *Journal of Parallel and Distributed Computing*, 14(4):431–435, April 1992.

[99] S. L. Johnsson and C.-T. Ho. Spanning graphs for optimum broadcasting and personalized communication in hypercubes. *IEEE Transactions on Computers*, 38(9):1249–1268, September 1989.

[100] M. T. Jones and P. E. Plassmann. Parallel algorithms for the adaptive refinement and partitioning of unstructured meshes. In *Proceedings of 1994 Scalable High Performance Computing Conference*, pages 478–485, May 1994.

[101] L. V. Kale. Comparing the performance of two dynamic load distribution methods. In *Proceedings of International Conference on Parallel Processing*, pages 8–12, 1988.

[102] L. V. Kale. The Chare kernel parallel programming language and system. In *Proceedings of International Conference on Parallel Processing*, volume 2, pages 17–25, 1990.

[103] R. M. Karp and Y. Zhang. A randomized parallel branch-and-bound procedure. In *Proceedings of 20th ACM Symposium on Theory of Computing*, pages 290–300, 1988.

[104] G. Karypis and V. Kumar. *Parallel multilevel graph partitioning*. University of Minnesota, Department of Computer Science, May 1995.

[105] P. Kermani and L. Kleinrock. Virtual cut through: A new computer communication switching technique. *Computer Networks*, 3:267–286, 1979.

[106] B. Kernighan and S. Lin. An efficient heuristic procedure for partitioning graphs. *Bell System Technical Journal*, 29:291–307, 1970.

[107] R. E. Kessler and J. L. Schwarzmeier. Cray T3D: A new dimension for Cray Research. In *Proceedings of COMPCON*, pages 176–182, February 1993.

[108] J. De Keyser and D. Roose. A software tool for load balanced adaptive multiple grids on distributed memory computers. In *Proceedings of 6th Distributed Memory Computing Conference*, pages 122–128, April 1991.

[109] J. De Keyser and D. Roose. Multigrid with solution-adaptive irregular grids on distributed memory computers. In D. J. Evans, G. R. Joubert, and H. Liddell, editors, *Parallel Computing*, pages 375–382. Elsevier Science Publishers, 1992.

[110] J. De Keyser and D. Roose. Load balancing data parallel programs on distributed memory computers. *Parallel Computing*, 19:1199–1219, November 1993.

[111] K. Kimura and N. Ichiyoshi. Probabilistic analysis of the optimal efficiency of the multi-level dynamic load balancing schems. In *Proceedings of 6th Distributed memory computing Conference*, pages 145–152, April 1991.

[112] S. Kirkpatrick, C. Gelatt, and M. Vecchi. Optimization by simulated annealing. *Science*, 220:671–680, 1983.

[113] O. Kremien and J. Kramer. Methodical analysis of adaptive load sharing algorithms. *IEEE Transactions on Parallel and Distributed Systems*, 3(6):747–760, November 1992.

[114] P. Krueger and M. Livny. Load balancing, load sharing and performance in distributed systems. Technical Report TR-700, Computer Science Department, University of Wisconsin at Madison, August 1987.

[115] P. Krueger and M. Livny. A comparison of preemptive and non-preemptive load distribution. In *Proceedings of International Conference on Distributed Computing Systems*, pages 123–130, 1988.

[116] D. W. Krumme, G. Cybenko, and K. N. Venkataraman. Gossiping in minimal time. *SIAM Journal on Computing*, 21(1):111–139, February 1992.

[117] D. Kumar. Development of a class of distributed termination detection algorithms. *IEEE Transactions on Knowledge and Data Engineering*, 4(2):145–155, April 1992.

[118] V. Kumar, A. Grama, A. Gupta, and G. Karypis. *Introduction to Parallel Computing*. The Benjamin/Cummings Pub. Co., 1994.

[119] V. Kumar, A. Y. Grama, and N. R. Vempaty. Scalable load balancing techniques for parallel computers. *Journal of Parallel and Distributed Computing*, 22(1):60–79, July 1994.

[120] T. Kunz. The influence of different workload descriptions on a heuristic load balancing scheme. *IEEE Transactions on Software Engineering*, 17(7):725–730, 1991.

[121] E. L. Lawler and D. E. Wood. Branch and bound methods, a survey. *Operations Research*, 14:699–719, 1966.

[122] A. Liestman and D. Richards. Network communication in edge-colored graphs: Gossiping. *IEEE Transactions on Parallel and Distributed Systems*, 4(4):438–445, April 1993.

[123] D. J. Lilja. *Architectural Alternatives for Exploiting Parallelism*. IEEE Computer Society Press, 1991.

[124] INMOS Limited. *ANSI C Toolset User Manual*. INMOS Limited, 1990.

[125] INMOS Limited. *Networks, Routers and Transputers: Functions, Performance and Applications*. IOS Press, 1993.

[126] F. C. H. Lin and R. M. Keller. The gradient model load balancing method. *IEEE Transactions on Software Engineering*, 13(1):32–38, January 1987.

[127] H.-C. Lin and C. S. Raghavendra. A dynamic load balancing policy with a central job dispatcher (LBC). *IEEE Transactions on Software Engineering*, 18(2):148–158, February 1992.

[128] B. Litow. The influence of graph structure on generalized dimension exchange. *Information Processing Letters*, 54:347–353, 1995.

[129] B. Litow, S. H. Hosseini, and K. Vairavan. Performance characteristics of a load balancing algorithm. *Journal of Parallel and Distributed Computing*, 31(2):159–165, December 1995.

[130] R. Lüling and B. Monien. Load balancing for distributed branch and bound algorithm. In *Proceedings of 6th International Parallel Processing Symposium*, pages 543–5448, March 1992.

[131] R. Lüling and B. Monien. A dynamic distributed load balancing algorithm with provable good performance. In *Proceedings of 5th ACM Symposium on Parallel Algorithms and Architectures*, pages 164–172, 1993.

[132] R. Lüling, B. Monien, and F. Ramme. Load balancing in large networks: A comparative study. In *Proceedings of 3th IEEE Symposium on parallel and distributed processing*, pages 686–689, December 1991.

[133] V. A. Lo. Heuristic algorithms for task assignment in distributed systems. *IEEE Transactions on Computers*, 37(11):1384–1397, November 1988.

[134] B. Lubachevsky and D. Mitra. A chaotic asynchronous algorithm for computing the fixed point of a nonnegative matrix of unit spectral radius. *Journal of the ACM*, 33(1):130–150, 1986.

[135] N. Mansour and G. C. Fox. Allocating data to multicomputer nodes by physical optimization algorithms for loosely synchronous computations. *Concurrency: Practice and Experience*, 4(7):557–574, October 1992.

[136] F. Mattern. Algorithms for distributed termination detection. *Distributed Computing*, 2:161–175, 1987.

[137] F. Mattern. Asynchronous distributed termination: Parallel and symmetric solutions with echo algorithms. *Algorithmica*, pages 325–340, May 1990.

[138] S. F. McCormick. *Multilevel Adaptive Methods for Partial Differential Equations*. SIAM, 1989.

[139] P. Mehra and B. W. Wah. *Load Balancing: An Automated Learning Approach*. World Scientific Publishing Co. Pte. Ltd., 1995.

[140] R. Mirchandaney and J.A. Stankovic. Using stochastic learning automata for job scheduling in distributed processing systems. *Journal of Parallel and Distributed Computing*, 3:527–552, 1986.

[141] J. Mohan. Experience with two parallel programs solving the traveling salesman problem. In *Proceedings of International Conference on Parallel Processing*, pages 191–193, 1983.

[142] B. Moon and J. Saltz. Adaptive runtime support for direct simulation monte carlo methods on distributed memory architectures. In *Scalable High Performance Computing Conference*, pages 176–183, May 1994.

[143] F. J. Muniz and E. J. Zaluska. Parallel load-balancing: An extension to the gradient model. *Parallel Computing*, 21:287–301, 1995.

[144] L. M. Ni and K. Hwang. Optimal load balancing in a multiple processor system with many job classes. *IEEE Transactions on Software Engineering*, 11:491–496, May 1985.

[145] L. M. Ni and P. K. McKinley. A survey of wormhole routing techniques in direct networks. *IEEE Computer*, 26:62–76, February 1993.

[146] L. M. Ni, C.-W. Xu, and T. B. Gendreau. A distributed drafting algorithm for load balancing. *IEEE Transactions on Software Engineering*, 11(10):1153–1161, October 1985.

[147] D. M. Nicol and Saltz J. H. Dynamic remapping of parallel computations with varying resource demands. *IEEE Transactions on Computers*, 37(9):1073–1087, September 1988.

[148] D. M. Nicol and D. R. O'Hallaron. Improved algorithms for mapping pipelined and parallel computations. *IEEE Transactions on Computers*, 40(3):295–306, March 1991.

[149] D. M. Nicol and J. H. Saltz. An analysis of scatter decomposition. *IEEE Transactions on Computers*, 39(11):1337–1345, November 1990.

[150] D. M. Nicol, R. Simha, and D. Towsley. Static assignment of stochastic tasks using majorization. *IEEE Transactions on Computers*, 45(6):730–740, June 1996.

[151] Convex Technology Center of Hewlett-Packard Company. HP-Convex Exemplar. `http://www.convex.com/prod_serv/exemplar/`.

[152] R. H. J. Otten and L. P. P. P. van Ginneken. *The Annealing Algorithm*. Kluwer Academic Publishers, 1989.

[153] C.-W. Ou and S. Ranka. Parallel remapping algorithms for adaptive problems. Technical Report SCCS-652, School of Computer and Information Science, Syracuse University, 1995.

[154] J. F. Palmer. The NCUBE family of parallel supercomputers. In *Proceedings IEEE International Conference on Computer Design*, page 107, 1990.

[155] A. Panconesi and A. Srinivasan. Parallel randomised edge coloring. In *Proceedings of Symposium on Principles of Distributed Computing*, 1990.

[156] D. Peleg and E. Upfal. The token distribution problem. *SIAM Journal on Computing*, 18(2):229–243, April 1989.

[157] G. F. Pfister. *In Search of Clusters—The coming battle for lowly parallel computing*. Prentice-Hall, 1995.

[158] C. G. Plaxton. Load balancing, selection and sorting on the hypercube. In *Proceedings of ACM Symposium on Parallel Algorithms and Architectures*, pages 64–73, 1989.

[159] J. Protić, M. Tomasević, and V. Milutinović. Distributed shared memory: Concepts and systems. *IEEE Parallel and Distributed Technology*, Summer 1996:63–79, 1996.

[160] X.-S. Qian and Q. Yang. Load balancing on generalized hypercube and mesh multiprocessors with LAL. In *Proceedings of 11th International Conference on Distributed Computing Systems*, pages 402–409, 1991.

[161] M. J. Quinn. Analysis and implementation of branch-and-bound algorithms on a hypercube multicomputer. *IEEE Transactions on Computers*, 39(3):384–387, March 1990.

[162] M. O. Rabin. Probabilistic algorithms. In J. F. Traub, editor, *Algorithms and Complexity: New Directions and Recent Results*, pages 21–39. Academic Press, 1976.

[163] G. Ramanathan and J. Oren. Survey of commercial parallel machines. *ACM Computer Architecture News*, 21(3):13–33, June 1993.

[164] S. P. Rana. A distributed solution of the distributed termination problem. *Information Processing Letters*, 17:43–46, 1983.

[165] S. Ranka, Y. Won, and S. Sahni. Programming a hypercube multicomputer. *IEEE Software*, 5:69–77, September 1988.

[166] V. N. Rao and V. Kumar. Parallel depth-first search on multiprocessors—Part I: Implementation; and Part II—Analysis. *Interational Journal on Parallel Programming*, 16(6), 1987.

[167] D. A. Reed and R. M. Fujimoto. *Multicomputer Networks: Message–Based Parallel Processing*. The MIT Press, 1987.

[168] C. G. Rommel. The probability of load balancing success in a homogeneous network. *IEEE Transactions on Software Engineering*, 17(9):922–933, September 1991.

[169] S. Rönn and H. Haikkonen. Distributed termination detection with counters. *Information Processing Letters*, 34:223–227, 1990.

[170] K. W. Ross and D. D. Yao. Optimal load balancing and scheduling in a distributed computer system. *Journal of the ACM*, 38(3):676–690, July 1991.

[171] Y. Shih and J. Fier. Hypercube systems and key applications. In K. Hwang and D. Degroot, editors, *Parallel Processing for Supercomputers and Artifical Intelligence*, pages 203–243. McGraw-Hill Publishing Co., 1989.

[172] K. G. Shin and Y.-C. Chang. Load sharing in distributed real-time systems with state-change broadcasts. *IEEE Transactions on Computers*, pages 1124–1142, August 1989.

[173] K. G. Shin and Y.-C. Chang. Load sharing in hypercube multicomputers for real-time applications. In *Proceedings of Conference on Hypercube Concurrent Computers and Applications*, pages 617–621, 1989.

[174] N. G. Shivaratri, P. Krueger, and M. Singhal. Load distribution for locally distributed systems. *IEEE Computer*, pages 33–44, December 1992.

[175] W. Shu and L. V. Kale. A dynamic scheduling strategy for the Chare kernel systems. In *Proceedings of Supercomputing*, pages 389–398, 1989.

[176] W. Shu and M.-Y. Wu. Runtime incremental parallel scheduling (RIPS) on distributed memory computers. *IEEE Transactions on Parallel and Distributed Systems*, 7(6):637–649, June 1996.

[177] A. B. Sinha and L. V. Kale. A load balancing strategy for prioritized execution of tasks. In *Proceedings of 7th International Parallel Processing Symposium*, pages 230–237, 1993.

[178] M. Snir et al. *MPI: The Complete Reference*. MIT Press, 1996.

[179] S. Sofianopoulou. The process allocation problem: A survey of the application of graph–theoretic and integer programming approaches. *Journal of Operational Research*, 43(5):407–413, 1992.

[180] J. Song. A partially asynchronous and iterative algorithm for distributed load balancing. *Parallel Computing*, 20(6):853–868, June 1994.

[181] J. A. Stankovic. Stability and distributed scheduling algorithms. *IEEE Transactions on Software Engineering*, 11(10):1141–1152, October 1985.

[182] J. A. Stankovic and I. S. Sidhu. An adaptive bidding algorithm for processes, clusters and distributed groups. In *Proceedings of 4th International Conference on Distributed Computer Systems*, pages 49–59, May 1984.

[183] S. C. Su, P. Biswas, and R. Krishnaswamy. Experiments in dynamic load balancing of parallel logic programs. In *Proceedings of Conference on Hypercube Concurrent Computers and Applications*, pages 623–626, 1989.

[184] R. Subramanian and I. D. Scherson. An analysis of diffusive load-balancing. In *Proceedings of 6th ACM Symposium on Parallel Algorithms and Architectures*, 1994.

[185] H. Sullivan, T. R. Bashkow, and D. Klappholz. A large scale homogeneous, fully distributed parallel machine. In *Proceedings of 4th Annual IEEE Symposium on Computer Architecture*, 1977.

[186] B. Szymanski, Y. Shi, and S. Prywes. Synchronized distributed termination. *IEEE Transactions on Software Engineering*, SE-11(10):1136–1140, October 1985.

[187] A. N. Tantawi and D. Towsley. Optimal static load balancing in distributed computer systems. *Journal of the ACM*, 32(2):445–465, April 1985.

[188] S. Taylor, J. R. Watts, M. A. Rieffel, and M. E. Palmer. The Concurrent Graph: Basic technology for irregular problems. *IEEE Parallel and Distributed Technology*, 4(2):15–25, 1996.

[189] A. Trew and G. Wilson. *Past, Present and Parallel: A Survey of Available Parallel Computer Systems*. Springer–Verlag, 1991.

[190] S. Tschöke and T. Polzer. Portable parallel branch-and-bound library: User manual. Technical report, University of Paderborn, 1995.

[191] T. Tschöke, R. Lüling, and B. Monien. Solving the traveling salesman problem with a distributed branch-and-bound algorithms on a 1024 processor network. In *Proceedings of 9th International Parallel Processing Symposium*, 1995.

[192] J. N. Tsitsiklis and M. Athans. Convergence and asymtpotic agreement in distributed decision problems. *IEEE Transactions on Automatic Control*, 29:42–45, 1984.

[193] A. Üresin and M. Dubois. Parallel asynchronous algorithms for discrete data. *Journal of the ACM*, 37(3):588–606, July 1990.

[194] L. G. Valiant and G. J. Brebner. Universal schemes for parallel communication. *ACM Symposium on Theory of Computing*, pages 263–277, 1981.

[195] R. S. Varga. *Matrix iterative analysis*. Prentice-Hall, 1962.

[196] B. W. Wah and C. F. Yu. Stochastic modeling of branch-and-bound algorithms with best-first search. *IEEE Transactions on Software Engineering*, 11:922–934, 1985.

[197] D. W. Walker. The design of a standard message passing interface for distributed memory concurrent computers. *Parallel Computing*, 20(4):657–674, April 1994.

[198] C. Walshaw and M. Berzines. Dynamic load-balancing for PDE solvers on adaptive unstructured meshes. *Concurrency: Practice and Experience*, 7(1):14–28, 1995.

[199] Y.-T. Wang and R. J. T. Morris. Load sharing in distributed systems. *IEEE Transactions on Computers*, 34(3):204–217, March 1985.

[200] J. Watts, M. Rieffel, and S. Taylor. Practical dynamic load balancing for irregular problems. In *Proceedings of IRREGULAR'96*, 1996.

[201] M. Willebeek-LeMair and A. P. Reeves. Distributed dynamic load balancing. In *Proceedings of Conference on Hypercube Concurrent Computers and Applications*, pages 609–612, 1989.

[202] M. Willebeek-LeMair and A. P. Reeves. Local vs. global strategies for dynamic load balancing. In *Proceedings of International Conference on Parallel Processing*, volume 1, pages 569–570, 1990.

[203] M. Willebeek-LeMair and A. P. Reeves. Strategies for dynamic load balancing on highly parallel computers. *IEEE Transactions on Parallel and Distributed Systems*, 4(9):979–993, September 1993.

[204] R. D. Williams. Performance of dynamic load balancing algorithms for unstructured mesh calculations. *Concurrency: Practice and Experience*, 3(5):451–481, October 1991.

[205] W. I. Williams. Load balancing and hypercubes: A preliminary look. In *Proceedings of 2th Conference on Hypercube Multicomputers*, pages 108–113, 1987.

[206] R. P. Wilson et al. *An Overview of the SUIF System*. `http://suif.stanford.edu/suif`.

[207] M.-Y. Wu and W. Shu. The direct dimension exchange method for load balancing in k-ary n-cubes. In *Proceedings of 8th IEEE Symposium on Parallel and Distributed Processing*, October 1996.

[208] M.-Y. Wu and W. Shu. A load-balancing algorithm for N-cubes. In *Proceedings of International Conference on Parallel Processing (ICPP'96)*, pages 148–155, 1996.

[209] C.-Z. Xu and F. C. M. Lau. Analysis of the generalized dimension exchange method for dynamic load balancing. *Journal of Parallel and Distributed Computing*, 16(4):385–393, December 1992.

[210] C.-Z. Xu and F. C. M. Lau. Termination detection for loosely synchronized computations. In *Proceedings of 4th IEEE Symposium on Parallel and Distributed Processing*, pages 196–203, December 1992.

[211] C.-Z. Xu and F. C. M. Lau. Optimal parameters for load balancing using the diffusion method in the k-ary n-cube networks. *Information Processing Letters*, 47(5):181–187, September 1993.

[212] C.-Z. Xu and F. C. M. Lau. Decentralized remapping of data-parallel computations with the generalized dimension exchange method. In *Proceedings of 1994 Scalable High Performance Computing Conference*, pages 414–421, May 1994.

[213] C.-Z. Xu and F. C. M. Lau. Iterative dynamic load balancing in multicomputers. *Journal of Operational Research Society*, 45(7):786–796, July 1994.

[214] C.-Z. Xu and F. C. M. Lau. Optimal parameters for load balancing with the diffusion method in mesh networks. *Parallel Processing Letters*, 4(2):139–147, June 1994.

[215] C.-Z. Xu and F. C. M. Lau. The generalized dimension exchange method for load balancing in k-ary n-cubes and variants. *Journal of Parallel and Distributed Computing*, 24(1):72–85, January 1995.

[216] C.-Z. Xu and F. C. M. Lau. Efficient termination detection for loosely synchronous applications in multicomputers. *IEEE Transactions on Parallel and Distributed Systems*, 7(5):537–544, May 1996.

[217] C.-Z. Xu, S. Tschoeke, and B. Monien. Performance evaluation of load distribution strategies in parallel branch-and-bound computations. In *Proceedings of 7th Symposium of Parallel and Distributed Systems*, pages 402–405, October 1995.

[218] M. K. Yang and C. R. Das. Evaluation of a parallel branch-and-bound algorithm on a class of multiprocessors. *IEEE Transactions on Parallel and Distributed Systems*, 5(1):74–86, January 1994.

[219] S. Zhou. A trace-driven simulation study of dynamic load balancing. *IEEE Transactions on Software Engineering*, 14(9):1327–1341, September 1985.

[220] S. Zhou et al. Utopia: A load sharing facilities for large, heterogeneous distributed computer systems. Technical Report CSRI-257, Computer Systems Research Institute, University of Toronto, April 1992.

[221] T. F. Znati, R. G. Melhem, and K. R. Pruhs. Dilation-based bidding schemes for dynamic load balancing on distributed processing systems. In *Proceedings of 6th Distributed Memory Computing Conference*, pages 129–136, April 1991.

Index

Copyright Permissions

Some figures and part of the text in Chapter 9 originally appeared in the article "Performance evaluation of load distribution strategies in parallel branch-and-bound computations", *Proceedings of 7th IEEE Symposium on Parallel and Distributed Processing,* October 1995. The material is reprinted here by permission of the publisher, Institute of Electrical and Electronics Engineers.

MIX
Papier aus verantwortungsvollen Quellen
Paper from responsible sources
FSC® C105338

If you have any concerns about our products,
you can contact us on
ProductSafety@springernature.com

In case Publisher is established outside the EU,
the EU authorized representative is:
Springer Nature Customer Service Center GmbH
Europaplatz 3, 69115 Heidelberg, Germany

Printed by Libri Plureos GmbH
in Hamburg, Germany